BasicSynth

Creating a Music Synthesizer in Software

Daniel R. Mitchell

BasicSynth: Creating a Music Synthesizer in Software
by Daniel R. Mitchell

ISBN: 978-0-557-02212-0

First Edition

http://basicsynth.com

Table of Contents

Dedication

I have had many good teachers over the years, each one adding something to my understanding. But there was one teacher in particular that shaped my understanding of music more than any other. From January 1980 until his death in the summer of 1981, I studied composition and electronic music with Merrill Ellis. It was one of those rare occurrences where teacher and student "clicked" and my abilities as a composer increased rapidly during that relatively short period. Merrill Ellis was a first-rate composer, an exceptional teacher, and a true pioneer in the field of electronic music. More important to me personally, it was Merrill Ellis that encouraged me to hear with the inner ear that is the heart and soul of a musician, and helped me develop the confidence I needed to write what I heard.

This book is filled with technical details out of necessity. Without them we could not implement a working synthesizer. Unfortunately, the technical nature of electronic and computer music can be dangerous to a composer. We can get caught up in the equations, algorithms and clever programming techniques to the point we forget what it is all about. When reading this book, it is good to remember what Mr. Ellis taught me shortly before he passed away:

When making music, it doesn't matter what you do or how you do it...as long as it sounds good.

Preface

My first exposure to synthesized sounds was through the *Switched on Bach* recordings by Walter Carlos. Those recordings opened up a whole new world of sounds for me. My fascination with synthesized sounds eventually led me to build my own synthesizer from a PAIA kit. It wasn't much of a synthesizer. I had one VCO, one VCA, one VCF, AR envelope generator, LFO and keyboard, and soon discovered that without a multi-track recorder there wasn't much I could do except make interesting sound effects. Nevertheless, that little synthesizer allowed me to gain an understanding of how synthesizers make sounds. A few years later I enrolled for graduate study at the University of North Texas and was able to work with two powerful synthesizers, a Moog analog synthesizer and a Synclavier II digital synthesizer.

Later, after I had left school and begun work as a computer programmer, I began to purchase my own synthesizers. A bonus check from my job was spent as a down payment on a Yamaha DX7, a remarkable synthesizer for its time. Hooked up to my Commodore C64 computer through a home-built MIDI interface, it gave me a way to continue to use computers and synthesizers to make music. Not having any commercial music software available, I wrote a simple sequencing program named Notelist. Notelist didn't do much more than convert text into MIDI events, but it became the foundation and starting point for the score language described later in this book.

Eventually the keyboards were set aside in favor of software synthesis using Barry Vercoe's CSound, a direct descendant of the original software synthesis system, MUSIC by Max Matthews. As flexible and powerful as a program like CSound is, I always missed the interactive creation of sound through a keyboard like the DX7. Being able to hear how the tweaks affect the sound is very useful. I eventually decided to create some synthesis software routines so that I could get a more immediate result. The software in this book is a direct outgrowth of that endeavor. Just as I discovered when building my own synthesizer as a teenager, I found that having to program the synthesis system myself improved my understanding of the underlying equations and algorithms that are used to create sound on a computer. Hopefully, documenting how I went from simple sound generators to complex instruments will help others gain a better understanding as well.

A variety of software synthesis systems with large libraries of patches and almost unlimited sequencing are now available for a home computer. These systems are inexpensive, produce high quality sound, and can make music synthesis relatively easy even for those with limited knowledge of computer programming or digital signal processing. With all of that capability readily available it may seem that creating a synthesizer of your own is a lot of unnecessary work. However, just because you have a thousand patches in your sound library doesn't mean you have the sound available that you hear in your head. If the synthesis system won't allow you to easily change patches, or you don't understand how tweaking the controls will change the sound, you can get stuck. The more you know about how the synthesizer works, the better chance you have of realizing what you hear in your mind. But, even if you know how you want to produce the sound, the software may not provide a convenient way for you to do so. Having your own synthesis software available allows you to extend and adapt it to fit your particular needs.

Sound generation software can also be used to enhance a wide variety of computer applications. For example, an interactive music tutorial needs to produce sounds beyond playback of recordings. Computer game programming is another application that can benefit by having the ability to generate sound directly. There are potentially many such applications for sound generation, if you have the right software libraries available to you as a programmer. A commercial software synthesizer, or an existing library, may not be in a form you can easily adapt to your application. For that you need your own sound generation library.

If you are not an experienced programmer, developing your own synthesizer in software may seem like an unrealistic goal. Although both sound generation and sound modification are well described by the mathematics of digital signal processing (DSP), if you browse through a book on DSP your first impression is likely to be, "it's incomprehensible." Fortunately, it turns out that most of what we need to know to generate sound on a computer is very easy to understand.

It is not the purpose of this book to describe signal processing theory or synthesis techniques in detail. In the case of signal processing, we can take it for granted that the mathematicians and engineers got it right, and use the derived equations. Likewise, this book does not explore any new or original methods of sound synthesis. The examples shown in this book are the way most synthesis software is implemented and has been implemented since the 1960s. Instead, the primary purpose of this book is to understand and address the practical problems of programming the sound generation routines and combining them in a way to produce an efficient working synthesizer.

Each chapter begins with an introduction to the necessary theory and then proceeds to develop actual programs to implement the theory. The first chapters concentrate on sound generation and processing functions. Later chapters use the sound generation and processing code to develop instruments that implement various synthesis methods. An example score language is then described and combined with the synthesis instruments to create a complete synthesizer.

In order to use the information in this book you will need to understand basic algebra and trigonometry and some basic computer programming techniques. Significant features of the software are discussed, but for the most part it is assumed that you can read the example code and understand it. The examples in the book are shown in C++ but can be adapted to most computer programming languages. In addition, the examples are fragments of code with variable declarations, data type conversions, and error checking left out. The complete source code is available on-line and should be downloaded and studied along with each chapter. The example source code is available at http://sourceforge.net/projects/basicsynth for download. The latest information on the source code is available at http://basicsynth.com.

Chapter 1

Synthesis Overview

The sounds we hear are the result of a mechanical vibration that creates pressure waves in the air. Sound synthesis refers to the creation of sounds by some electronic means, either electronic circuits that directly generate electrical signals, or a computer that calculates the amplitude values for the signals. When the electronic signals are sent to a loudspeaker, they are converted into a mechanical vibration that produces sound.

When we say that something is synthetic, we mean that it is a replacement for a natural substance or process. Likewise, many musicians consider a synthesizer to be substitute for traditional musical instruments or other physical devices that make sound. However, we can also think of a synthesizer as a musical instrument in its own right with the goal of producing sounds that could not otherwise be heard. Both views are valid, and a well designed synthesizer can be used for both purposes. Fortunately, the software routines used to imitate natural sounds are the same as those used to produce completely new sounds.

We can think of a synthesizer as either a performance instrument or as a compositional tool. When used for performance, the focus of the instrument is on real-time response to the musician and we want sounds to occur immediately when we press a key on a keyboard, vary a control, or strike an input pad. Because it requires immediate response, a synthesizer used for live performance will usually have a limited range of sounds available at any moment and also be limited in the number of simultaneous sounds it can produce. When used as a compositional tool, the synthesizer does not have to respond in real-time, and can therefore be used to generate almost any sound the musician can imagine. In addition, the synthesizer can generate complex polyphonic textures that would be next to impossible for human players to perform. The compositional tool approach requires some kind of automated sequencer that controls the selection of instruments and their performance. In effect, the synthesizer becomes an "orchestra in a box" with a computer acting as both conductor and performer. However, the synthesizer does not have to be limited to one or the other use. A synthesizer designed mainly for live performance may also include a sequencer for automated playback.

A synthesizer can be designed to have a fixed number of easy to use preset sounds, or can be designed for maximum flexibility in sound generation. Preset synthesizers are usually intended for live performance, but are sometimes useful for quick composition as well. With a large library of preset sounds, the composer can spend more time on arranging the sounds as opposed to creating new sounds. Synthesizers with maximum variability in sound generation require the musician to set numerous parameters of each instrument and are usually intended as composition or research tools.

We can also consider a synthesizer to be replacement for a traditional musical instrument. This is often the case when a composer wants to preview a composition that is intended for performance by human players on traditional musical instruments. It can also be the case when the synthesizer is used to reduce the cost of commercial music production. In contrast, the synthesizer can be viewed as an instrument in its own right, and may be used stand-alone or combined with traditional musical instruments to create an ensemble.

Combining the various features listed above, we can produce a diagram showing potential synthesizer applications. Where we locate the synthesizer application on this diagram will determine the set of features that are most important in the design of the synthesizer (See Figure 1 below).

At the top of the circle, we have a combination of features suited to an instrument that can switch quickly between a limited number of emulated sounds. Such an instrument may be performed live, or set up with sequences much like an electronic player piano, but is mainly used for the purpose of duplicating several instruments in one. An electronic piano that can also switch to an organ or harpsichord sound is one example. Along the right side are applications such as commercial film and video production where the musician needs to produce sound effects, reproduce traditional musical instrument sounds at low cost, and also be able to closely synchronize the music with images. The left side area fits well with small ensemble and recording studio applications where the range of sound varies from traditional to new, but is typically performed live. Along the bottom of the circle we have a combination aimed more towards composition of purely electronic music and research into new synthesis techniques.

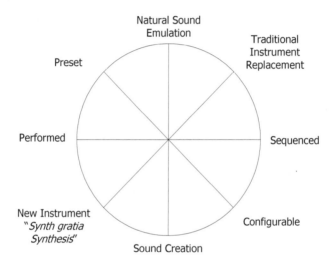

Figure 1 - Synthesizer Applications

An advantage of a software synthesis system, as opposed to a hardware synthesizer, is that it can potentially sit right in the middle of the circle. Such a system would be quite large and require considerable forethought, but is not beyond the capabilities of a typical personal computer. More commonly, the programmer will have in mind a specific application and design the synthesis system around those specific needs.

Synthesis Methods

Over the years many sound synthesis techniques have been developed, each with unique advantages and disadvantages. In many cases, the synthesis technique grew directly from the technology available at the time. Although this book is not intended as a tutorial on synthesis techniques, it is useful to review the most basic techniques in terms of possible software implementation so that we have a starting point for development of the synthesizer.

Additive synthesis creates complex sounds by adding together more than one signal. Usually, although not always, each signal is a simple sinusoid waveform with each sinusoid defined by relative frequency, amplitude and phase. When the signal amplitudes are relatively close to each other we hear a combination of tones. However, when the relative amplitudes of the higher frequencies are small compared to the lowest frequency, the signals blend together and we hear a single complex tone. The frequencies and amplitudes of the signals used for additive synthesis are often determined by analysis of recorded sounds with the goal of reproducing those sounds as exactly as possible. Additive synthesis can also be done "by ear" by interactively adjusting the frequency and amplitude values of each sinusoid until the desired sound is heard. Additive synthesis is the most straight-forward synthesis method, but requires a large number of signal generators to be usable. In the past, this requirement prevented additive synthesis from being widely used. However, with the ability to generate signals in software, we can implement additive synthesis methods very easily by running the same signal generator routine multiple times. The only additional cost for each signal is the time it takes to execute the signal generator software.

Subtractive synthesis is the inverse of additive synthesis. Where additive synthesis builds up a complex waveform one signal at a time, subtractive synthesis starts with a complex waveform and then attenuates frequencies by filtering the waveform. Subtractive synthesis requires only a few signal generators and filters to produce sounds similar to an additive synthesis system requiring many signal generators. For that reason it was the preferred method in early synthesizer design. A software synthesis system can easily produce complex waveforms and filters for use in subtractive synthesis. However, it is difficult to exactly reproduce a natural sound by filtering alone. Consequently, subtractive synthesis is more commonly used to generate unique electronic sounds.

FM and AM synthesis, distortion synthesis and non-linear synthesis are all variations of the same basic technique. Modulation involves continuous variation of one signal (the carrier) by another signal (the modulator). When both the carrier and modulator are in the audio frequency range, the two signals combine to produce sum and difference tones that sound similar to a sum of sinusoids. The spectrum that results from modulation can be as complex as a sum of dozens of individual sinusoid signals. Changing the amplitude and frequency relationship of the signals produces nearly unlimited variety of sounds. Because this technique requires so few signal generators, and produces such a wide range of sounds, it has been widely used in both analog and digital synthesizers. However, the complex interaction of the modulator and carrier creates a frequency spectrum that is difficult to control precisely and traditional signal synthesis based on spectrum analysis does not easily translate into a set of carriers and modulators. The relationship of the carrier, modulator and resulting spectrum is anything but intuitive. Consequently, simulating natural sounds with modulation is usually done by tweaking the modulator and carrier until an acceptable sound is heard. However, the ability to create very unnatural sounds makes non-linear synthesis especially appropriate for creating new and unusual sounds.

Wavetable synthesis is a technique that sits somewhere between additive and non-linear synthesis. Like additive synthesis, the wavetables combine to produce complex sounds. However, the transition from one waveform to another is a result of modulating multiple wavetables with a non-periodic function. Put another way, wavetable synthesis "morphs" the waveform between several sounds. Wavetable synthesis can use pre-recorded sounds to fill the wavetables. However, this introduces the same difficulties as a sampling system (see below). The main advantage of wavetable synthesis is that it allows a dynamic spectrum with only one signal generator constructed from a set of phase integrators. That advantage is less important when the signal generator exists only in computer memory. Nevertheless, wavetable synthesis can be implemented fairly easily in software, and is a good addition to a software synthesis system.

Granular synthesis is a unique, and specialized, synthesis technique. It produces a varying sound by stringing together very short sounds, often only a few milliseconds in length. The effect can be anything from a "bubbling" sound to a sound that slowly shifts in timbre over time. Granular synthesis was developed originally by physically splicing together small segments of sound recordings. The same technique can be performed very easily in software by concatenating recorded sounds, but can also be extended to use grains directly created with software signal generators.

A sampler synthesis system uses recorded sounds instead of internally generated waveforms. Such a system can get very close to exact reproduction of natural sounds. However, there are some limits that complicate a sampler system. If we only need to generate a sound effect, such as a buzzer or bell, the program is very simple. However, to reproduce musical instruments, the pitch, duration and timbre of the sound need to be variable. This introduces several potential problems. First, we need to know the fundamental frequency of the signal and analyzing an arbitrary signal to determine the actual pitch can be difficult. Second, changing the pitch by playing the recording at different rates introduces changes in envelope and spectrum of the signal. In addition, a sampler must be able to loop over the sustained portion of the sound without producing discontinuities in the waveform. Consequently, different recordings are used for different ranges of the instrument's sound, and the attack and decay portions of the sound are handled separately from the sustain portion. In short, a complete sampler requires many sound files and very careful preparation of the files in order to be usable. Implementing playback of the recorded sounds is easy, but creating a good set of sounds is very difficult.

A newer and potentially very powerful synthesis technique is known as physical modeling and waveguide synthesis. Rather than trying to analyze and then reproduce the spectrum of a sound, physical modeling creates a model of the sound as a combination of impulses, resonators and filters. In theory, any sound that can be produced by initiating a vibration in some physical object can be modeled in this manner. The basic software functions needed to model the sound are surprisingly simple. This is a method that has a great deal of potential, but one that also requires a significant amount of analysis of the sound and its controlling parameters.

Any or all of these common synthesis techniques can be used for any application described above. However, some synthesis techniques are more appropriate to each category than others. For example, additive synthesis usually requires the greatest number of calculations and is thus more appropriate for creating sound files for playback than live performance. In contrast, FM synthesis can produce a wide variety of sounds with a relatively small number of calculations and works well for both pre-recorded sound and live performance. Subtractive synthesis, along with wavetable distortion, granular synthesis and related techniques, are good for producing very distinctive artificial sounds, and, although they can simulate natural sounds, are better suited to new-sound categories than emulation of natural sounds. Sampled systems, physical modeling and waveguide synthesis are focused on efficient simulation of natural sounds, but can also be used to create arbitrary and artificial sounds if appropriate adjustable parameters are provided.

Expressive Music Synthesis Systems

The discussion above, like most writings on music synthesis, concentrates on methods for producing sounds. This is understandable since the unique feature of a synthesizer is its ability to produce a wide range of sounds from one instrument. Unfortunately, there is another important feature of a music synthesizer that often gets ignored.

Music is more than interesting *sounds*. Interesting *music* has an almost mystical quality that we call *expressive*. Sounds performed on traditional instruments are not static, but vary from note to note and over the duration of a single note as the performer varies the sounds during performance and from one performance to another. To get the same musical expression, a musician using a computer synthesis system needs more than a large catalog of interesting sounds. He must also have a way to control the expressive aspects of the composition. In traditional music notation, this can be done with a few short instructions to the performer, such as dynamics, tempo changes, accents, etc. We need something analogous for our computer music system if we want to create expressive music with it.

This is the area where synthesis systems most often fall short. The synthesizer is capable of producing a vast range of interesting sounds, but the musician or composer cannot easily introduce all the subtle variations to the sound that make the music expressive. Keyboard synthesizers have improved considerably in this area through the use of velocity and touch sensitive keyboards. However, trying to simulate all of the subtle variations of performance in software requires considerable effort and can be tedious. As a result, many software synthesis systems rely heavily on input from keyboards or other devices rather than providing a pure software solution. Furthermore, it is not intuitively obvious how changing a parameter, such as the value that controls the attack rate of an envelope generator, will affect the musical expressiveness. When we construct a synthesizer in software, with the computer acting as performer, we have to be aware of the need to be able to parameterize these subtle interactions between musician and sound in such a way that they are both available and meaningful for musical expression.

Whatever the application or synthesis technique, all synthesis systems rely on a common set of sound generation and processing functions that can be combined in various ways. The first section of this book steps through the process of understanding and creating those basic sound generation and processing functions. Later, we will look at designing instruments and automatic sequencing of the music with the goal of producing a synthesizer suited to expressive music composition. The additional features needed for simulation of traditional sounds and live performance are not covered in detail. However, the synthesis system described in this book can be extended to include those features.

Chapter 2

Sound in Software

We can represent any audio signal as a set of discrete values if we make each value a sample of the amplitude of the signal at a discrete time and make the time between samples a constant interval. This process, called *quantization*, is shown in the following figures. Figure 2 shows an input signal, in this case a sine wave.

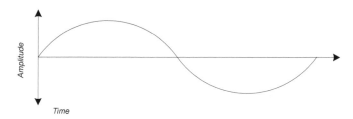

Figure 2 - Continuous signal

We can sample the amplitude of the signal at a regular interval to obtain the instantaneous amplitude values shown in Figure 3, and store those values in a computer file.

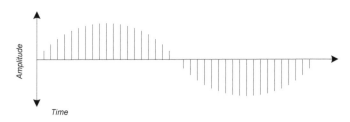

Figure 3 - Sampled waveform

The recorded samples can later be sent through a digital to analog converter (DAC) to produce a varying voltage that will drive an audio amplifier and loudspeaker. The output from the DAC is a series of steps as shown in Figure 4. When the stepped output is passed through a smoothing filter, the final output is a continuous signal, as was the original input signal.

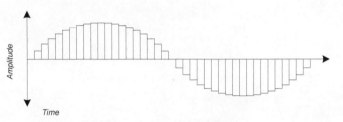

Figure 4 - Sample Output

The representation of a signal by a set of samples equally spaced in time is the foundation of digital audio systems, including both CD audio and digital sound synthesizers. Since the sound is represented by a set of numbers, a computer can also calculate the sample values directly rather than by sampling an analog input signal. Simply put, a digital sound synthesizer produces sound by generating a series of samples representing the instantaneous amplitude of the signal at a constant time interval. Samples can be directly calculated, taken from a recorded sound, or any mixture of the two. In addition, samples can be processed with filters and other sound effects by direct calculations on the samples. Thus a digital synthesis system can produce a wide variety of sounds, both natural and artificial, limited only by capacity of the computer system and the imagination of the musician.

Time and Amplitude

Before proceeding to develop sound generation software, we need to select the time interval between samples and the representation of amplitude.

Frequency (what musicians call pitch) is specified in cycles per second, abbreviated Hz. If we have a signal at 100Hz, the cycle repeats 100 times per second. Thus the time of one cycle (or period) is the inverse of the frequency, 1/100 sec. Consequently, we can express frequency as either f or $1/t$, where f is the frequency and t the time of one period. Given a time interval between samples, or *sample time*, the frequency of the samples, the *sample rate,* is the reciprocal:

$$t_s = \frac{1}{f_s} \tag{2.1}$$

$$f_s = \frac{1}{t_s} \tag{2.2}$$

The sample rate will ultimately determine the range of frequencies we can produce. In order to represent a periodic signal, we need at minimum one value above and one value below the zero level of amplitude for each cycle. In other words, we need at least two samples per cycle:

$$f_{max} = \frac{1}{t_{max}} = \frac{1}{2t_s} = \frac{f_s}{2} \tag{2.3}$$

The frequency at one-half the sampling rate is called the Nyquist frequency, or limit. For the sample rate, we must choose a value at least twice the highest frequency we want to reproduce. The accepted upper limit for audible sound is around 20,000Hz. In fact, most adults can't hear much above 12,000Hz, but the 20,000Hz upper limit is typical for audio equipment specifications and makes a reasonably good maximum. Any sampling rate over 40,000Hz will be able to represent the audio frequency range.

Sampling rates higher than the minimum do have some benefit, however. If we resample a digital sound file, we can change the frequency of the sound. But changing the frequency in that way means that we have to interpolate or discard some samples. If the sound is recorded at a minimum sampling rate, we can end up with distortion, noise, and a poor representation of higher frequencies. The same is true for signals that we generate internally. It might be a benefit, therefore, to have a higher internal sampling rate and also to be able to generate and read sound files at higher rates. Nevertheless, an equally important consideration is compatibility with existing audio equipment and software. The sample rate of 44,100Hz is currently the standard for both CD audio and computer sound files. That is the sample rate we will want to produce at the output of the program. If we are careful in our program design, we can change the sample rate at any time, or use a higher rate internally and only convert to the standard rate when we write out samples.

Almost all of our time values are non-integer values and we need to choose a data type to represent time that can represent both fractions of a second and the multiple-seconds duration of music. Normally this means using a floating point representation for duration, but a fixed point representation can also be used.

The number of samples we generate for a given sound is the duration in seconds multiplied by the sample rate. Internally, we need to convert time into a sample number. The sample number is the time in seconds multiplied by the number of samples per second.

$$S = T \cdot f_s \qquad\qquad (2.4)$$

Since we cannot generate a fraction of a sample, we can use an integer value to represent sample numbers. If we use a 32-bit signed integer, we can represent up to 2^{31}-1 samples. At a rate of 44,100 samples per second, that would be enough to represent a duration of 48,695 seconds, or about 13.5 hours. A 64-bit integer or a double precision floating point data type could represent durations much longer than that if needed, but in most cases a 32-bit value is sufficient.

To choose a representation for amplitude, we have to think in terms of the precision needed to accurately represent the dynamic range of audio signals. The nominal range for the data type is not critical since we can always normalize the values and treat the maximum value as 1 and the minimum value as -1. In fact, normalization to the range of [-1,+1] is typical for many of the equations used to represent periodic signals. Trigonometric functions, for example, are defined in terms of a unit circle. However, the number of bits we use to represent amplitude significantly affects the accuracy of our amplitude values. Given n bits in our computer data type, we can only represent 2^n different values. If we need to represent signed values, our absolute value is limited to 2^n-1.[1] For

---

[1] Rigorously defined, the range is $[-2^n,+2^n-1]$ due to the anomaly of "minus zero" sitting in the middle of a twos-complement representation. Programmers generally ignore that slight discrepancy, however, and think in

example, if a 16-bit word is used, the sample value can represent 65,536 different amplitudes. Since the amplitude is both positive and negative, the amplitude is limited to ±32,767 steps. Any amplitude values that fall in between those steps will be slightly inaccurate. An inaccuracy in the amplitude value is known as quantization error and is the digital equivalent of noise and/or distortion in the signal. The more bits we use, the more accurately we can represent the amplitude, and the less noise we will introduce into the signal. We need to be sure we choose a word size that will be practical, yet limit noise to an acceptable level.

A good way to analyze the requirement for amplitude values is to consider the dynamic range of hearing. We want to have a dynamic range that can represent what we can hear, and, if the range is large enough, the noise level will be small enough that it won't have a significant effect on the audio quality. The range of hearing is quite large, a ratio of about 10^{12} to 1. Fortunately, the number of discrete steps in amplitude we can detect is considerably smaller. For this reason, amplitude is represented using a logarithmic scale known as the decibel scale. The decibel scale uses 1dB to represent the average smallest change in amplitude we can hear. A decibel is defined as:[2]

$$A_{dB} = 20\log_{10}(A_1 / A_0)$$ (2.5)

Each bit in a data word represents a power of 2 increase in range. Thus a one bit value can represent $20 \log_{10}(2/1) \cong 6$dB. Each additional bit adds 6dB to the dynamic range (peak-to-peak). An 8-bit sample size would only produce 48dB dynamic range. A 16-bit value would give us 96dB, while a 32-bit sample size would provide 192dB. Since the dynamic range of music is around 100dB, the 16-bit value is very close to what we need. A 16-bit sample size is also the standard for commercial digital audio at the present time. Systems that use larger word sizes do gain a benefit by minimizing quantization error during calculations and thus potentially have lower noise in the signal. As with sampling rate, we can use one representation internally and convert to the standard on output.

---

terms of the positive magnitude as the limit for both positive and negative values.
[2] There are actually two dB scales, one for power ratios and one for amplitude ratios, but the one for amplitude ratios is what concerns us.

When calculating samples it is necessary to add, subtract, multiply and divide values before reaching the final output sample. If we use a 16-bit integer internally, any fractional portion of the value is lost and it will be difficult to perform calculations without losing significant information. Thus we should use a floating point representation during calculations. Double precision floating point provides the greatest precision, but takes more processor time and memory. Single precision floating point produces nearly the same quality of samples, but consumes considerably less memory and processor time.

Chapter 3

From Equation to Code

Both periodic signals and digital signal generation are well defined mathematically and the necessary equations can be found in any DSP text. What is not always well described in those texts, and may at first seem incomprehensible, is how to convert those equations into a useful synthesizer program. However, as you will see, the equivalent program functions are usually short and simple. The complexity in a synthesis system is in the combinations of the basic functions (architecture), not the functions themselves. For sound generation functions, a few general rules for conversion can be developed that will work in almost all situations.

Good programming practice dictates that we write code that is clear and obvious, test for valid memory locations before writing to variables, and test for valid ranges of values during execution of the program. However, if we are not careful, following these practices can add an excessive amount of execution time to the program. Consider a synthesizer program to be constructed as two loops, an outer loop and an inner loop. The outer loop performs setup and initialization for each sound, while the inner loop generates the samples for the sound.

```
initialize for sound generation
for each sound
    initialize values for this sound
    for each sample
        generate and store the next sample
```

At a sample rate of *SR* samples per second, the inner loop will be executed *SR* times for each second of each sound. Suppose we want to play *N* sounds with an average duration of one-half second each.

The outer loop is executed N times, but the inner loop is executed $N \cdot (SR/2)$ times. The inner loop is obviously more critical to the execution speed of the program, and moving even a few instructions from the inner loop to the outer loop can significantly improve the program's execution speed. In general, we should precalculate as many values as possible and perform any range testing or other validation before executing the inner loop.

Most algebraic equations can be directly converted into a computer program statement. In general, we replace the variables in the equations with program variables and convert the operators into the program language equivalents. For some equations, especially periodic functions and series, we must write several program statements to implement the equation.

The first implementation step is to define the program variables that represent the variables in the equation. By convention, mathematicians use single letter variable names such as x and y to represent variable quantities. Many signal processing equations use x to represent time and and y to represent amplitude. However, when the equations represent processing an input signal, x represents the input and y represents the output, both of which are amplitude values. When writing a computer program, we are applying the equation to a specific case and can use names or abbreviations such as *amplitude, sample* and *duration* instead of x and y. Using the longer names will make the program easier to understand.

When defining variables we need to select an appropriate data type. Obviously, we use floating point types (*float, double*) when a calculation can produce a real value, and integer types (*short, int, long*) when only integer values are needed. The built-in type names are not always the best choice, however. When we see a variable of type *float* we don't immediately know if the variable refers to amplitude, time, or something else. For key data types it is helpful to define aliases for the types. For example, we could use *PhaseValue* for a signal phase and *AmpValue* for a sample amplitude rather than declaring the variables as *float*. Using aliases for types makes it easier to change from one internal representation to another. For example, if we later decide to use double precision instead of single precision floating point types for amplitude values, we only need to change the code where the alias is defined. Not all programming languages allow aliases for data types, but the C++ language used for the examples in the book provides several ways to do this.

We can replace the arithmentic operators for addition, subtraction, multiplication and division with the programming language equivalent (+ - * /). Some operators used in the equations may not be defined by the programming language, but are usually available as a library function. For example, exponentiation of the form $y=a^n$ is implemented in C++ as *y=pow(a,n)*. Likewise, trigonometric functions and logarithms convert into library function calls.

The equal sign (=) in an equation represents equality, but in C++ the '=' operator represents assignment, while the '==' is used for comparison. Not all equal signs in the equation represent assignment, and the appropriate C++ operator must be selected. When '=' is used in an equation to show that a value is the result of a function or calculation, we use the assignment operator in C++.

Some symbols used in mathematics don't have a direct equivalent in C++ and we must write a series of statements to implement them. Equations using summation are very common in signal processing.

$$y = \sum_{n=0}^{100} f(n) \tag{3.1}$$

Summation is implemented by a loop that repeatedly calls the function *f* with the limits used to set the values for the loop condition.

```
for (n = 0; n <= 100; n++)
    y = f(n);
```

We will sometimes see a limit in an equation expressed as *N-1*. In that case we can use the less-than operator and compare against *N* rather than perform the subtraction of 1 from *N* on every iteration.

We also implement a series using a program loop. For example, consider a simple arithmetic series.

$$y = n \cdot x, n = 0...m \tag{3.2}$$

This equation can be implemented as a program loop that repeatedly multiplies the value of *x*.

```
for (n = 0; n <= m; n++)
    y = n*x;
```

When possible, we should convert a series to the equivalent recursive form. The recursive form will almost always produce a more efficient program. Conversion to the recursive form is done by expanding the series, regrouping the terms, and substituting a group with a prior value.

$$y_0 = 0$$

$$y_1 = x$$

$$y_2 = x + x$$

$$y_3 = x + x + x$$

$$y_3 = x + (x + x) = x + y_2$$

$$y_n = x + y_{n-1} \tag{3.3}$$

We can now implement the series using the faster add operator in place of multiplication.

```
y=0;
for (n = 1; n <= m; n++)
    y += x
```

An exponential series is implemented in a similar manner using exponentiation in a loop.

$$y = x^n, n = 0...m \tag{3.4}$$

In C++, we use the *pow* function for exponentiation.

```
for (n = 0; n <= m; n++)
    y = pow(x,n);
```

An exponential series can also be converted to a recursive form.

$$y_0 = 1$$

$$y_1 = x$$

$$y_2 = x \cdot x$$

$$y_3 = x \cdot (x \cdot x) = x \cdot y_2$$

$$y_n = x \cdot y_{n-1} \tag{3.5}$$

We can now implement the loop using multiplication in place of the exponential function (*pow*).

```
y = 1;
for (n = 1; n <= m; n++)
    y *= x;
```

This expansion only works if x is constant throughout the loop and n is an integer value. By applying the rules for exponents we can make the same expansion work for any real n as well. We can represent any real value of n as a product of an integer value k and a real number j such that $n=k \cdot j$. For example, if $n=0.5$ we could use $k=10$ and $j=0.05$. From the laws for exponents, we know that:

$$x^{k \cdot j} = \left(x^j \right)^k$$

We can substitute x^j for x and k for n in equation (3.4) and the recursive form will be valid.

In some cases we use the current value of the series immediately, but in many cases we need to store the entire series and will declare an array for that purpose. The subscript on the variable in the equation becomes a subscript on the program array variable.

$$y_n = ax_n + bx_{n-1} \tag{3.6}$$

This is easily converted to a program, but we must check the boundaries of the subscript carefully. When used in a computer program, the subscript $n-1$ is only valid for $n > 0$ and we must treat $n=0$ as a special case. Rather than testing n on each iteration of the loop, we place code outside the loop and then begin the loop at $n=1$.

```
y[0] = a * x[0];
for (n = 1; n < m; n++)
    y[n] = (a * x[n]) + (b * x[n-1]);
```

The parentheses in the program are not necessary, but they are often included to make the programmer's intent clear. Relying on the default order of evaluation may make for a more compact program, but tends to lead to programming errors.

There is one significant difference between the mathematical representation of sound and the software implementation that can produce unexpected errors in the program output. The math assumes an infinite precision in the representation of numbers while a computer program is always limited to a finite number of bits to represent a number. The limited precision of a computer data type can result in one of three errors: overflow, underflow, and round-off.

Overflow and underflow occur when the magnitude of a value exceeds the maximum or minimum value for the computer data type. Using a signed 16-bit integer data type, values outside the range ±32,767 will fold over to a value inside that range. In other words, integer calculations are always performed "modulo the word size." When overflow happens on a sample value, the value does not simply clip to a limit value. Adding 2 to 32,767 (0x7fff) produces -32,767 (0x8001) and results in severe distortion of the waveform.

Round-off occurs when the fractional portion of the value cannot be represented exactly. In the case of an integer data type, we cannot represent the fractional portion at all. Thus 10/3 produces a value of 3, not 3.33333… A naïve programmer will think that using a floating point data type will solve the problem. However, floating point representation also has a limited number of bits to store the fractional value, and at some point the value must be truncated.

Round-off can result in an incorrect value when we use iteration to calculate a sum or product. If the increment value cannot be precisely represented, it will either be rounded to the nearest available value, or simply truncated. In either case, the iterative operation may not end on the final value. In other words, repeatedly summing the increment may not produce the same value as multiplying the increment by a count. Usually the error is so small that it can be safely ignored. But when we iterate over several thousand samples, the error may accumulate and produce audible distortion.

Failure to consider the potential overflow, underflow, and round-off error can result in a program that produces distorted sound or no sound at all. This is an unavoidable issue, but there are ways to minimize the problem, and in some cases eliminate it.

Often we can avoid or reduce numerical errors by rearranging the order of operators. For example, calculating ten percent of 12345 using 16-bit integers must be done in a specific order to produce a usable result. We cannot use 12345*(10/100) since the division will truncate to 0. We could multiply first then divide with (12345*10)/100 but the intermediate product (123,450) would exceed the maximum value for a 16-bit integer. We can, however, use (12345/100)*10 and get a result. The result will lose two digits of precision, but at least we have a usable value (1230), perhaps even close enough for what we need to do.

Another common method of avoiding overflow and underflow is to normalize the values. Normalization is the process of scaling values to a convenient range, performing the calculations, and then rescaling them to the desired range. For example, by normalizing the range of a variable to [-1,+1] we can multiply values together as many times as we want without exceeding the normalized range. We still need to be careful when adding, but multiplication is far more likely to produce overflow than addition. Multiplying two n-bit words will potentially require $2n$ bits to represent the product. Adding two n-bit words will never require more than $n+1$ bits to represent the sum. Normalization does not avoid round-off error, however.

One way to eliminate round-off error is to force the value to a known value whenever possible. If we know that after n iterations a calculation should end with the value 100, we can explicitly set the value to 100 at the end of the loop. We can also rearrange the order of operations as shown above with integers. This may require thinking of a value as a ratio rather than a single constant. For example, a ratio such as 2/3 represents a repeating fraction. We can multiply by 0.6667 and possibly lose precision, or, multiply by 2 and then divide by 3 and get a more accurate result at the cost of one additional arithmetic operation.

The additional processing time required for floating point can also be a potential problem. As a rule, integer calculations are faster than floating point, and with the large number of calculations that must be made to produce sound, using integers can result in a large performance gain. Where appropriate, or when needed for performance reasons, we can use a *fixed point* representation.

Technically, all integers are fixed point representations, but here we mean a specific use of integers to represent fractional quantities. Fixed point representation uses an integer data type with each value scaled by some power of two. The most significant bits represent the integer part and the least significant bits represent the fractional part. We can treat the values as integers and perform integer operations so long as we remember to shift the result by an appropriate amount. For example, a 16 by 16 multiply produces a 32-bit result. For a 16-bit fixed point system, we would need to produce a 32-bit product and then extract the 16 bits containing the appropriately scaled result.

The example in Figure 5 shows adding 123.45 and 67.89 using fixed point representation. The fixed point values are obtained by multiplying each number by 2^{16} and then adding them as integers. Note that the final result has a slight error, but when rounded to two significant digits, is the same value as the sum of the real numbers.

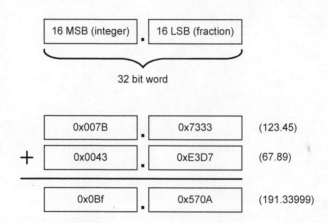

Figure 5 - Fixed Point Addition

Fixed point multiplication is shown in Figure 6. We first multiply each half of the number separately to avoid overflow, then sum the results with the appropriate shift value so that the binary point is aligned. As with addition, the result has a slight round-off error, but is accurate to three significant digits.

Most 32-bit processors can produce a 64-bit result in a register pair. For example, on the Intel Pentium® processor, the result of a 32-bit multiply is a 64-bit value in the AX,DX register pair. Adding AX, shifted right by 16, with DX, shifted left by 16, produces the 32-bit result. Thus only one multiply, two shifts and one add, all performed in registers, are needed to perform the fixed point multiply.

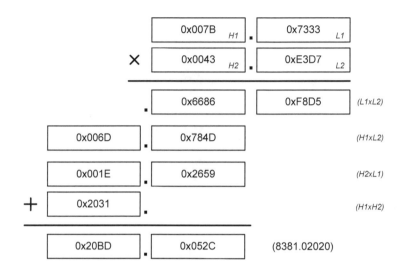

Figure 6 - Fixed Point Multiply

Although efficient, fixed point programming can be complicated and error prone. The programmer must be aware of when the results must be shifted and by how much, and must also be careful about overflow during intermediate calculations. The resulting code can become cluttered and difficult to understand. For most applications, processor speeds are now sufficiently fast that even a floating point representation can work in real-time. A good rule of programming is, "*FIRST* make it work, *THEN* make it work fast." After all, a slow system that produces correct output is worth far more than a system that produces errors very quickly. Thus the examples in this book will use a floating point representation for amplitude, frequency, and phase. If better performance is needed, we can convert the floating point calculations to fixed point in time critical areas.

BasicSynth Library

The defined types *PhsAccum, FrqValue* and *AmpValue* are used whenever the code must refer to a signal phase, frequency or amplitude, respectively. The default for these types are *double, float* and *float*. To change the phase, frequency or amplitude representation, only these definitions need to be altered. The *SampleValue* type is defined appropriately for the size of output samples. Constants for commonly used values such as π and 2π are also defined.

Some values are used globally in the synthesizer system and it is useful to put these together into a single global object for reference. The *SynthConfig* class is used for this purpose. The *sampleRate* member is used to hold the sample rate, default 44100. The *sampleScale* value is used to convert an *AmpValue* to the appropriate range for output samples (*SampleValue*) and is 32767.0 for signed 16-bit output. The other member variables will be described in the appropriate chapters.

Thie *SynthConfig* class definition must be included in all programs that use the *BasicSynth* library and a single global instance of the class named *synthParams* must be defined somewhere in the program. The library defines an instance of this class so that when the library is linked with the main program, the necessary object is automatically available. The object will be initialized in its constructor to reasonable default values. It can also be initialized by calling either the *Init* member function or the global *InitSynthesizer* function if a different sample rate is desired.

Files:

```
Include/SynthDefs.h
Src/Common/Global.cpp
```

Chapter 4

Output File Format

Before we generate any samples, we need to determine the format for the output file that will be produced. If we are developing the software for personal use, we can define a private format that meets the minimum requirements of our system. However, if we use a standard format, the output of the program can be used by other sound processing and playback systems. Compatibility with other systems allows us to leverage the abilities of those systems and thus automatically gain features for our own system without having to write additional code.

Several standard sound file formats are widely used. The MP3 format is often used for sound files on the Internet as well as video and audio players. However, MP3 is a compressed format that requires additional processing, cannot be sent directly to many sound devices, and also loses some fidelity due to compression. The WMF format is similar to MP3. Another standard format is the WAVE file format. This format can be used for direct playback or for production of audio CDs, and it can also be converted to MP3, WMF and other formats using a stand-alone utility program. Any off-the-shelf software should be able to read WAVE files as well. Most important, the samples are in raw form without any compression or equalization required. We can read, process, and write the files as many times as desired without loss of fidelity.

The WAVE file format allows specification of the sampling rate, sample size, and number of channels. However, these values are ultimately controlled by the sound output device and it is best to produce WAVE files that already meet the requirements for direct playback. For most computer sound output devices, and CD audio, the standard sampling rate is 44,100Hz; samples are sixteen bit signed integers, with two channels (stereo). Newer computers also support twenty-four bit samples at rates up to 192kHz. In either case, we can use any internal format as long as the output is converted to the standard before writing values to the output file or device.

WAVE File Format

A WAVE file is a type of RIFF file.[3] The RIFF specification defines the file as a set of nested "chunks" of data. Each chunk begins with an 8-byte chunk header. The chunk header identifies the chunk type with a 4-character ID followed by the chunk size as a 4-byte binary value in little-endian format. Figure 7 shows the structure of a typical WAVE file. Each gray box represents a chunk header containing the chunk ID along with the size of the chunk. The white boxes represent the chunk data, which includes any nested chunks.

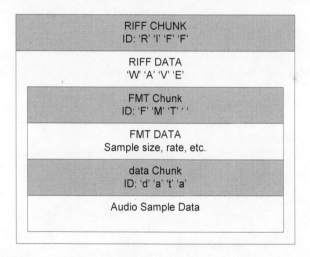

Figure 7 - WAVE File Structure

A WAVE file can contain other chunk types in addition to the two shown here. A WAVE file can contain multiple sets of samples along with cue information, description, etc. In addition, the chunks are not required to be in the order shown. However, most WAVE files

---

[3] RIFF stands for *Resource Interchange File Format*.

contain only two data chunks, one containing format information and one containing sample data, and those chunks are located first in the file. This allows us to create a simplified representation of a WAVE file. Doing so will make the code specific to one form of file, but is sufficient for the synthesizer we will develop, is simple to program, and is very fast to save or load. The file is readable by other sound processing systems without any problems.

Taking this approach, we can consider the WAVE file as a file with a fixed length header and variable length block of samples. To create a WAVE file, we fill in a header, write it to the file, then write the sample data, converting to the file sample representation if needed. Each sample is one sixteen bit word per channel. For stereo, the sample for the left channel is written followed immediately by the sample for the right channel. In other words, the two channels are interlaced in the file. The following code shows a general purpose WAVE file write function in C++. Note that this code is for a little-endian processor. For big-endian processors, the byte order must be swapped before writing to disk.

```
struct WavHDR {
    uint8  riffId[4];    // 'RIFF' chunk
    uint32 riffSize;     // filesize - 8
    uint8  waveType[4];  // 'WAVE' type of file
    uint8  fmtId[4];     // 'fmt ' format chunk
    uint32 fmtSize;      // format chunk size (16)
    uint16 fmtCode;      // 1 = PCM
    uint16 channels;     // 1 = mono, 2 = stereo
    uint32 sampleRate;   // 44100
    uint32 avgbps;       // samplerate * align
    uint16 align;        // (channels*bits)/8;
    uint16 bits;         // bits per sample (16)
    uint8  waveId[4];    // 'data' chunk
    uint32 waveSize;     // size of sample data
};

void WriteWaveFile(int16 *sampleBuffer,
    uint32 sampleTotal,
    int channels)
{
// two bytes per value and one value per channel
    uint32 byteTotal = sampleTotal * 2 * channels;
```

```
WavHDR wh;
wh.riffId[0] = 'R';
wh.riffId[1] = 'I';
wh.riffId[2] = 'F';
wh.riffId[3] = 'F';
wh.riffSize = byteTotal + sizeof(wh) - 8;
wh.waveType[0] = 'W';
wh.waveType[1] = 'A';
wh.waveType[2] = 'V';
wh.waveType[3] = 'E';
wh.fmtId[0] = 'f';
wh.fmtId[1] = 'm';
wh.fmtId[2] = 't';
wh.fmtId[3] = ' ';
wh.fmtSize = 16;
wh.fmtCode = 1;
wh.channels = (uint16) channels;
wh.sampleRate = 44100;
wh.bits = 16;
wh.align = (wh.channels * wh.bits) / 8;
wh.avgbps = (wh.sampleRate * wh.align);
wh.waveId[0] = 'd';
wh.waveId[1] = 'a';
wh.waveId[2] = 't';
wh.waveId[3] = 'a';
wh.waveSize = byteTotal;

FILE *f = fopen("out.wav", "wb");
fwrite(&wh, 1, sizeof(wh), f);
fwrite(sampleBuffer,2*channels,sampleTotal,f);
fclose(f);
}
```

The *WriteWaveFile* function requires the entire sample buffer to be passed in as an argument. For a minimal program that generates sound into a memory buffer, this will work fine. For a more general WAVE file output function we would like to be able to pass samples in as they are generated without having to store the entire sound file in memory. For the *BasicSynth* library, the function shown above is implemented as a class that incorporates an internal buffer and provides methods for adding samples to that buffer.

When reading a WAVE file we read each chunk header, check the id, type and information fields to make sure it is a file we can process, allocate a buffer, then read the chunk data into the buffer. Reading a WAVE file containing more than one sample data chunk, or other types of chunks, involves reading a chunk header and then either descending into the chunk, ascending out of the current chunk, reading the chunk data, or stepping over the chunk as appropriate. The code for reading wave files is shown in a later chapter.

BasicSynth Library Classes

The *BasicSynth* library contains classes to read and write files in WAVE format. Three WAVE file classes are defined, one that manages the sample buffer (*WaveOutBuf*), one to manage file output (*WaveOut*), and one to load wave files (*WaveFileIn*). The file output class inherits from the buffer class.

These classes do not use the standard C library FILE type for I/O. Since the *WaveFile* class contains its own internal buffer, the buffering provided by the standard library is redundant. The *FileWriteUnBuf* class will perform direct writes using the operating system API. Likewise, the file input operations rely on the *FileReadBuf* class in place of the standard file I/O functions.

Files:

```
Include/WaveFile.h
Include/SynthFile.h
Src/Common/WaveFile.cpp
Src/Common/SynthFile.cpp
```

Chapter 5

Signal Generator

The most straightforward method of sound generation in software is to evaluate a periodic function for each sample time. A periodic function is any function that repeats at a constant interval, called the period. Consider the circle in the figure below. Starting at the 3:00 position and then sweeping around the circle counter-clockwise, we make a complete cycle in 2π radians. If we plot the points on the circumference at equally spaced time intervals we produce a waveform as shown in Figure 8.

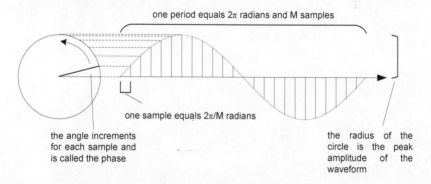

one period equals 2π radians and M samples

one sample equals $2\pi/M$ radians

the angle increments for each sample and is called the phase

the radius of the circle is the peak amplitude of the waveform

Figure 8 - Periodic Function

To generate a signal we need to know the number of samples in one period and the phase increment for one sample time. The period is the time it takes for the waveform to repeat and is the reciprocal of the frequency ($1/f$). In other words, a frequency of 100Hz repeats every $1/100$ second. Multiplying the sample rate (f_s) by the time of one period ($1/f$) will give us the samples per period. The period is equal to 2π radians, thus the phase increment for one sample (φ) is 2π divided by the number of samples in one period.

$$\varphi = \frac{2\pi}{f_s / f} \tag{5.1}$$

The amplitude for any given sample is the amplitude value of the phase at that point in time multiplied by the radius of the circle. In other words, the amplitude is the sine of the phase angle and we can also derive the phase increment from the sine function.

$$s_n = A_n \cdot \sin \theta_n \tag{5.2}$$

The value s_n is the nth sample, A_n the peak amplitude (volume) at sample n, and θ_n the phase at sample n. To calculate θ_n for any sample n, we must multiply the phase increment for one sample time by the sample number.

$$\theta_n = \varphi \cdot n \tag{5.3}$$

To calculate φ, we need to determine the radians for one sample time at a given frequency. As there are 2π radians per period, we multiply the frequency by 2π to get the radians per second. The time of one sample is the reciprocal of the sample rate, thus the phase increment for one sample time is the radians per second divided by the sample rate.

$$t = \frac{1}{f_s} \tag{5.4}$$

$$\omega = 2\pi f \tag{5.5}$$

$$\varphi = \omega \cdot t = \frac{2\pi f}{f_s} = \frac{2\pi}{f_s} \cdot f \tag{5.6}$$

The calculation for ω (5.5) is used extensively in signal processing equations. It represents the frequency of the signal as radians per second and is called the *angular frequency*.

A closer examination of (5.6) can show us why the frequency f must be less than 1/2 the sample rate (the Nyquist limit). Consider the frequency as a fraction of the sampling rate (x):

$$\varphi = \frac{2\pi}{f_s} \cdot \frac{f_s}{x} = \frac{2\pi}{x} \qquad (5.7)$$

For any value of x less than 2, the phase increment will be greater than π. Consequently, the resulting waveform will have fewer than two values for each period and will produce an incorrect frequency as shown in Figure 9.

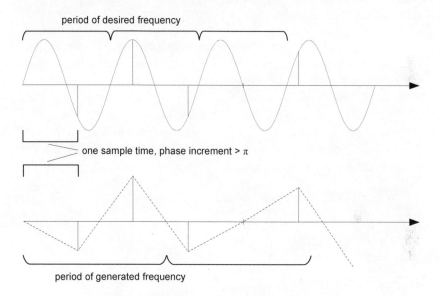

period of desired frequency

one sample time, phase increment > π

period of generated frequency

Figure 9 - Alias Frequency

The resulting frequency is less than the expected frequency and is called an *alias* frequency. Because the frequency decreases rather than increases as the phase increment increases beyond π, this phenomenon is also called *foldover*.

Equation (5.1) is obviously equivalent to (5.6) and either version can be used to produce the program. The third form of (5.6) is generally preferred for programming purposes since the value of $2\pi/f_s$ is constant during the program's execution. We can calculate that ratio once at initialization and avoid the calculation on each frequency change.

Substituting for θ_n in the original equation produces:

$$s_n = A_n \cdot \sin(\varphi \cdot n) = A_n \cdot \sin(\frac{2\pi}{f_s} \cdot f \cdot n) \qquad (5.8)$$

Equation (5.8) is easily implemented as a counted program loop:

```
frqRad = twoPI / sampleRate;
totalSamples = duration * sampleRate;
for (n = 0; n < totalSamples; n++)
   sample[n] = volume * sin(frqRad*frequency*n);
```

The calculation of the phase increment (*frqRad* * *frequency*) is loop invariant, and we can move that calculation out of the loop to improve performance. Furthermore, the product of the phase increment and *n* is a series that we can replace with repeated summation. Finally, although the *sin* function will automatically fold the phase to the range of [0,2π], we should prevent the phase from going out of range by testing after each increment. Applying these changes produces the basic program for sound generation.

```
frqRad = twoPI / sampleRate;
phaseIncr = frqRad * frequency;
phase = 0;
volume = 1;
totalSamples = duration * sampleRate;

for (n = 0; n < totalSamples; n++) {
   sample[n] = volume * sin(phase);
   phase += phaseIncr;
   if (phase >= twoPI)
      phase -= twoPI;
}
```

To complete the implementation, we need to allocate a buffer large enough to hold the samples and write the buffer to a WAVE file after calculating the sample values.

The standard WAVE format uses signed 16-bit integers to represent each sample and we need to scale the peak output amplitude to the range of $\pm 2^{15}-1$ ($\pm 32,767$). The *sin* function returns a value in the range [-1,+1] and we will usually specify the volume as a value in the range of [0,1] to keep all samples normalized to [-1,+1] during intermediate calculations. The final sample must be scaled at some point to the output sample size, usually when writing the sample to the output file buffer.

The *duration* value is specified in seconds and must be multiplied by the sample rate to determine the number of samples. Duration can alternatively be specified directly as number of samples. A music program will need to convert rhythm values into seconds (or samples) based on the desired tempo. For example, a quarter note at 60 beats per minute has a duration of one second, or 44,100 samples. In the case where duration values are the result of recording keyboard key on/off events, the duration is already a time value, but may need to be converted to seconds of duration in order to easily calculate the number of samples.

The *frequency* variable is in Hz. Musicians express frequency as a pitch or possibly as a number representing a key on a keyboard. For an equal-tempered scale, the frequency can be calculated directly from the pitch or key number. Each half-step between notes in the musical scale represents a frequency ratio of $2^{1/12}$ (~1.059). Given a known pitch of frequency f_0 and the number of half-steps between pitches h, the frequency of any pitch is $(f_0 \cdot 2^{h/12})$. To save processing time, the frequency values for the standard musical scale are usually calculated during program initialization and stored in a table. The pitch can then be quickly converted into frequency by using the pitch value as an index into the frequency table.

We can replace the *sin* function with any periodic function that returns an amplitude for a given phase. Thus this small piece of code can be used to produce a very wide range of sounds. Functionally it is the software equivalent of an oscillator, the basic building block of almost all synthesizers. In a later chapter we will develop this basic oscillator into a C++ class that is capable of producing a variety of waveforms.

Example Program

The *Example01* directory contains a complete program that produces one second of sound at middle C and writes the output to a wave file. The duration and pitch can be changed by supplying command line arguments. The example oscillator code uses the *sampleRate* and *frqRad* members of the global parameters object to calculate phase. These values are set automatically when the *synthParams* object is initialized. If desired, the *Init* method can be called directly to change the sample rate. The *synthParams* object also contains a table of frequencies for the standard musical pitches. The table is initialized such that middle C has an index of 48. The *GetFrequency* method converts a pitch number to frequency using the table. Alternate tuning systems can be used by filling the *tuning[]* array with the appropriate frequency values.

BasicSynth Library

The example program implements the oscillator code inline for simplicity. The oscillator described in this chapter is also implemented by the *GenWave* class. *GenWave* defines methods to set the frequency of the oscillator, reset the oscillator phase, and retrieve the next sample. This *GenWave* class is the base class for all other oscillators described in this book. *GenWave* inherits from an abstract base class named *GenUnit* that defines generic methods required by all signal generators. The name is a variation of "unit generator," the term commonly used in software synthesis systems to indicate anything that can produce an output signal.

Files:
```
Include/SynthDefs.h
Include/GenWave.h
Src/Common/Global.cpp
```

Chapter 6

Envelope Generators

In the example code shown above, volume is constant for the duration of the sound. However, musical instruments make sounds that vary in volume over the duration of the sound, and synthesized sounds do the same. A typical sound has an initial rise time (attack), a steady state portion (sustain), and a final segment that decays to silence (release) as shown in Figure 10.

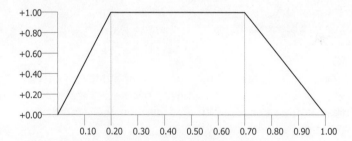

Figure 10 - Amplitude Envelope

The graph shows the peak amplitude of the signal over time. The peak amplitude has both positive and negative values, and if we were to graph the entire signal and connect the peak amplitude values, the resulting line would form a border, or *envelope* around the sound. Since our waveform values are both positive and negative, we only need to calculate the positive side of the envelope and then multiply the envelope values by the waveform values.

The final decay segment is called the release. The term release is adopted from analog synthesizers where the envelope generator is triggered when a key on the keyboard is pressed. When the key is released, the final decay begins. For some sounds, there is no sustain portion. Plucking a string, striking a metal plate or wooden bowl produces an envelope with only attack and decay portions. The decay begins at the end of the attack, whether or not the key has been released. In those cases, the release segment is more appropriately called the decay, but the term release is used generally for the final decay section even when there is no sustain portion to the envelope.

Applying an amplitude envelope to the signal can be achieved if we set the *volume* value with a series of line segments that calculate the amplitude based on the beginning and ending values over the duration of a segment. We can represent an envelope attack or decay with the equation for a line.

$$y = a \cdot x + b \tag{6.1}$$

To implement equation (6.1) as a program, we first need to decide what the variables represent. The obvious association is that y represents amplitude and x represents time. The range of values for x is $[0,d]$ where d is the total duration of the segment in samples. The range for y is $[A_{start}, A_{end}]$ where A is the amplitude. The starting amplitude is when $x=0$, thus:

$$y = a \cdot 0 + b = b$$

In other words, b must be the starting amplitude value (A_{start}). If we normalize our envelope to $[0,1]$, then b becomes 0 and we can ignore it. When x is equal to the duration of the segment, y must be at its end value and thus the value of a is:

$$1 = a \cdot x$$

$$a = 1/x \tag{6.2}$$

If we have a starting value other than zero, or an ending value other than 1, we could do the same thing and get:

$$y_{end} = a \cdot x + y_{start}$$

$$y_{end} - y_{start} = a \cdot x$$

$$a = (y_{end} - y_{start})/x \tag{6.3}$$

In other words, we calculate a as the range of the segment divided by the number of samples and then multiply the sample number by a to get each amplitude value.

```
segSamples = segDuration * sampleRate;
amp = (ampEnd - ampStart) / segSamples;

for (n = 0; n < segSamples; n++)
   volume = (n * amp) + ampStart;
```

If we convert equation (6.1) to the recursive form we can replace the multiplication with incremental addition.

To program the envelope generator we convert the duration of the attack and decay times into number of equivalent samples, and then calculate the increment value at the beginning of the respective segments. For each sample, we multiply the amplitude by the waveform value for the sample to produce the output value. Combining the amplitude envelope with the oscillator from the previous chapter produces the following program.

```
phaseIncr = frqRad * frequency;
phase = 0;
totalSamples = duration * sampleRate;
attackTime = attackRate * sampleRate;
decayTime = decayRate * sampleRate;
decayStart = totalSamples - decayTime;
if (attackTime > 0)
   envInc = peakAmp / attackTime;
volume = 0;

for (n = 0; n < totalSamples; n++) {
   if (n < attackTime || n > decayStart)
      volume += envInc;
   else if (n == attackTime)
      volume = peakAmp;
   else if (n == decayStart)
      envInc = -volume / decayTime;
   sample[n] = volume * sin(phase);
   if ((phase += phaseIncr) >= twoPI)
      phase -= twoPI;
}
```

This code executes quickly and can be easily extended to include additional envelope segments. Code should be added to insure the combined attack and decay times do not equal or exceed the total duration. Otherwise, the attack time will be greater than or equal to the decay start time and the statement that calculates the decay segment decrement will never execute.

The increment of *volume* is performed before the sample is calculated, skipping over the starting volume value. Assume we have 100 samples in the attack segment and a *peakAmp* value of 1. The *envInc* value is 1/100=0.01. If we increment before calculating the sample, *volume* will be 0.01 at n=0 and 1 at n=99. If we increment after calculating the sample, the volume will be 0 at n=0 and 0.99 at n=99. Since we are using a starting volume value of 0, we can skip the start value without any noticeable difference in sound and end precisely on the final value at the end of the attack segment. However, it may be important to use both the initial and final values if an envelope generator segment begins or ends with values other than 0 and 1. To handle either case, the code explicitly sets the volume to the peak value at the end of the attack segment to insure we reach the peak value. Doing so also eliminates any accumulated round-off error in the volume level at the end of the attack segment. However, the code uses the current volume level to calculate the decay decrement in case the peak level is not reached.

The data type used to calculate the attack and decay times sets a limit on the duration of any segment. A 16-bit integer and 44,1000Hz sampling rate would only allow durations up to 0.74 seconds. We should use a 32-bit integer or a floating point data type to allow for longer durations.

For longer durations, the step between amplitude values can be smaller than the minimum change in amplitude. For example, at a sampling rate of 44,100Hz and a duration of 0.77 seconds, the increment between amplitude values would be $1/(44100*0.77) = 0.000029449$. When scaled to a 16-bit output range, the resulting amplitude change is 0.9649, less than one bit in the output sample. As a result, for durations longer than 0.77 seconds, we are calculating the amplitude on every sample even though the result of the calculation makes no difference to the final amplitude. We can gain a slight performance improvement by only calculating a new amplitude every n samples with n chosen as the point where we have a minimum change in output. For practical music synthesis systems, envelope segments are often relatively short and sub-dividing the segment will not produce a significant performance improvement. A slower computer system that needs to reduce the number of calculations can take advantage of this fact and only calculate envelope values every 10 samples or so.

Curved Segments

A linear change in amplitude does not produce a linear change in perceived loudness. In order to double the loudness of a sound, we need to double the power of the sound, and that requires an exponential increase in amplitude. Thus synthesis systems typically include envelope generators that produce curved segments in place of straight lines. Curved segments often have a more natural sound, although the difference can be subtle and almost imperceptible when the attack or decay times are very short. Linear segments are faster to calculate and will work fine in many cases, but, if desired, we can replace the line function with an exponential function to produce curved envelope segments. The equation to produce an exponential curve is:

$$y_n = a \cdot (x_n)^b + c \qquad\qquad (6.4)$$

As above, the value for y represents the amplitude, and x represents time. We would like to normalize y to the range of $[0,1]$ such that $(x_0)^b = 0$ and $(x_n)^b = 1$. We know that $0^b = 0$ and $1^b = 1$ for any value of b, and thus x should vary over the interval of $[0,1]$. Since x represents time, the value of x is $n \cdot 1/d$ where d is the duration in samples. We can generate the exponential curve as an incremental calculation of x which is then raised to some power b.

If we want to vary the amplitude over some other range, we calculate the range and offset as:

$$a = (y_{\text{end}} - y_{\text{start}}) / n \qquad\qquad (6.5)$$

$$c = y_{\text{start}} \qquad\qquad (6.6)$$

Assuming that the envelope begins and ends on 0, we can implement the envelope as shown in the following program.

```
range = peakAmp / totalSamples;
offset = 0;
expIncr = 1 / attackTime;
expX = 0;
expB = 2;

for (n = 0; n < totalSamples; n++) {
    if (n < attackTime || n > decayStart) {
        volume = range * pow(expX, expB);
        expX += expIncr;
    } else if (n == decayStart) {
        expIncr = -1 / decayTime;
        expX = 1;
    }
    sample[n] = volume * sin(phase);
    if ((phase += phaseIncr) >= twoPI)
        phase -= twoPI;
}
```

Calculation of *phase*, *attackTime* and *decayTime* is the same as for the linear segment example. Tests for zero length segments also need to be included. This code will produce an envelope similar to that shown in Figure 11.

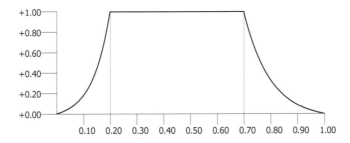

Figure 11 - Exponential Envelope (b > 1)

The value of *b* controls the depth of the curve. For values greater than 1, the curve becomes increasingly steeper. For values between 0 and 1, the curve changes to a logarithmic curve, similar to that shown in Figure 12. A logarithmic amplitude curve produces a sharper attack but with a smoother transition to the final value. Note that when *b*=1 the output is a straight line, and we could use the same code for both linear and curved segments.

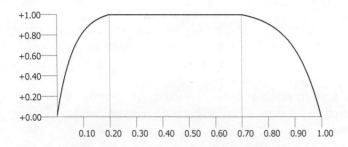

Figure 12 - Logarithmic Envelope (0 < b < 1)

This implementation requires calling the exponential function on every sample, a time consuming operation. If we limited the value of *b* to small integers, such as 2 or 3, we could replace the call to the exponential function with a multiply, but would lose considerable flexibility by doing so. To get the best performance while retaining the ability to vary the curve shape, we should remove the exponential function and replace it with an iterative calculation. Unfortunately, we cannot easily convert equation (6.4) into the recursive form. However, we can use a different form of the exponential equation:

$$y = a \cdot b^n + c, \ n=0...k \tag{6.7}$$

For now, we can set $a=1$ and $c=0$, and produce:

$$y = b^n, n=0...k$$

$$y_n = b^n \cdot y_{n-1}$$

$$y_k = b^k \cdot y_0$$

$$y_k / y_0 = b^k$$

$$b = (y_k / y_0)^{1/k} \tag{6.8}$$

If wet set *k* to the number of samples to generate, we now have an iterative solution. However, we no longer have a curve that ranges from [0,1] since at $n=0$, the value of $y=1$. We also have a problem if we want the minimum value $y_0=0$ since we can't divide by 0. We can get around these problems if we set *c* to something other than 0.

$$y = b^n + c, n=1...k$$

$$y = c, n=0$$

$$b = ((y_k + c) / c)^{1/k} \qquad\qquad (6.9)$$

If the value of y when $n=0$ is set equal to c, we can set c to any value greater than 0 and then produce a volume range of [0,1] by subtracting c from the volume value. Increasing the value of c will change the y intercept, move the curve left along the x axis and produce an increasing flatness to the curve, just as we did earlier by varying the exponent. Thus we have the same capability as before, but can now implement the generator in the recursive form.

We can now implement the exponential volume curve by multiplying the last amplitude value with the value of b. We initialize b for the attack segment, and at the transition to the decay segment recalculate b to produce an inverse curve. Calculation of *phase*, *attackTime* and *decayTime* is the same as in the previous examples.

```
expMin = 0.2; // adjust to change curvature
expMul = pow((expMin+1)/expMin, 1/attackTime);
expNow = expMin;

for (n = 0; n < totalSamples; n++) {
    if (n < attackTime || n > decayStart) {
        expNow *= expMul;
        volume = (expNow - expMin) * peakAmp;
    } else if (n == attackTime) {
        volume = peakAmp;
    } else if (n == decayStart) {
        expNow = 1+expMin;
        expMul = pow(expMin/(1+expMin),1/decayTime));
    }
    sample[n] = volume * sin(phase);
    if ((phase += phaseIncr) >= twoPI)
        phase -= twoPI;
}
```

For a log curve, we must invert the curves and translate the value to a positive range. In other words, invert the exponent and subtract y from 1.

```
expMin = 0.2; // adjust to change curvature
expMul = pow(expMin/(expMin+1), 1/attackTime);
expNow = expMin+1;
```

```
for (n = 0; n < totalSamples; n++) {
   if (n < attackTime || n > decayStart) {
      expNow *= expMul;
      volume = (1 - (expNow - expMin)) * peakAmp;
   } else if (n == attackTime) {
      volume = peakAmp;
   } else if (n == decayStart) {
      expNow = expMin;
      expMul = pow((expMin+1)/expMin,1/decayTime));
   }
   sample[n] = volume * sin(phase);
   if ((phase += phaseIncr) >= twoPI)
      phase -= twoPI;
}
```

To vary a segment between two values other than 0 and *peakAmp* we must calculate a range and offset and then multiply the *volume* value accordingly.

```
range = (endAmp - startAmp);
offs = startAmp; // for attack
offs = endAmp;   // for decay
volume = ((expNow - expMin) * range) + offs;
```

State Machine Implementation

Rather than testing each time period against the attack and decay times, we can use a state machine to keep track of segments. In state 0, the envelope is in the attack ramp and the volume value is incremented for each sample. When the end of the segment is reached, we transition to state 1 and force the volume to the maximum value to compensate for any round-off error. We remain in state 1, returning the maximum value, until the decay start point is reached. At that point we transition to state 2 and begin subtracting the decay step from the volume. When we reach the end of the decay segment, we transition to state 3 and continue to return the final value.

```
envState = 0;
envCount = attackTime;
for (n = 0; n < totalSamples; n++) {
   switch (envState) {
   case 0:
      if (--envCount > 0) {
         volume += envInc;
      } else {
         volume = peakVolume;
         envCount = sustainTime;
         envState = 1;
      }
      break;
   case 1:
      if (--envCount < 0) {
         envCount = decayTime;
         envInc = volume/decayTime;
         envState = 2
      }
      break;
   case 2:
      if (--envCount > 0) {
         volume -= envInc;
      } else {
         volume = 0;
         envState = 3;
      }
      break;
   case 3:
      break;
   }
   sample[n] = volume * sin(phase);
   if ((phase += phaseIncr) >= twoPI)
      phase -= twoPI;
}
```

As with the previous example we can use an exponential curve instead of a line.

This implementation enters each state for at least one sample time. If that is not desired, we can add tests to each state and skip forward if the next state has a time of 0.

The state machine lends itself well to live performance systems. In a live performance system, we do not know the total duration of the sound in advance and must wait for the performer to release the note before beginning the decay segment. We can replace the count for the sustain segment with a test of a signal or flag that is set by a note off event. The state machine remains in state 1 until that notification is received.

```
case 1:
   if (noteOffSignaled) {
      envCount = decayTime;
      envInc = volume/decayTime;
      envState = 2;
   }
   break;
```

This technique can be useful for playback of a score as well. Because the envelope generator waits on an external signal before entering the release state, the score playback code, rather than the envelope generator, controls note duration. This allows us to specify the note duration without regard to the release time, a more intuitive way of thinking of note duration.

Variable Number of Segments

A basic envelope can be produced with only attack, sustain and release segments, but we often need to produce more complex envelopes. A typical sound has an initial peak that settles back to a slightly lower level similar to the envelope in Figure 13. This is the 'ADSR' envelope found on many synthesizers.

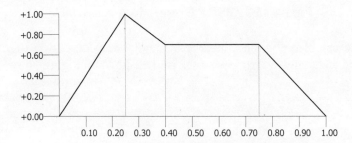

Figure 13 - ADSR Envelope

The envelope in the figure is shown with linear segments, but often exponential attack and decay are used.

Another very useful envelope is one with three attack segments. If the first attack segment has a constant level of 0, it will delay the onset of the sound.

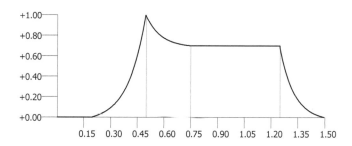

Figure 14 - A3SR - Delayed Attack

Alternatively, the third attack segment can slowly rise, producing a crescendo effect prior to the sustain portion.

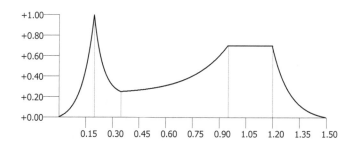

Figure 15 - A3SR - Crescendo After Attack

We can also combine linear, exponential and log curves together to produce complex envelopes such as that shown in Figure 16.

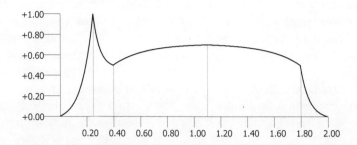

Figure 16 - Combined Exp/Log Envelope Segments

Because we are generating the envelope in software, we can add as many segments as desired with little additional code if we specify each segment with level and duration values stored in arrays. When the duration of the current segment is finished, we move to the next array entry.

```
envCount = 0;
envIndex = -1;
endVolume = 0;

for (n = 0; n < totalSamples; n++ {
   if (--envCount <= 0) {
      volume = endVolume;
      if (++envIndex < maxEnvIndex) {
         endVolume = envLevel[envIndex];
         envCount = envTime[envIndex];
         envInc = endVolume - volume;
         if (envCount > 0)
            envInc /= envCount;
      }else {
         envInc = 0
      }
   } else {
      volume += envInc;
   }
   sample[n] = volume * sin(phase);
   if ((phase += phaseIncr) >= twoPI)
      phase -= twoPI;
}
```

We can combine this technique with the state machine to produce an envelope generator with a variable number of attack segments and a variable number of release segments, but indeterminate sustain length. We need two sets of arrays, one for attack values and one for release values. State 0 represents the attack portion of the envelope and we transition to state 1 when all attack segments are complete. State 1 represents the sustain and transitions to the release portion when the note off signal is received (or calculated). In addition, we can support a flag to indicate no sustain state is intended and transition from state 0 to state 2. State 3 is reached when all release segments are complete.

```
envCount = 0;
envIndex = -1;
envState = 0;
volume = 0;
endLevel = 0;


for (n = 0; n < totalSamples; n++ {
   switch (envState) {
   case 0:
      if (--envCount <= 0) {
         volume = endLevel; // optional
         if (++envIndex < maxAtkIndex) {
            endLevel = atkLevel[envIndex];
            envCount = atkTime[envIndex];
            envInc = endLevel - volume;
            if (envCount > 0)
               envInc /= envCount;
         } else {
            envCount = 0;
            envIndex = -1;
            if (susOn)
               envState = 1
            else
               envState = 2;
         }
      } else {
         volume += envInc;
      }
      break;
```

```
case 1:
    if (noteOffSignaled)
        envState = 2;
    break;
case 2:
    if (--envCount <= 0) {
        volume = endLevel;
        if (++envIndex < maxRelIndex) {
            endLevel = relLevel[envIndex];
            envCount = relTime[envIndex];
            envInc = endLevel - volume;
            if (envCount > 0)
                envInc /= envCount;
        } else
            envState = 3;
    } else {
        volume += envInc;
    }
    break;
}
sample[n] = volume * sin(phase);
if ((phase += phaseIncr) >= twoPI)
    phase -= twoPI;
}
```

It is also possible to force the state machine into the release state when the note-off signal is sent regardless of the current state and segment index. The envelope generator will skip any remaining attack or sustain segments and begin the final release immediately.

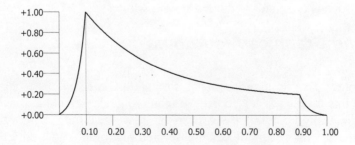

Figure 17 - Piano-like Envelope

This is useful when a note duration is less than the configured attack time and is also a good approximation of the way a piano works. When the key is held down, the sound has a long decay. When the key is released, the shorter, final decay begins.

Table Lookup Envelope Generators

The envelope generators shown above all perform incremental calculations on each sample. When the envelope does not change from sound to sound, we are performing the same calculations repeatedly. If we calculate the values once and store them in a table, we can then increment through the table one value per sample and produce the envelope without any additional calculations. The table can be initialized using the envelope generator functions already developed. However, the table can be filled with any curve desired, including periodic functions and complex splines.

Using a table fixes the time relationship of the attack and decay segments, and the overall duration of the envelope, to the pre-computed values in the table, thus making dynamic envelope changes difficult. Although it is possible to alter the overall duration by incrementing through the table with a value other than 1, the duration of attack and decay segments will be altered along with the overall time. Use of an envelope table is most effective for sounds where the duration and envelope of the sound never changes. Sound effects (e.g., buzzer, siren, fog-horn, door slamming), percussion sounds and plucked strings fall into this category of sounds. Using a table also consumes additional memory, and generally should only be used for short sounds or sounds without a sustain segment.

Using Graphics Algorithms

Computer graphic algorithms are similar to the envelope generator code that we have developed. Graphic routines calculate x and y coordinates representing pixel locations. If we treat the x axis as time and the y axis as amplitude, the graphic algorithm can be used to calculate an envelope.

Graphic algorithms are designed for maximum speed and we can borrow those algorithms if we need a faster envelope generator. One good example is the typical line drawing algorithm, the Bresenham midpoint algorithm. Because the Bresenham algorithm uses addition and subtraction of integer values to calculate points along the line segment, it is very fast. This method is especially appropriate for use on microprocessors that lack a floating point coprocessor.

A full description of the Bresenham algorithm can be found in any book on computer graphics, or by searching the Internet. For our purpose, we will skip the derivation and only look at how to adapt the Bresenham algorithm for use as an envelope generator. The y value will represent the amplitude, and the x value the sample number.

First, we can discard the parts of the algorithm that handle negative x increments (quadrants II and III), since our sample number is monotonically increasing.

Second, we can assume the line begins at (0,0). Any scaling or translation to another starting value can be performed by code that calls the line generation function.

Third, the Bresenham algorithm uses the slope of the line to determine whether to increment the x value or the y value on each iteration. When the slope of the line is > 1, it will produce multiple y values before the next x increment. For our application, we must always increment x by one no matter how many y increments are needed. Thus we have to adapt the algorithm slightly so that we get exactly one y value for each value of x. The simplest way to do this is to execute a loop until the next y value is reached.

Finally, when the envelope is in a decay segment, the slope of the line is negative. However, we can always calculate a line with a positive slope and then subtract the values from the maximum amplitude.

We will use two subroutines to implement the envelope generator. The first routine initializes the variables and is called whenever we begin a new segment. The second routine is a function that calculates the next y value. The variables *dx2, dy2, slopeFlag, linErr, linDir, linY,* and *linMax* must be persistent across subroutine calls. The value for *dx* is the number of samples we need to generate. The *dy* value is the ending volume level minus the beginning value, $|y_{max}-y_{min}|$. We test for the boundary conditions where *dx* or *dy* is 0 and always return the maximum value. Likewise, we can detect a line with slope of 1 and simply increment the y value for each call.

```
static int linDir;
static int linMax;
static int linY;
static int dx2;
static int dy2;
static int slopeFlag;

void InitLine(int dx, int dy, int dir) {
   linDir = dir
   linMax = dy
   linY = 0
   dx2 = dx + dx
   dy2 = dy + dy
   if (dx == 0 || dy == 0)
      slopeFlag = 0;
   else if (dx2 == dy2)
      slopeFlag = 1;
   else if (dx2 > dy2) {
      slopeFlag = 2;
      linErr = dy2 - dxl
   } else {
      slopeFlag = 3;
      linErr = dx2 - dy;
   }
}

int CalcLine() {
   switch (slopeFlag) {
   case 0:
      return linMax;
   case 1:
      return ++linY;
   case 2:
      if (linErr >= 0) {
         linErr -= dx2;
         ++linY;
      }
      linErr += dy2;
      break;
   case 3:
      while (linErr <= 0) {
         ++linY;
         linErr += dx2;
      }
```

```
        linErr -= dy2;
        break;
    }
    return (linDir < 0) ? linMax - linY : linY;
}
```

If desired, we can eliminate the *while* loop for case 3 by calculating a multiplier and applying it to the error variable and *y*.

```
mult = abs(linErr / dx2) + 1;
linY += mult;
linErr -= (dx2 * mult);
linErr -= dy2;
```

Since the value for *dx* must be an integer, we cannot use an amplitude value normalized to the range of [0,1]. We could set the range to the final output amplitude range [0, 2^{15}-1] and bypass scaling the volume level on output. Alternatively, we can normalize the volume range by using any arbitrary range that will produce a suitable number of divisions of the amplitude without integer overflow (e.g., [0,10000]), and then divide the return value from *CalcLine* by the maximum value to obtain a normalized volume value.

Incorporating these subroutines to the basic generator loop produces the following implementation.

```
linScale = 32767;
InitLine(attackTime, peakAmp * linScale, 1);

for (n = 0; n < totalSamples; n++) {
    if (n <= attackTime || n > decayStart)
        volume = CalcLine() / linScale;
    else if (n == decayStart)
        InitLine(decayTime, peakAmp, -1);
    sample[n] = volume * sin(phase)
    if ((phase += phaseIncr) >= twoPI)
        phase -= twoPI;
}
```

Other graphic line drawing algorithms for arcs and curves can be adapted in a similar manner.

Additional Applications

An envelope generator can be used for more than amplitude control. For example, we can apply the output of an envelope generator to the center frequency of a filter to produce varying spectrum, or apply the envelope to the base frequency of an oscillator to produce a pitch-bend effect. In these applications, the range of values will be other than [0,1], and we will need to scale and offset the output of the envelope generator accordingly.

If we automatically reset the envelope generator when it reaches the end it will function as an oscillator with a waveform consisting of arbitrary curves and a period equal to the duration of the envelope. A repeating envelope is useful for modulation effects, automatic panning, simulation of a cyclic sound such as a siren, etc.

Example Program

The *Example02* directory contains a complete program that generates seven sounds, each using a different envelope generator method.

1. AR, linear attack and decay.
2. AR, exponential attack and decay.
3. AR, log attack and decay.
4. AR, state machine
5. ADSR, multiple segments in arrays
6. Multiple attack, multiple decay segments, state machine.

The *Example02a* directory contains a program that uses the *BasicSynth* library classes described below.

The *Example02b* directory contains a program that uses the Bresenham midpoint line algorithm as the envelope generator.

BasicSynth Library Classes

Each of the envelope generator methods is available as a separate class. We have two basic forms of the envelope generators. The first form is the simple AR type with fixed duration. The second form is a multi-segment generator with indeterminate duration.

> *EnvGen* - linear attack and decay, base class for other types
> *EnvGenExp* - exponential attack and decay
> *EnvGenLog* - log attack and decay
> *EnvSeg* – base class for segment generators
> *EnvSegLin* – linear segment generator
> *EnvSegExp* – exponential segment generator
> *EnvSegLog* – log segment generator
> *EnvGenSeg* – variable number of segments, no sustain.
> *EnvGenSegSus* – variable number of segments, sustain.
> *EnvGenAR* – attack, sustain, release envelope
> *EnvGenADSR* – attack, decay, sustain, release envelope.
> *EnvGenMulSus* – variable number of attack, variable number of release segments with indeterminate sustain time.
> *EnvGenTable* – Produces a table from a variable number of segments.

Files:

```
Include/EnvGen.h
Include/EnvGenSeg.h
```

Chapter 7

Complex Waveforms

The examples shown so far have used the *sin* function to produce a waveform. However, useful sounds for music require waveforms with many varying overtones and we need to expand our oscillator to produce a wider range of waveforms.

Summing Sine Waves

As has been known since ancient times, a vibrating string produces a set of harmonics, tones that are integer multiples of the fundamental pitch.[4] Today, we know that any complex waveform created by harmonic motion can be calculated as a sum of sine and cosine waves, as shown by the Fourier theorem.[5] The discrete Fourier transform is represented by equation (7.1).

$$f(t) = \frac{a_0}{2} + \sum_{n=1}^{\infty} \left(a_n \cos(\omega nt) + b_n \sin(\omega nt) \right) \qquad (7.1)$$

In plain language, the Fourier transform produces a periodic waveform from a sum of cosine and sine functions evaluated at a constant interval. The first tem, $a_0/2$, represents the center amplitude and can be set to 0 for audio signals. In addition, we can represent the

---

[4] The higher frequencies are variously referred to as harmonics, overtones, or partials. Although each term has a specific meaning, musicians often use the terms interchangeably.

[5] The theorem was developed by the French mathematician J.B. Fourier in the early 19th century. It has many applications in digital signal processing beyond calculation of waveforms.

sum of sine and cosine as either a sine or cosine with the appropriate amplitude and phase offset.

$A \sin(x) + B \cos(x) = M \cos(x + \varphi)$

$A \sin(x) + B \cos(x) = M \sin(x + \varphi)$

Thus we can eliminate one of the two terms and produce complex waveforms by summing either sines or cosines of different frequencies, amplitudes and initial phase. The cosine is typically used alone, but the sine has the value of 0 when phase is 0, and that has some practical advantages in sound generation and modification. The term sinusoid is generally used in this case. We can't produce an infinite series of sinusoids, so we also have to limit the summation to some reasonable number. That leaves us with:

$$f(t) = \sum_{n=1}^{m} b_n \sin(\omega nt) \qquad (7.2)$$

The following code sums the first four partials to produce a waveform with the shape of a wiggly ramp. The amplitude of each partial is the inverse of its partial number resulting in lower amplitudes for higher frequencies.

```
phsIncr[0] = frqRad * frequency;
phsIncr[1] = frqRad * frequency * 2;
phsIncr[2] = frqRad * frequency * 3;
phsIncr[3] = frqRad * frequency * 4;
for (n = 0; n < totalSamples; n++) {
    value = 0
    for (p = 0; p < 4; p++) {
        value += sin(phase[p]) / (p+1);
        if ((phase[p] += phsIncr[p]) >= twoPI)
            phase[p] -= twoPI;
    }
    sample[n] = volume * (value / 1.53);
}
```

Because we are adding multiple waveforms, the peak amplitude varies depending on the number, phase and amplitude of the partials. To keep the amplitude normalized, the final value should be rescaled so that it covers the range [-1,+1]. We can use the sum of the amplitudes as the scale, but may have a reduced peak amplitude depending on the phase of the partials. The best way to determine the peak is to sum one period and save the largest value. For the examples, we will use an approximate constant value determined empirically.

In this example, the multiple and amplitude of each partial is fixed. For a more useful program, we can store the multiples and amplitudes of the partials in separate arrays. We can also set the initial phase of each partial, and/or change the sign of the amplitude, to represent a cosine value. The arrays, *partMult, partAmp*, and *phsInit,* would be filled with the partial numbers, amplitudes, and initial phase, respectively.

```
numPart = 1;
phsIncr[0] = frqRad * frequency;
phase[0] = 0;
for (p = 1; p < 4; p++) {
   phase[numPart] = phsInit[p];
   phsIncr[numPart] = phsIncr[0] * partMult[p];
   if (phsIncr[numPart] < PI)
      numPart++;
}

for (n = 0; n < totalSamples; n++) {
   value = 0;
   for (p = 0; p < numPart; p++) {
      value += sin(phase[p]) * partAmp[p];
      if ((phase[p] += phsIncr[p]) >= twoPI)
         phase[p] -= twoPI;
   }
   sample[n] = volume * (value / scale);
}
```

When summing sinusoids it is quite possible that multiples of the fundamental frequency will exceed the Nyquist limit. To prevent that from happening, we must test each partial against the Nyquist limit and eliminate any partials that would create alias frequencies. We do that in the code above by testing each phase increment to determine if it is greater than π and reduce the count of partials accordingly.

The shape of the waveform can be easily changed by varying the values stored in the two arrays. For example, a square wave can be produced by adding only odd numbered partials with the amplitude set to the inverse of the partial number.

```
partMult[0] = 1.0;
partAmp[0] = 1.0;
for (n = 1; n < maxPart; n++) {
    partMult[n] = (2*n) - 1;
    partAmp[n] = 1 / partMult[n];
}
```

If we increase the number of partials, the waveform gets richer, brighter and closer to the true sawtooth or square wave. However, a plot of these waveforms has a ripple rather than a straight line between peaks. In the case of a square wave there are little "horns" where the transition from peak to peak overshoots a little and then settles back. These effects are the result of summing a finite series of partials rather than the infinite series of partials specified by the Fourier transform. The ripple and overshoot is called the *Gibbs Phenomenon* after the engineer who identified the cause. The ripple in the waveform changes the sound slightly, but we can usually ignore it for audio signals. However, if we want to use the waveform for modulation or a low frequency oscillator (LFO) the ripple in the waveform might be troublesome.

We can eliminate much of the ripple and overshoot by using a larger number of partials and multiply the amplitude of all partials above the fundamental with a small value called the Lanczos *sigma* factor.

$$\sigma = \frac{\sin(x)}{x} \tag{7.3}$$

$$x = \frac{n\pi}{M}, n = 1...M \tag{7.4}$$

The value of M is the number of partials and n is the partial number. We can calculate *sigma* by defining a variable for π/M and multiply by the partial number.

```
sigmaK = PI / numPart;
for (p = 0; p < numPart; p++) {
    sigmaN = partMult[p] * sigmaK;
    sigma[p] = sin(sigmaN) / sigmaN;
}
```

```
for (n = 0; n < totalSamples; n++) {
   value = 0;
   for (p = 0; p < numPart; p++) {
      amp = partAmp[p] * sigma[p];
      value += sin(phase[p]) * amp;
      if ((phase[p] += phsIncr[p]) >= twoPI)
         phase[p] -= twoPI;
   }
   sample[n] = volume * (value / scale);
}
```

Sawtooth Waveform Generator

In addition to summing sinusoids, we can easily calculate some waveforms directly. For example, we can calculate the samples for a sawtooth wave directly from the phase.

$$s_n = \left(\frac{\phi_n}{\pi}\right) - 1 \tag{7.5}$$

Since the phase varies from $[0,2\pi]$, the first term varies from $[0,2]$. Subtracting 1 produces values over the range $[-1,1]$.

```
phaseIncr = frqRad * frequency;
phase = 0;
for (n = 0; n < totalSamples; n++) {
   sample[n] = volume * ((phase / PI) - 1);
   if ((phase += phaseIncr) >= twoPI)
      phase -= twoPI;
}
```

We can also produce the sawtooth by calculating an amplitude increment directly from the number of samples per period, similar to what we did for envelope generators. The amplitude increment per sample is the range of $[-1,+1]$ divided by the samples per period:

$$\frac{1-(-1)}{f_s/f} = \frac{2f}{f_s} \tag{7.6}$$

Equation (7.6) produces a very efficient program that only needs to increment the amplitude for each sample and test for the end of the period (i.e., when the amplitude is at its maximum).

```
sawIncr = (2 * frequency) / sampleRate;
sawValue = -1;
for (n = 0; n < totalSamples; n++) {
    sample[n] = volume * sawValue;
    sawValue += sawIncr;
    if (sawValue >= 1)
        sawValue -= 2;
}
```

Triangle Waveform Generator

A triangle wave is a linear increment or decrement that switches direction every π radians. It can be generated using equation (7.7).

$$s_n = 1 - \frac{2|\phi_n - \pi|}{\pi} \tag{7.7}$$

We can optimize the code by pre-calculating the value of $2/\pi$ and eliminate the subtraction of π by varying the phase from $[-\pi, \pi]$.

```
phaseIncr = (twoPI / sampleRate) * frequency;
phase = 0;
twoDivPI = 2.0/PI;
for (n = 0; n < totalSamples; n++) {
    triValue = (phase * twoDivPI);
    if (phase < 0)
        triValue = 1.0 + triValue
    else
        triValue = 1.0 - triValue;
    sample[n] = volume * triValue;
    if ((phase += phaseIncr) >= PI)
        phase -= twoPI;
}
```

Square Wave Generator

For a square wave, we only need to check whether the phase is less than or greater than the midpoint of the period and use +1 or -1 as the value. We can use a phase in radians as usual, or simply calculate the time of one sample and the time of one period and incrementally calculate the equivalent of phase in the time domain. To allow for a variable duty cycle square wave, we multiply the period by the duty cycle to obtain the midpoint.

```
sampleTime = 1 / sampleRate;
period = 1 / frequency;
midPoint = period * dutyCycle / 100.0;
phase = 0;

for (n = 0; n < totalSamples; n++) {
   if (phase < midpoint)
      sample[n] = volume;
   else
      sample[n] = -volume;
   phase += sampleTime;
   if (phase >= period)
      phase -= period;
}
```

Alternatively, we can calculate the period and midpoint in samples and use an integer value for the phase. However, this will produce a slight frequency error due to round-off.

```
period = (sampleRate / frequency) + 0.5;
midpoint = period * dutyCycle / 100;
phase = 0;

for (n = 0; n < totalSamples; n++) {
   if (phase < midpoint)
      sample[n] = volume;
   else
      sample[n] = -volume;
   if (++phase >= period)
      phase = 0;
}
```

The sawtooth, square and triangle waveforms make a sudden transition in the amplitude at one or more points in the waveform. Any round-off in the calculation of the phase will shift the transition point back and forth by one sample (phase jitter) and produce an alias frequency. At low oscillator frequencies, the alias frequency is below the audible range, but at higher frequencies it is readily apparent. We can eliminate the phase jitter by discarding the fractional part of the phase increment at the end of the period, but this produces a frequency error. The amount of error for any given frequency is the fractional part of the sample count divided by the number of samples in a period. The period is longer at low frequencies, and the frequency error is small, but increases as frequency increases, and the oscillator gets increasingly out of tune as the frequency increases. In either case, the useful frequency range for these oscillators is only a portion of the audible frequency range.

A sharp corner in a waveform indicates a large number of partials, including frequencies beyond the Nyquist limit, that can create problems when the signal is passed through various processing stages. However, unlike waveforms created by summation of partials, direct calculation produces waveforms that do not have any ripple. The absence of ripple makes them ideal for pitch bend, vibrato and similar low frequency modulation effects.

Frequency Modulation

Frequency modulation (FM) is another technique for generating complex waveforms.[6] FM is produced by using one oscillator (the modulator) to vary the frequency of a second oscillator (the carrier).

$$f(t) = A_c \cdot \sin(\omega_c t + (A_m \cdot \sin \omega_m t)) \qquad (7.8)$$

The modulator amplitude (A_m) determines the peak variation in frequency of the signal while the modulator frequency determines the rate at which the frequency changes. When the frequencies of both

---

[6] The use of FM for audio synthesis was discovered and developed by John M. Chowning in the late 1960's and described in *"The Synthesis of Complex Audio Spectra by Means of Frequency Modulation"*, JAES 21:526-534, 1973. Chowning was awarded U.S. Patent 4018121, which became the basis for the Yamaha DX series of synthesizers. The patent expired in 1995.

oscillators are in the audible range, modulation produces sum and difference tones (sidebands) that are also in the audible range. The result is a rich spectrum consisting of the original frequency plus the sidebands.

Modulator frequency is usually specified as a multiple of the carrier and identified by the term *c:m ratio*. In general, integer multiples produce a harmonic spectrum while non-integer multiples produce an inharmonic spectrum.

We can implement FM by calculating two waveforms simultaneously and then use the value from the first waveform to calculate the phase increment of the second waveform.

```
modIncr = frqRad * modFrequency;
modPhase = 0;
modAmp = 100;
carPhase = 0;

for (n = 0; n < totalSamples; n++) {
    sample[n] = volume * sin(carPhase);
    modValue = modAmp * sin(modPhase);
    carIncr = frqRad * (carFrequency + modValue);
    if ((carPhase += carIncr) >= twoPI)
       carPhase -= twoPI;
    if ((modPhase += modIncr) >= twoPI)
       modPhase -= twoPI;
}
```

We can re-factor the calculation of the carrier phase as:

```
carIncr = frqRad * carFrequency;
modValue = (frqRad * modAmp) * sin(modPhase);
carPhase += carIncr + modValue
```

In this form, the values for *frqRad*carFrequency* and *frqRad*modAmp* are loop invariant and can be calculated once. If we pre-calculate these values, we can simply add the modulator value to the carrier phase for each sample.

```
modIncr = frqRad * modFrequency;
carIncr = frqRad * carFrequency;
modAmp = frqRad * 100;
modPhase = carPhase = 0;
```

```
for (n = 0; n < totalSamples; n++) {
   sample[n] = volume * sin(carPhase);
   modValue = modAmp * sin(modPhase);
   carPhase += carIncr + modValue;
   if (carPhase >= twoPI)
      carPhase -= twoPI;
   if ((modPhase += modIncr) >= twoPI)
      modPhase -= twoPI;
}
```

In the first example we modified the phase increment, while in the second example we modified the phase directly. For that reason the second form is usually called *phase modulation* rather than frequency modulation. However, both programs produce the same result.

The only significant difference between the two programs is in how we specify the modulator amplitude. The modulator amplitude affects the change in frequency of the carrier (Δf). When using the frequency modulation form, the *modAmp* value represents change in frequency and is limited to the maximum frequency range. When using the phase modulation form, the *modAmp* value represents change of phase increment and we need to convert the value from frequency to radians.

The value for modulator amplitude must be chosen carefully to avoid driving the carrier past the Nyquist frequency while also providing a good range of sum and difference tones. Although we could test each modulator on each sample, it would be much more efficient to insure the peak amplitude of the modulators is within range before calculating samples, similar to what was done with summation of sine waves. In addition, a high value for modulator amplitude will produce a noisy signal, which can sometimes be used as a special sound effect. However, a useful maximum for Δf is around 2,000, or about $1/10^{th}$ of the Nyquist frequency.

A fixed modulator amplitude affects the spectrum differently at different carrier frequencies. For example, a carrier of 100Hz and a modulator amplitude of 50 will vary the carrier over the range of 50-150Hz, or 50% of the carrier frequency. However, with a carrier at 1000Hz, a modulator amplitude of 50 will only vary the frequency from 950-1050Hz, or 5% of the frequency. The spacing of the sidebands will vary as a result and the timbre will vary considerably over the entire frequency range when we have a fixed modulator amplitude. For this reason, a good FM instrument uses the value of the *index of modulation* to calculate the modulator amplitude. Index of modulation is defined as $I=\Delta f/f_m$ where Δf is the peak frequency deviation and f_m is the modulator frequency. The modulator amplitude determines the variation in frequency and is thus the same as Δf. We then calculate modulator amplitude as $A_m=I{\cdot}f_m$.

We can extend the basic two-oscillator FM generator by adding an additional modulator and using two parallel modulating signals on the carrier:

```
mod1Value = mod1Amp * sin(mod1Phase)
mod2Value = mod2Amp * sin(mod2Phase)
carPhase = carIncr + mod1Value + mod2Value
```

Or we can use two or more modulators in series:

```
mod1Value = mod1Amp * sin(mod1Phase);
mod2Phase += mod2Incr + mod1Value;
mod2Value = mod2Amp * sin(mod2Phase);
carPhase += carIncr + mod2Value;
```

Thus by adding only a few lines of code, we can produce a very wide range of dynamically varying timbres. Note, however, that if we add multiple modulators to a single carrier, the index increment can potentially exceed the maximum phase increment even if the individual modulator amplitudes are low. When adding multiple phase increments the *total value* must be checked if we are to avoid producing an alias frequency.

We are not limited to using sine waves for the carrier and modulator waveforms. We can start with a carrier that is produced as a sum of sine waves and then modulate that signal to produce an even more complex spectrum. In addition, applying a separate envelope to each modulator allows modulation effects to grow or diminish over the duration of the sound and on a note to note basis. The wide variety of sounds available from only a few lines of programming is the reason so many synthesizer systems rely heavily on FM synthesis techniques.

Amplitude Modulation

Where frequency modulation varies the frequency of the carrier with a periodic function, amplitude modulation varies the amplitude of the carrier. We have already seen one type of amplitude modulation in the form of envelope generators. In that case the period of the modulator was equal to the duration of the sound. When the period of the modulating signal is in the audio frequency range, the result is a complex spectrum created by the sum and differences of the two signals. We can generalize amplitude modulation by modifying the basic signal equation as follows.

$$f(t) = A_c \sin(\omega_c t) \cdot A_m \sin(\omega_m t) \tag{7.9}$$

The values for A_c and A_m are the peak amplitudes of the carrier and modulator, respectively. The values for ω_c and ω_m are the frequencies expressed in radians. In terms of the resulting spectrum, the sum of the modulator and carrier frequencies will determine the frequency of the sidebands. The amplitude of the modulator will control the amplitude of the sidebands.

We can replace the *sin* function with any periodic function. However, as with the envelope generator, the range of values for the modulator should be [0,1].

Equation (7.9) as shown will actually produce *ring modulation* with the carrier frequency absent from the final signal. To produce true amplitude modulation, the amplitude of the modulator must be offset to produce a positive value. Using a sine function for the modulator, the modulator amplitude will vary from $[-A_m, +A_m]$. Assuming the amplitude values are normalized to [-1,+1], we can add an offset of 1 and the values will be in the positive range between $[1-A_m, 1+A_m]$. The maximum peak amplitude range will be the same. In order to normalize the peak amplitude, we need to rescale the value at some point by dividing by $1+A_m$. Putting it all together, we have the following equation for amplitude modulation.

$$f(t) = \frac{A_c \sin(\omega_c t) \cdot (1 + A_m \sin(\omega_m t))}{1 + A_m} \tag{7.10}$$

Converting to a program is straightforward.

```
carIncr = frqRad * carFrequency;
carPhase = 0;
modIncr = frqRad * modFrequency;
modAmp = 0.75;
modScale = 1.0 / (1.0 + modAmp);
modPhase = 0;

for (n = 0; n < totalSamples; n++) {
   modValue = 1.0 + (modAmp * sin(modPhase));
   carValue = volume * sin(carPhase);
   sample[n] = carValue * modValue * modScale;
   if ((carPhase += carIncr) >= twoPI)
      carPhase -= twoPI;
   if ((modPhase += modIncr) >= twoPI)
      modPhase -= twoPI;
}
```

Ring modulation is also straightforward. The program is essentially the same, but we do not need to offset and scale the amplitude values.

```
for (n = 0; n < totalSamples; n++) {
   modValue = modAmp * sin(modPhase);
   carValue = volume * sin(carPhase);
   sample[n] = carValue * modValue;
   if ((carPhase += carIncr) >= twoPI)
      carPhase -= twoPI;
   if ((modPhase += modIncr) >= twoPI)
      modPhase -= twoPI;
}
```

Noise

Although noise in a signal is generally considered something to avoid, many sounds we might want to produce consist primarily of noise. The sound of wind, for example, can be simulated with filtered noise.

White noise is defined as an equal probability distribution of all frequencies and we can simulate white noise by generating random values for the samples. Computers cannot generate a true random number, but can generate a pseudo-random sequence that works well enough for the purpose of generating noise. Most programming languages have a built-in function that returns a random number using a pseudo-random function. To generate noise, we simply call that function and then scale the value to the range [-1,+1]. For the standard C++ library function, the following code will work. Because the function returns a positive integer value over the range [0,0x7FFF], we need to shift the values to a positive and negative range and scale appropriately.

```
for (n = 0; n < totalSamples; n++) {
   value = rand();
   value -= (RAND_MAX/2);
   value /= (RAND_MAX/2);
   sample[n] = volume * value;
}
```

If the programming language used to implement the synthesizer does not include a random number function, we can define such a function and include it in the program. Various equations for generating a pseudo-random number sequence can be found on the Internet and books on computer programming. One other interesting possibility is to sample several seconds of a white noise source, such as a noisy diode or a radio tuned between stations, and then load the sampled data to obtain a random number sequence.

Using the random number sequence produces the familiar hiss of white noise. However, not all noise sounds have a full spectrum distribution of frequencies. A low rumble, for example, has very little high frequency content. Later, we will look at using various filters to affect the frequency content, but there are other very simple ways to filter the high frequency content from white noise. One easy method is to lower the rate at which random numbers are generated to a rate less than the sampling rate. The result is a value that holds over the duration of many samples, and thus changes more slowly, producing a lower frequency content.

```
float GetRand() {
   return (rand()-(RAND_MAX/2)) / (RAND_MAX/2);
}

hcount = sampleRate / hfreq;
count = hcount;
```

```
for (n = 0; n < totalSamples; n++) {
   if (++count >= hcount) {
      value = GetRand();
      count = 0;
   }
   sample[n] = volume * value;
}
```

In this example, *hfreq* sets the rate at which the random sequence is sampled and thus how long the previous value is held. We can also interpolate between successive random values rather than simply holding the previous value.

```
hcount = sampleRate / hfreq;
count = hcount;
next = GetRand();
for (n = 0; n < totalSamples; n++) {
   if (++count >= hcount) {
      last = next;
      next = GetRand();
      incr = (next - last) / hcount;
      count = 0;
   } else {
      value += incr;
   }
   sample[n] = volume * value;
}
```

Note that the value for *hfreq* must be less than or equal to f_s. Otherwise, truncation to an integer count value will result in a zero count. If desired, we can use a floating point for *hcount*.

It is also possible to create a pitched noise sound by ring modulation of a sine wave oscillator with the interpolated noise generator. The resulting sound is similar to passing noise through a narrow band filter.

```
phsIncr = frqRad * freq;
phs = 0;
for (n = 0; n < totalSamples; n++) {
   sample[n] = volume * GetRandI() * sin(phs);
   if ((phs += phsIncr) > twoPI)
      phs -= twoPI;
}
```

The *GetRandI* function would perform the calculation shown in the previous example.

Example Code

The program in the *Example03* directory produces a sound using each of the methods described above.

BasicSynth Library Classes

The *GenWave* class defines the basic waveform generator method inherited by all waveform generators in the *BasicSynth* library. Other classes derived from this class produce complex waveforms. The direct waveform generation classes are listed below.

GenWave - sine wave generator using *sin* function
GenWaveSaw - sawtooth wave generator
GenWaveTri - triangle wave generator
GenWaveSqr - square wave generator
GenWaveSqr32 - square wave generator, integers

The *GenNoise* class generates white noise by calling the random number generator. Other noise generators derive from this class. The filtered noise generators will be discussed in a later chapter.

GenNoise – white noise generator
GenNoiseH – held value noise generator
GenNoiseI – interpolated noise generator
GenNoisePink1 – filtered noise generator
GenNoisePink2 – filtered noise generator

Files:

```
Include/GenWave.h
Include/GenNoise.h
```

Chapter 8

Wavetable Oscillators

Direct sound generation using the *sin* function can be used to produce almost any waveform we want and can be used as the starting point for a synthesizer. However, direct sound generation requires a large number of computations and those computations must be performed for each sample. (As programmers say, it is computationally expensive.)

A general principle of computer programming is that we can trade memory for computational speed. In other words, if we store a waveform in a table, we can retrive the amplitude values from the table rather than repeatedly calculating them. For complex waveforms we can calculate one period of a sum of sinusoids once, an even greater savings. We produce a sound by looping through the table using an index, incrementing the index modulo the table length.

```
period = sampleRate / frequency;
phaseIncr = frqRad * frequency;
phase = 0;
for (index = 0; index < period; index++) {
    wavetable[index] = sin(phase);
    phase += phaseIncr;
}

for (index = n = 0; n < totalSamples; n++ {
    sample[n] = volume * wavetable[index];
    if (++index >= period)
        index = 0;
}
```

Pre-calculating the waveform moves the *sin* function call out of the sample generation loop and thus eliminates a lengthy computation on each sample, saving us considerable execution time. However, we are still recreating the wavetable for each sound. Moreover, we have lost the ability to easily vary the oscillator frequency during the sound and cannot use frequency modulation to produce complex waveforms. We need to be able to vary the frequency without recalculating the values in the table.

We can accomplish a change in frequency by incrementing the table index by a value other than one. For example, if we increment by two, we scan the table in half the time and produce a frequency twice the original frequency. Other increment values will yield proportionate frequencies. In order to use a fixed length table for all frequencies, we calculate the number of steps through the table for one period and then increment the table index by one step for each sample. As stated before, the number of samples per period is calculated as the sample rate divided by the frequency (f_s/f). The index increment for a given frequency is the table length divided by the number of samples per period:

$$i = \frac{L}{f_s/f} = \frac{L}{f_s} \cdot f \qquad\qquad (8.1)$$

Assuming all our waveform tables are one period in length and are all the same length, we only need to calculate (L/f_s) once at the point in the program where we initialize the wave table.

Given that the table contains one complete cycle (or period) of the waveform, the table length represents 2π radians. To initialize the table, we calculate a phase increment as 2π divided by the table length and then iterate over one period.

```
phaseIncr = twoPi / tableLength;
phase = 0;
for (index = 0; index < tableLength; index++) {
   wavetable[index] = sin(phase);
   phase += phaseIncr;
}
```

Generating the sound is reduced to calculating an index increment and retrieving the sample values from the table.

```
frqTI = tableLength / sampleRate;
indexIncr = frqTI * frequency;
index = 0;
for (n = 0; n < totalSamples; n++ {
    sample[n] = volume * wavetable[index];
    if ((index += indexIncr) >= tableLength)
        index -= tableLength;
}
```

The wavetable does not have to be filled with a sine wave. We can sum sine waves together when we initialize the table, calculate the waveform as a series of curve segments, or even load the waveform from a file to playback a pre-computed waveform. We can also change between wavetables during sound generation to produce a varying waveform. Furthermore, the wavetable does not have to be limited to one cycle of the waveform. If we have a waveform that varies over some regular number of periods, we can still build a table for that waveform if we include multiple periods. However, when more than one period is included, the increment must be multiplied by the number of periods to produce the correct frequency. In any case, the beginning and ending values in the table must represent adjacent phases in order to avoid a discontinuity in the signal.

A complex waveform produced as a sum of sinusoids can be created by calculating the sum once and storing it in the wave table. However, we can also dynamically sum the sinusoids as we did before and allow the amplitude of the partials to vary over time. Dynamic summing of the partials also allows checking each partial to insure that it does not exceed the Nyquist limit. A static table must always be a compromise between a reasonable number of partials and the maximum fundamental frequency allowed for the table.

```
numPart = 0;
incr = frqTL * frequency;

for (p = 0; p < N; p++) {
    indexIncr[numPart] = incr * partMult[p];
    index[numPart] = (phsInit[p]/twoPI)*tableLength;
    if (indexIncr[numPart] < (tableLength/2))
        numPart++;
}
```

```
for (n = 0; n < totalSamples; n++) {
   value = 0;
   for (p = 0; p < numPart; p++) {
      value += wavetable[index[p]] * partAmp[p];
      index[p] += indexIncr[p];
      if (index[p] >= tableLength)
         index[p] -= tableLength;
   }
   sample[n] = volume * value;
}
```

Frequency modulation is accomplished by reading two values from the wave table, one for the carrier and one for the modulator, and then adding the modulator value to the carrier index. Since the modulator value will vary from positive to negative, we will subtract from the index for some samples. If the current value of the carrier index is less than the absolute value of the modulator index, we will have a negative index value. Thus we must check for a negative index as well as an index past the end of the table and adjust the index appropriately

```
incrCar = frqTI * frequency;
incrMod = frqTI * modFreq;
modAmp = frqTI * indexOfMod * modFreq;
indexCar = 0;
indexMod = 0;

for (n = 0; n < totalSamples; n++) {
   sample[n] = volume * wavetable[indexCar];
   modVal = modAmp * wavetable[indexMod];
   indexCar += incrCar + modVal;
   if (indexCar >= tableLength)
      indexCar -= tableLength;
   else if (indexCar < 0)
      indexCar += tableLength;
   indexMod += incrMod;
   if (indexMod >= tableLength)
      indexMod -= tableLength;
}
```

The value for the modulator amplitude must be less than one-half the table length minus the carrier index increment in order that the sum of the modulator and carrier does not exceed the Nyquist limit. As before, we can specify the modulator amplitude as a frequency displacement or as the index of modulation, but must now convert from frequency to table index range.

Amplitude modulation is much the same as frequency modulation. We index into a wavetable twice and multiply the amplitude values.

```
carIncr = frqTI * carFrequency;
carPhase = 0;
modIncr = frqTI * modFrequency;
modAmp = 0.75;
modScale = 1.0 / (1.0 + modAmp);
modPhase = 0;

for (n = 0; n < totalSamples; n++) {
    modValue = 1.0 + (modAmp * wavetable[modPhase]);
    carValue = volume * wavetable[carPhase];
    sample[n] = carValue * modValue * modScale;
    carPhase += carIncr;
    if (carPhase >= tableLength)
       carPhase -= tableLength;
    modPhase += modIncr;
    if (modPhase >= tableLength)
       modPhase -= tableLength;
}
```

Interpolation

Few frequencies will result in an integer increment of the table index. Thus the table index and increment must be able to represent fractional values, and the table index must be truncated or rounded to an integer during a table lookup. Conversion to an integer index is equivalent to altering the phase and will result in an amplitude value slightly different from the one we would calculate directly. We are introducing a quantization error into the signal as a result. The error in the sample value is equivalent to distortion and we should minimize or eliminate it if possible.

The true sample value lies somewhere between the value at the current index and the next value in the table. Rounding the table index will help, but will still produce errors up to one-half the difference between table entries. We can reduce the error if we interpolate between adjacent table entries as shown in Figure 18.

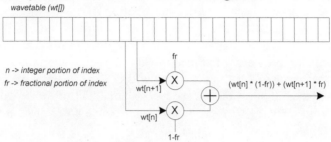

Figure 18 - Wavetable Interpolation

The value of *n* is the integer portion of the table index and varies from 0 to *tableLength-1*. The value of *fr* is the fractional portion and varies from 0 to 1. The equation shown at the output is the two-multiply form. We can rearrange the equation and eliminate one multiply operation.

```
wt[n] + ((wt[n+1] - wt[n]) * fr)
```

Because we are using a non-integer index increment, we effectively resample the table to get different frequencies. More sophisticated interpolation is usually required for resampling in order to avoid loss of fidelity in the signal. However, more sophisticated forms of interpolation also require significant calculation time and effectively defeat the purpose for wavetable scanning. Thus a simple linear interpolation as shown in the diagram is normally used for wavetable oscillators. The following code shows the calculation of the sample using linear interpolation.

```
indexBase = floor(index);
indexFract = index - indexBase;
value = wavetable[indexBase];
value2 = wavetable[indexBase+1];
value = value1 + ((value2 - value1) * indexFract);
```

Note that when *indexBase* is equal to *tableLength-1* we will be reading beyond the end of the table for the lookup of *value2*. The table needs to have one additional entry added beyond *tableLength* to avoid testing for an index at the end of the table. The wavetable memory must be allocated as size *tableLength+1* and the last value in the table set to the same value as index zero.

Using interpolation adds some computation time, but is still much faster than repeatedly calculating the waveform. However, there is a possibility to get nearly the same results without interpolation. The amount of error in the sample value will depend in large part on the table length. For short tables, we have a small set of index values to select from and will be more likely to introduce an error than with a longer table.

Optimal Table Length

The length of the table can be as large as the precision of the index and as small as the number of samples needed to accurately represent the waveform. For example, with a single precision floating point index (24-bits precision) the table could be as large as 16 million entries, far more than is needed. At the other extreme, a square wave could be represented with only two values. An ideal table length would be one where all frequencies we want to produce will result in an integer table index increment. Obviously, that is not practical either. What we would like to do is to find a good compromise that allows efficient memory use and accurate representation of waveforms without interpolation.

The table index value has a fixed number of bits available to represent the integer and fractional parts of the index. With longer tables, the index varies over a larger range and more bits are contained in the integer portion of the index. For example, with a table of 256 values, only 8 bits of the index are used for the integer portion. For a table of 512 values, 9 bits are used, etc. With each doubling of the table length we gain one bit of precision in the index and are discarding one less bit of precision to obtain an integer index. This results in a smaller variation between the lookup value and the directly calculated value. In effect, lengthening the table is much like performing interpolation on a shorter table once rather than for each sample. Note that to make best use of the index range, table length should be a power of two.

We can write a short test program to see what happens when we increase the table length. The test program computes a block of samples using a direct call to the *sin* function and then compares that value with wavetable lookup using round-off and interpolation.

```
phaseIncr = (twoPI * frequency) / sampleRate;
tableIncr = (tableLen * frequency) / sampleRate;

for (n = 0; n < totalSamples; n++) {
   sDirect = sin(phaseIndex);
   sRound  = wavetable[tableIndex + 0.5];
   fract = tableIndex - floor(tableIndex);
   s1 = wavetable[tableIndex];
   s2 = wavetable[tableIndex+1];
   sIntrp = s1 + ((s2 - s1) * fract);
   // compare sDirect, sRound, sIntrp
   phaseIndex += phaseIncr;
   if (phaseIndex >= twoPI)
      phaseIndex -= twoPI;
   tableIndex += tableIncr;
   if (tableIndex >= tableLen)
      tableIndex -= tableLen;
}
```

The output of this program shows that for tables less than 4K in length, and using a single precision floating point phase accumulator, interpolation has a significant advantage. However, as the table length gets longer, the round-off method improves while the interpolation method degrades. At 16K table length and longer, there is only a small difference between interpolation and round-off of the index. What has happened is that we have shifted bits from the fractional part to the integer part of the table index. At the point where fewer bits are available in the fractional part than in the integer part, interpolation gets worse while round-off gets better. However, if we use a double precision table index, interpolation remains better than rounding regardless of the table length. Using a double precision index, interpolation, and a table length of 2K or longer produces samples where the maximum error is 1 bit and only occurs in about 1.5% of the samples. At 4K table length, the number of samples with 1-bit error is less than 0.4%. In other words, it is virtually the same as direct calculation using the *sin* function. Round-off errors when accumulating the phase will produce significant quantization error.

We find that the accuracy of the phase accumulator is more important than the table length.

Looking at the error for non-interpolated values, we find that at table length of 16K about 80% of the samples have quantization errors. But about 30% of the samples will have a 1-bit error, and the greatest quantization error is only ± 3 bits. Given that we multiply most samples by a peak amplitude level less than 1, the low order bits will tend to have less effect on the final signal. In fact, if the program is run with the peak amplitude set to 0.5, the quantization error is cut in half as well. In addition, some errors are positive, while others are negative. When generating sounds for music, we usually add the output of multiple oscillators together, causing quantization errors to average out in the final signal. Although interpolation does provide much better theoretical results, for actual music, a long wave table with round-off of the index is nearly equivalent. In other words, as the overall complexity of the sound increases, noise and distortion are masked and tend to be less noticeable.

This gives us two guidelines for table length. If the desire is maximum accuracy, then we should use a double precision phase accumulator and a table of 4K or greater length with interpolation. For best speed with good accuracy, use a fixed point accumulator (described below) with a table of 16K or greater length.

Longer tables will require more memory. Assuming we are using either a 32-bit integer or single precision floating point for amplitude values, ten tables of 16K length will consume 640K bytes of memory and 100 tables about 6.4MB. That seems wasteful, but with the large amount of memory now available in computers, the added memory consumption is usually not a problem. Older synthesis programs used interpolation primarily because they were designed when computer memory was limited. Tables in those systems were small out of necessity and interpolation made a significant improvement in sound quality. Today, we can simply allocate a large table, 16K or greater in length, and then do direct lookup by rounding the fractional portion of the table index. Interpolation is needed when designing for a small system with limited memory, where a very large number of tables must be created, or for applications where the smallest possible distortion is important. In any case, table lookup is a performance optimization and those systems that need more accurate representation of the waveform can use direct waveform calculation with the *sin* function and accept the lower performance.

Fixed Point Table Index

As noted above, the table index must store a fractional value. As we scan the table, the index increment is repeatedly added to the index, modulo the table length. Any error in the increment value will result in quantization error. In those cases where very precise waveforms are required, it is best to use a double precision type to calculate the table index.

However, the increment and wrapping of the table index must be performed for every sample in every generator and is thus a critical factor in execution time. Optimizing that calculation could potentially result in a large performance gain. One strategy to gain performance is to use a fixed point representation of the table index. For example, we can use a 32-bit integer value and scale the table index so that the integer portion of the index is in the upper bits and the fractional portion in the lower bits.

With a table length of 8k, we need at least 13 bits to store the integer portion. We need a sign bit if we are going to allow the index to move backward, as it will do in FM synthesis. We also need to allow summation of the index increment without losing information, so we need at least 1 bit for overflow as well. We typically don't need more bits for overflow because we know the index increment can never be more than one-half the table length. Larger values would exceed the Nyquist limit. However, if we are doing FM synthesis, we will add the modulator value to the index. So long as the combined upper limit of the modulator amplitude and the carrier increment is less than the table length, we will be within the 1-bit overflow limit. This condition must be true to avoid alias frequencies, but to be on the safe side, we can allow 2 bits overflow.

The easiest way to implement the fixed-point index is to use the upper 16 bits for the integer portion and the lower 16 bits for the fraction. To calculate the index step, we need to multiply the increment by 2^{16}. We can extract the integer index portion by dividing by 2^{16}, which can be accomplished by the simple expedient of a right shift by 16. To round the index, we add 0.5, which in our fixed point representation is 0x8000.

```
i32Length = tableLength * 65536;
i32Incr = (long) (frTI * frequency * 65536);
i32Index = 0;
for (n = 0; n < totalSamples; n++) {
   samples[n] = wavetable[(i32Index+0x8000) >> 16];
   if ((i32Index += i32Increment) >= i32Length)
      i32Index -= i32Length;
}
```

This implementation avoids using floating point in the interior of the loop and only adds a single right shift operation in its place. In addition, it provides as good or better precision than a single precision floating point data type, which only has 24 significant bits in the index. On a 64-bit processor, we can use a 64-bit integer data type for the index and increment and get the same precision as a double precision floating point data type. With a 64-bit value, we can use a shift of up to 48 bits rather than 16. Note, however, that when using a 64-bit value, the multiplier needed to convert index increment to fixed point will be 2^{48} and can potentially exceed the precision (not the maximum range) of a double precision data type when multiplied by long table sizes. A smaller shift, such as 40 bits, can prevent the overflow. Since we are not using the fractional portion of the index for interpolation, a 32-bit value is very nearly as good as a 64-bit value. Unless the native word size of the computer is 64-bits, or table lengths exceed 64K entries, there is no great advantage to using a 64-bit value.

One final optimization is possible when using fixed point index values. We can mask off the upper bits beyond the bits used for the index rather than testing against the limits to the index value. For a table length that is a power of two, the mask is 2^n-1, which is *tableLength* shifted into the high word minus one.

```
i32Increment = frTI * frequency * 65536;
i32Index = 0;
i32Mask = (tableLength << 16) - 1;
for (n = 0; n < totalSamples; n++) {
   samples[n] = wavetable[(i32Index+0x8000)>>16];
   i32Index = (i32Index + i32Increment) & i32Mask;
}
```

This is as optimal as we can get without resorting to assembly language. Note that we can only safely go up to 16K in table size using 16 bits as the index. We can, however, use larger tables by changing the shift value. In other words, we move the binary point to allow for more index bits. A 64k table will work if we use 14 bits for the fractional part. Alternatively, if we don't need to subtract from the index, we can use an unsigned 32-bit data type for the index and set the shift value so that the index is located in the MSB. In that case, there is no need to mask the index at all since it will overflow at modulo the table length.

A Micro-Synth

In the chapter on envelope generators we saw that we can produce an envelope generator using a table of stored values. Such an envelope generator is nearly identical to a wavetable oscillator. We can, in fact, use identical code for both by constructing the envelope table to be the same length as the oscillator wavetable. We must calculate the table increment for the envelope generator by treating the duration of the sound as the period of the waveform. In other words, the frequency of the envelope is $1/d$ where d is the duration of the sound.

Using the same table scanning code for signal and envelope generation allows us to develop a very small synthesis routine that can generate sounds of different frequencies and timbre without adding any significant amount of code to a program. Such a routine is useful as a simple sound generator in a larger program, or on an embedded processor where memory and processor speed are limited.

Combining the wavetable oscillator and wavetable envelope generator produces the following code, which we can call the *micro-synth*. The tables can be filled using the routines from the envelope generator and sine wave summing code shown before. The tables need to be re-initialized when the waveform, envelope or amplitude changes. If a fixed waveform and envelope are sufficient, the tables can be initialized at compile time.

```
long waveTable[TL];
long envTable[TL];
float frqTI = TL / sampleRate;
long indexMask = (TL << 16) - 1;
```

```
long GenSound(float freq, float dur, short *out) {
   long totalSamples = (dur * sampleRate);
   long wavIncr = ((frqTI * freq) * 65536.0);
   long envIncr = ((frqTI / dur) * 65536.0);
   long wavNdx  = 0;
   long envNdx = 0;
   for (int n = 0; n < totalSamples; n++) {
      out[n] = ((waveTable[(wavNdx+0x8000)>>16]
            * envTable[(envNdx+0x8000)>>16])
            >> 15);
      wavNdx = (wavNdx + wavIncr) & indexMask;
      envNdx = (envNdx + envIncr) & indexMask;
   }
   return totalSamples;
}
```

This code uses fixed point values for both the envelope and oscillator phase increment and thus completely avoids floating point operations inside the sample generation loop. It is also possible to pass the frequency and duration values as fixed point values and eliminate the floating point code altogether.

On a historical note, early synthesis systems often used a wavetable oscillator as an envelope generator, and numerous examples of instruments found in the literature show two stacked oscillators rather than an envelope generator and oscillator combination.

Example Code

An example program that uses the wavetable oscillators is contained in the *Example04* directory. This example uses the classes from the *BasicSynth* library for oscillators and envelope generators.

BasicSynth Library Classes

Several wavetable oscillator classes are defined in the library.

GenWaveWT –non-interpolating wavetable generator.
GenWaveI - wavetable generator with linear interpolation

GenWave32 – fast wavetable generator, 32-bit fixed point index
GenWave64 – fast wavetable generator, 64-bit fixed point index

These classes share a set of wavetables maintained in the *WaveTableSet* class. A global instance of this class is defined in the library and initialized by the *InitSynthesizer* function. The pre-defined waveforms are as follows.

WT_SIN – sine wave
WT_SAW – sawtooth wave, sum of first 16 partials.
WT_SQR – square wave, sum of first 8 odd partials.
WT_TRI – triangle wave, sum of first 8 odd partials.
WT_PLS –pulse wave, sum of first 16 partials, equal amplitude.
WT_SAWL – sawtooth wave, direct calculation.
WT_SQRL – square wave, direct calculation.
WT_TRIL – triangle wave, direct calculation.
WT_SAWP – sawtooth wave, direct calculation, 0-1.
WT_TRIP – triangle wave, direct calculation, 0-1.

The sawtooth, square, pulse and triangle waveforms created by summation are not necessarily bandwidth limited. For high-pitched sounds the upper partials may exceed the Nyquist limit. The number of partials are limited so that they may be used safely up to about 1.2kHz fundamental frequency (i.e., two octaves above Middle C) with a 44.1kHz sampling rate.

The waveforms designated with a *L* or *P* suffix are intended for LFO use. These waveforms are calculated directly and are not bandwidth limited. The waveforms with a *P* suffix have positive only values (i.e., amplitude 0-1) so that they may be used easily for amplitude control.

In addition to the basic WT generator classes, classes that implement various synthesis techniques are defined.

GenWaveSum – sum of waveforms.
GenWaveFM – two oscillator frequency modulation generator
GenWaveAM – amplitude modulation generator.
GenWaveRM – ring modulation generator.
GenWaveNZ – ring modulation of sine wave and noise generator.

Files:

```
Include/WaveTable.h
Include/GenWaveWT.h
Include/GenWaveX.h
```

Chapter 9

Mixing and Panning

In order to play simultaneous notes we need to combine samples from multiple generators before output. In other words, we need the equivalent of an audio mixer. A mixer for digital audio is simply a set of buffers that accumulate samples for the current sample time. When all samples for the current time have been generated, the mixer adds all the buffers together to produce the current sample.

The mixer buffer can be as simple as a single variable for each input channel. In order to produce stereo output we will need two variables, or a two element array, for each mixer input. As the current sample for each sound is generated it is added to the buffer. Because we are summing values together, we will need to attenuate the sample before adding it to the buffer, when removing it from the buffer, or both.

```
value *= inBuf[input].volume;
inBuf[input].left  += value;
inBuf[input].right += value;
```

When all inputs are set with the current samples, the combined input buffers are transferred to the output buffer. The input buffer is then cleared back to zero in preparation for the next sample.

```
for (i = 0; i < mixInputs; i++) {
   outLeft  += inBuf[i].left * lftOutVol;
   outRight += inBuf[i].right * rgtOutVol;
   inBuf[i].left = 0;
   inBuf[i].right = 0;
}
```

Panning

Panning refers to an apparent angle of displacement from a position directly in front of the listener.

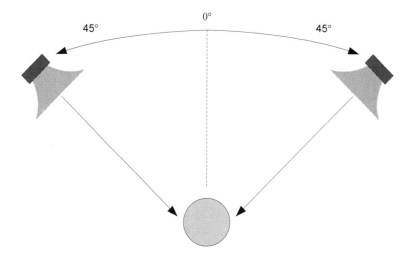

Figure 19 - Panning

As each sample is written to the mixer input buffer, we can vary the apparent spatial location of the sound by setting a different volume level for left and right channels. The difference in relative loudness will cause the listener to perceive the sound location to the left or right of the center position.

```
inBuf[input].left += value * leftVol;
inBuf[input].right += value * rightVol;
```

The simplest way to implement panning is to provide a different value for left and right volume as shown above. However, if we want to alter the overall volume level of a mixer input, we must change both values while keeping the same ratio. Usually we would prefer to set panning independently of the volume level. We can then move the spatial location of the sound by varying only one parameter. We can let the pan parameter vary over the range of [0,1] where 0 indicates full-left and 1 indicates full-right. This produces a simple calculation for the left and right output values.

```
value *= volume;
inBuf[input].left += value * (1 - panSet);
inBuf[input].right += value * panSet;
```

We can also let the pan setting range from -1 to +1 where a value of -1 indicates a sound all in the left and a value of +1 represents a sound all in the right. A value of zero sends the same amount to both outputs. We can then calculate volume levels for the left and right channels as follows.

```
value *= volume;
leftPan = (1 - panSet) / 2;
rightPan = (1 + panSet) / 2;
inBuf[input].left += value * leftPan;
inBuf[input].right += value * rightPan;
```

Either range will work equally well and which is chosen is a matter of preference. The *BasicSynth* library uses the range [-1,+1]. The resulting left and right volume multipliers values for different pan settings from -1 to +1 are shown in the following table.

Pan Value	Left Multiplier	Right Multiplier
+1.00	0.000	1.000
+0.50	0.250	0.750
+0.25	0.375	0.625
+0.00	0.500	0.500
-0.25	0.625	0.375
-0.50	0.750	0.250
-1.00	1.000	0.000

Note how the amplitudes change from 0 to 1 in each channel while the combined amplitude remains the same (1.0). With the pan set to 0, we have split the amplitude equally between the two output channels. When the pan value is non-zero, the total amplitude for the sample remains the same, but one channel will sound louder and we will hear this as a spatial movement of the sound.

The linear calculation of the pan amplitude is simple and efficient but produces the well-known "hole in the middle" effect due to a linear variation in peak amplitude in each channel. The greater intensity at one side or the other causes us to perceive the sound to have moved away from or towards the listener instead of only moving side-to-side.

To improve the smoothness of the panning effect, we can use a non-linear calculation. A common way to do this is to calculate the pan value by taking the *sin* of the apparent angle of the sound location. In the figure above, the pan location can vary from -45 to +45 degrees. At a value of 0 the sound is centered. We can normalize this angle to [-1,+1] and convert the pan setting to radians. The left and right amplitude values are then calculated as follows.

```
leftPan  = sin((1 - panSet)/2 * PI/2);
rightPan = sin((1 + panSet)/2 * PI/2);
```

The following table shows the resulting multipliers for left and right channels at various pan settings. This method produces a non-linear change in the amplitude values with combined amplitude ranges from 1 to 1.414, producing a greater amplitude at center than at full pan left or right. This compensates for the apparent forward and backward movement of the sound as it is panned.

Pan Value	Left Multiplier	Right Multiplier
+1.00	0.000	1.000
+0.50	0.383	0.924
+0.25	0.556	0.831
+0.00	0.707	0.707
-0.25	0.831	0.556
-0.50	0.924	0.383
-1.00	1.000	0.000

An alternative method of equalizing the intensity is to take the square root of the pan setting.

```
leftPan  = sqrt((1 - panSet)/2);
rightPan = sqrt((1 + panSet)/2);
```

This results in a slightly different curve, but one that also produces a nearly equal sound intensity as the pan setting is changed.

Pan Value	Left Multiplier	Right Multiplier
+1.00	0.000	1.000
+0.50	0.500	0.866
+0.25	0.612	0.791
+0.00	0.707	0.707
-0.25	0.791	0.612
-0.50	0.866	0.500
-1.00	1.000	0.000

In order to keep the amplitude range such that each channel is half amplitude at middle pan position, we can scale the pan values by multiplying them with $(\sqrt{2})/2$ (0.707..). This produces a lower sound intensity at full left and full right, but keeps the center value at 0.5.

All three methods will result in an apparent spatial movement of the sound and which method is chosen is partly a matter of preference. If desired, we can implement the pan function with multiple panning methods, including pan off, and then provide a parameter setting on the mixer to choose the method at runtime. Linear panning is obviously faster, but this is only a consideration if the panning position is changed continuously. In situations where the pan setting is fixed over the duration of a sound, the calculation of left and right amplitude multipliers can be made only when the pan setting is changed, avoiding the calculation on every sample. Furthermore, we can calculate the sin and square root values once and store them in a table. The panning code then only needs to retrieve the values from the table at runtime.

Typically, panning is incorporated into a mixer input channel. However, we can separate out the panning implementation and place it in a subroutine (or class) so that we can also incorporate panning in other places, such as a sound generator. Panning in a sound generator allows fine-grained, note-by-note control over the spatial location, including sending slightly different sounds to each channel. Dynamic panning can be controlled by an oscillator or envelope generator so that the sound sweeps back and forth while it is sounding. When panning is controlled outside the mixer, we need a way to bypass the mixer panning if desired. The library implementation of the mixer provides a method that allows the caller to set the left and right values directly.

Effects

Most commercial mixers include a separate in/out bus for effects such as reverb, flanging, and echo. Each of these effects will be described in subsequent chapters. For now, we can look at how generic effects can be incorporated into the mixer. With a generic effects interface, we can later add as many effects processors as desired.

In a typical mixer, each input channel includes an effects send level. When a signal is sent to the input it is also passed to the effects unit, attenuated by the send level. An effects unit receive level on the mixer acts as a sub-mixer that adds each effects unit, possibly with panning, to the summed output of the input channels. Thus each effects unit needs a buffer to accumulate the current sample, the input level for each mixer input channel, a pan value, and an output level. We can add an array of effects unit objects to the main mixer to hold these settings.

We apply the effects when we add the input channels together to produce the final output samples of the mixer. As each input channel is processed, the value is added to the effects unit buffer, attenuated by the send level for the input channel.

```
for (i = 0; i < mixInputs; i++) {
   value = inBuf[i].value;
   for (f = 0; f < fxUnits; f++)
      fx[f].value += fx[f].in[i] * value;
   outLeft  += value * inBuf[i].panleft * lftVol;
   outRight += value * inBuf[i].panright * rgtVol;
   inBuf[i].left = 0;
   inBuf[i].right = 0;
   inBuf[i].value = 0;
}
```

As an alternative, we can store the effects level values as an array in the input channel buffer and use:

```
fx[f].value += inBuf[i].fx[f] * value;
```

Once all inputs have been processed, we retrieve the processed sample from the effects unit and add it to the final output.

```
for (f = 0; f < fxUnits; f++) {
   value = fx[f].Process() * fx[f].outLvl;
   outLeft += value * fx[f].panleft * lftVol;
   outRight += value * fx[f].panright * rgtVol;
}
```

The *Process* method is a placeholder for the code that sends the current input value through the effects unit and returns the processed sample. Typically, this method will invoke the *Sample* method on the effects unit.

As with the input channel panning, we should add a capability to send values directly to a specific effects unit, bypassing the input channel.

Example Code

The program in the *Example06* directory shows various panning methods using the *BasicSynth Mixer* class.

BasicSynth Library Classes

The *Mixer* class implements a multiple input channel, stereo output mixer. The number of input channels is dynamically allocated at runtime. Each channel is represented by a *MixChannel* object. Effects unit channels are also dynamically allocated. A *Panning* class encapsulates the calculation of the left and right amplitude scaling values and may be used independently as well.

Files:

```
Include/Mixer.h
```

Chapter 10
Digital Filters

In the broadest sense, a filter is any function that takes input samples, modifies them in some way, and produces output samples. However, in music applications, we usually think of filters as those functions that alter the spectrum of the sound by amplifying or attenuating selected frequencies.

The mathematics involved in understanding and designing filters is complex and beyond the scope of this book. For those who need to design filters, that information can be found in books on digital signal processing. For the purposes of this book, we will take a simpler, more intuitive approach to understanding digital filters. *Note*: the equations for filters use the x variable to represent the input and the y variable for the output. This is slightly different from the use of these variables in describing signal generators where x typically represents time or frequency and y represents amplitude.

If we add a sinusoid to itself the resulting signal will be of the same phase and frequency but doubled in amplitude as shown in Figure 20.

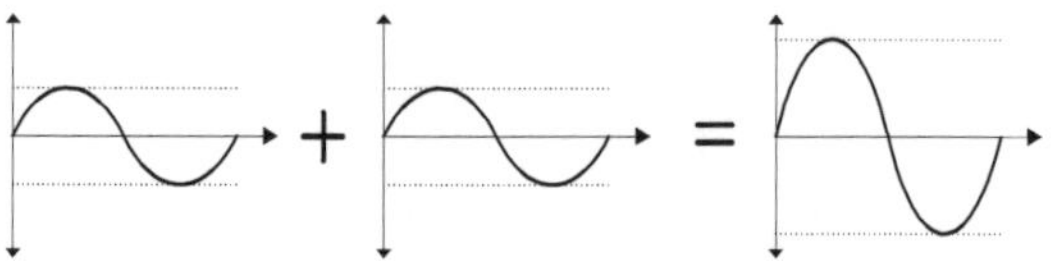

Figure 20 - Sum of sin waves

If we shift the input signal by 180° before adding, the input values cancel and produce no output (Figure 21).

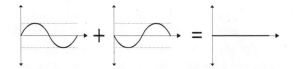

Figure 21 - Sum of sin waves, 180° phase shift

As the phase difference of the two waveforms increases from 0 to 180°, the amplitude of the sum decreases from 2 to 0. For example, at 90° phase difference, the amplitude of the output signal is 1.4142 (Figure 22). The phase of the output signal is shifted as well.

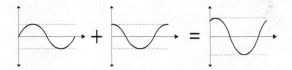

Figure 22 - Sum of sin waves, 90° phase shift

For a digitized signal, we can sum waveforms by adding samples together and a phase shift can be created by delaying the samples one or more sample times. If we store each sample in a buffer and then later add that sample back to the current sample, we have summed the signal with a phase-shifted version of itself. We can represent the sum of the signal and delayed sample with a diagram as shown in Figure 23. The delayed sample is represented by the box labeled z^{-1}. An amplitude multiplier is shown by a triangle.

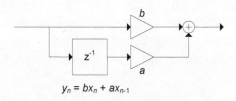

$$y_n = bx_n + ax_{n-1}$$

Figure 23 - Filter Diagram

When a delayed sample is summed with the current sample, the amount of phase shift is dependent on the sample rate and frequency of the signal. For example, at a sample rate of 10kHz, one sample delay is equal to the sample time of 0.0001 seconds. For a signal of 100Hz, the time of one period is 0.01 seconds and a one sample delay represents 1/100 of the period, or 3.6° of phase difference. A signal at 1000Hz has a period of 0.001 seconds and a one sample time delay is 1/10 of the period, or 36°. The larger phase difference results in a lower amplitude and the higher frequency signal is attenuated more than the lower frequency signal. The effect is that of a low-pass filter.

With the multipliers set to 1, the low-pass filter created by summing a one sample delay will have an amplitude of 2 at zero frequency and amplitude of 0 at $f_s/2$. This is easy to see since at $f_s/2$ the period of the waveform is only 2 samples long and a one sample delay represents half the period, or 180° phase shift. The peak amplitude for any frequency in between varies from 2 to 0.

With a two sample delay, the amplitude will be 0 at $f_s/4$ and will then increase back to 2 at $f_s/2$. The effect is a notch filter with a center frequency at 1/4 the sample rate.

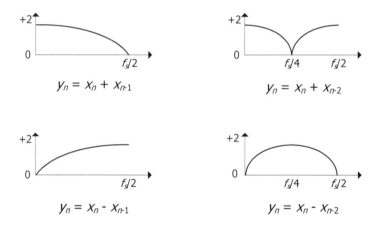

$$y_n = x_n + x_{n-1}$$

$$y_n = x_n + x_{n-2}$$

$$y_n = x_n - x_{n-1}$$

$$y_n = x_n - x_{n-2}$$

Figure 24 - Frequency Response of Simple Filters

If we subtract the delayed sample rather than add, the amplitude will be 0 when the phase difference is 0° and increase to a maximum of 2 at 180° phase difference. The effect is that of a high-pass filter. When we subtract the waveforms with a two sample delay, the result is a band-pass filter with the center frequency at $f_s/4$. The frequency responses of the various filters are shown in Figure 24.

The curves shown in the diagrams stop at zero and one-half the sample rate. If we were to continue the curves in the left column they would look like the curves on the right, but with a portion of the frequency range negative or above the one-half sampling rate point. In fact, all of these filters have a continuing series of peaks and zeros spaced at regular frequency intervals. As additional delay times are added, the filter output develops additional zeros within the audible range and the plot of the frequency response begins to look like a comb. Thus a filter created by multiple delays is referred to as a *comb filter*.

We can multiply the current and delayed samples by a value less than one in order to further affect the output amplitude. As the amplitude of the delayed sample is reduced, the filtering effect is reduced as well and the curve becomes flatter.

Implemented as a computer program, a digital filter is simply a sum of the input and delayed samples multiplied by their respective coefficients.

```
output = (input * ampIn) + (delay * ampDel);
delay = input;
```

We can implement a filter very simply by taking the average of the current sample and the previous sample, ($a=b=0.5$). This filter has a frequency response from 0Hz to $f_s/2$ with a very slow roll-off. As a general audio filter it has limited usefulness. However, there are a few situations where it is quite useful, despite its simplicity. Earlier we created a white noise generator by calling the *rand* function and scaling the output. If we apply a one-sample averaging filter to the noise signal we can reduce the upper frequencies and produce an approximation of pink noise. We can call it a *pinkish* noise generator.

```
value = (rand() - (RAND_MAX/2)) / (RAND_MAX/2);
out = (value + prev) / 2;
prev = value;
```

In addition to adding more delays, we can vary the filter response by adding multiple delay times together as shown in Figure 25.

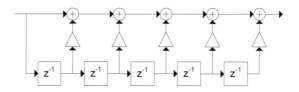

Figure 25 – Multiple Delay Filter

If we set the amplitude multipliers such that each successive delay is one-half the previous amplitude then send a sample at amplitude 1 through the filter followed by samples at 0 amplitude, the first output sample will be equal to 1, the next 1/2, the next 1/4, the next 1/8 and so on. In other words, our single input pulse has produced a series of decaying amplitude pulses as output. The output pulse will continue until it falls below the minimum amplitude level we can represent, or until we no longer add the delayed pulse into the input. The series of output pulses is known as the filter's impulse response. Because we eventually stop adding the impulse response into the signal, this type of filter is known as a Finite Impulse Response, or FIR.

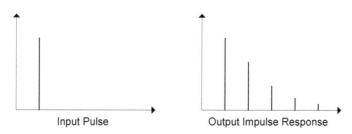

Input Pulse   Output Impulse Response

Figure 26 - Impulse Response

Since a digital signal can be considered a series of impulses at varying amplitudes, if we know the impulse response of the filter, we can sum the impulse response produced by each input sample and produce a digital filter with any frequency response we want. This process is called *convolution* and is the foundation of many digital signal processing techniques.

To implement a filter using convolution we must multiply the impulse response by each input sample. Since the current input sample multiplied by the impulse response affects future output samples, we need to do something like the following. (Array *a* contains the impulse response.)

```
for (n = 0; n < totalSamples; n++) {
   for (m = 0; m < impLen; m++)
      out[n+m] += a[m]*in[n];
}
```

However, this program will only work when we have buffers containing all input and output samples. If we only have the current input samples available, we can still perform convolution if we multiply the impulse response by prior samples. In DSP terminology, we must "flip" the impulse response relative to the prior input samples.

```
for (n = 0; n < totalSamples; n++) {
   for (m = 0; m < impLen; m++)
      out[n] += a[m] * in[n-m];
}
```

The program must match the first impulse with the current sample, the next impulse with the previous sample, etc. In other words, as the impulse subscript increases, the input sample index decreases. The easiest way to do this is to push the input samples into the front of an array so that sample *n* is at index 0, sample *n*-1 is at index 1, etc. We then loop through the two arrays and multiply them without actually "flipping" the stored impulse response. We can also shift the input samples as we scan the array and avoid looping over the delayed samples twice.

```
for (n = 0; n < totalSamples; n++) {
   in = samples[n];
   out = a[0] * in;
   for (m = impLen-1; m > 0; m--) {
      delay[m] = delay[m-1];
      out += a[m] * delay[m];
   }
   delay[0] = in;
   samples[n] = out;
}
```

This code will also work incrementally on samples as they are generated and does not need to have the entire input signal available. Although shown storing the values into the *sample* array, we can just as easily send the sample to another processor, output file or device.

Notice how the series of delays keeps adding prior samples to the current input. When the amplitude coefficient is reduced by the same amount for successive delay times, we can do the same thing if we take the output of the filter, attenuate it, and then add it back in. This is similar to how we converted a series equation into a recursive form, and this form of the comb filter is called a *recursive* filter. The diagram for this filter is shown in Figure 27.

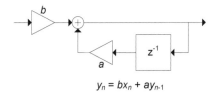

$$y_n = bx_n + ay_{n-1}$$

Figure 27 – Recursive (IIR) Filter

The feedback loop in this filter keeps summing the previous inputs and thus is an effective way to replace a series of delayed samples with a single delay buffer. More important, it eliminates the need to multiply and add each impulse response value for each sample. Because this filter can potentially continue to affect the output indefinitely, it is called an Infinite Impulse Response filter, or IIR. In order to be stable, the feedback coefficient must be less than 1. The frequency response of this filter is shown below. Notice that it is the inverse of the feedforward (FIR) filter.

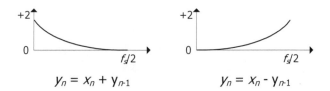

$$y_n = x_n + y_{n-1} \qquad\qquad y_n = x_n - y_{n-1}$$

Figure 28 - IIR Filter Frequency Response

The implementation of the IIR filter is nearly identical to the FIR filter. We only need to change the code so that we store the last output in the delay buffer instead of the last input.

```
output = (input * ampIn) + (delay * ampDel);
delay = output;
```

More complex filters can be constructed by combining the different filters shown above. By varying the number of delays, and the coefficients for the delays, a variety of filters can be created. A commonly used combination is the *bi-quad* filter. The bi-quad filter combines one and two sample feedforward delays (FIR) with one and two sample feedback delays (IIR).

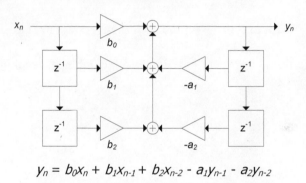

$$y_n = b_0 x_n + b_1 x_{n-1} + b_2 x_{n-2} - a_1 y_{n-1} - a_2 y_{n-2}$$

Figure 29 - Bi-Quad Filter, Direct Form I

We can convert this into a computer program as follows.

```
out = (ampIn0 * in)
    + (ampIn1 * dlyIn1)
    + (ampIn2 * dlyIn2)
    - (ampOut1 * dlyOut1)
    - (ampOut2 * dlyOut2);
dlyOut2 = dlyOut1;
dlyOut1 = out;
dlyIn2 = dlyIn1;
dlyIn1 = in;
```

We can also implement the bi-quad filter by swapping the FIR and IIR sections as shown in Figure 30.[7]

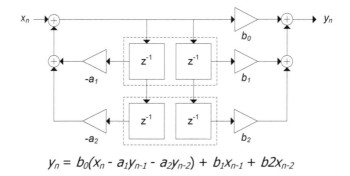

$$y_n = b_0(x_n - a_1 y_{n-1} - a_2 y_{n-2}) + b_1 x_{n-1} + b2 x_{n-2}$$

Figure 30 - Bi-quad Filter, Direct Form II

In this form, the delay buffers can be combined, resulting in the following code.

```
tmp = in
    - (ampOut1 * dlyBuf1)
    - (ampOut2 * dlyBuf2);
out = (ampIn0 * tmp)
    + (ampIn1 * dlyBuf1)
    + (ampIn2 * dlyBuf2);
dlyBuf2 = dlyBuf1;
dlyBuf1 = tmp;
```

Filter Coefficients

To create a filter with a specific frequency response it is necessary to calculate the appropriate coefficients for each delay. There are a variety of programs available that will calculate the coefficients given the type of filter, cutoff frequency, pass-band, gain, sample rate, etc.

---

[7] We can do this because the filter sections are both time-invariant and linear. In other words, they have the same effects independent of the order in which they are applied. This also means we can combine filters in series to get a sharper frequency response.

In those situations where the desired filter has a fixed frequency response, we can use a filter design program and then compile the values into the synthesizer program.

For dynamic filtering, such as that used in subtractive synthesis, we need to calculate the coefficients at runtime. This limits using filter design programs since they calculate the coefficients for a pre-defined set of frequencies. If we need to, we can pre-calculate the coefficients for a variety of frequencies and store them in a table. However, that limits the cutoff frequencies available. For a general purpose synthesizer, we need to recalculate the coefficients whenever the center frequency of the filter is changed, potentially on every sample.

For a low-pass FIR filter, the impulse response of the filter can be calculated using a windowed *sinc* function. In the following equation, f_c is the cutoff frequency, f_s is the sampling rate, N is an even number representing the number of delayed samples and k varies from 0 to N, inclusive. The expression in brackets containing two constants calculates a Hamming window.

$$a_k = \frac{\sin(2\pi(f_c/f_s)(k - N/2))}{\pi(k - N/2)} \cdot \left[0.54 + 0.46\cos\left(\frac{2\pi(k - N/2)}{N} \right) \right]$$

Although complicated at first glance, this equation is not that difficult to program. First, we can see that the expression $(k-N/2)$ will vary from $-N/2$ to $+N/2$. For example, with $N=6$, the expression will evaluate to values covering the range [-3,+3]. We know that $sin(x)$ and $sin(-x)$ have the same magnitude with differing sign and, because the divisor is also negative, the series of values produced will be a reflection around the middle value where $k=N/2$. When $k=N/2$ the value of the first term will be $sin(0)/0$ and cannot be calculated with a computer. We simply set this sample to a value of $(2 \cdot f_c/f_s)$. We can then calculate one-half of the series with $k=1...n/2$ and duplicate the values into the appropriate array positions.

The arguments to the *sin* and *cos* functions, as well as the divisor of the *sinc* function, can be calculated incrementally, as we did with oscillators.

We can also convert the low pass filter response into a high pass by spectral inversion. This is accomplished by inverting the sign on all coefficients and adding 1 to the middle coefficient.

```
impResp = new float[N+1];
n2 = N/2;
ndx1 = n2 + 1;
ndx2 = n2 - 1;
w1 = twoPI * (cutoff / sampleRate);
w2 = PI;
w3 = twoPI / N;
phs1 = w1;
phs2 = w2;
phs3 = w3;
impResp[n2] = 2 * (cutoff / sampleRate);
for (k = 0; k < n2; k++) {
    value = (sin(phs1) / phs2)
          * (0.54 + (0.46 * cos(phs3)));
    impResp[ndx1++] = value;
    impResp[ndx2--] = value;
    phs1 += w1;
    phs2 += w2;
    phs3 += w3;
}
if (hipass) {
    for (k = 0; k <= N; k++)
        impResp[k] = -impResp[k];
    impResp[n2] += 1.0;
}
```

As we did with oscillators, we can improve performance if we replace the calls to the *sin* and *cos* functions with a table lookup. The resulting coefficients may be slightly inaccurate, but will be sufficient for most synthesizer applications. If desired, interpolation of the table entries can improve the accuracy of the calculations.

The one-pole IIR filter can be used as an efficient low-pass filter, with some limitations. The roll-off is very sharp with low cutoff frequencies, and much flatter as the frequency is increased. The *a* and *b* coefficients are calculated as:

$$x = e^{-2\pi f}$$

$$a = -x$$

$$b = 1-x$$

The value of f is a fraction of the sample rate between 0.0 and 0.5, typically specified as a cutoff frequency and calculated as f_c/f_s.

```
x = exp(-twoPI*(cutoff/samplerate);
ampIn = 1 - x;
ampDel = -x;
```

The bi-quad filter can be used to realize a wide variety of filters. One filter type good for audio is the Butterworth filter. This filter has a flat pass-band and can easily be adapted to low-pass, high-pass, band-pass and band-reject operation. A second order filter will produce 12dB/oct response and is good enough for many applications while requiring a minimum of calculations. The calculations of coefficients for different filter types are shown below.

	Low Pass	High Pass	Bandpass
c	$1/\tan((\pi \cdot f)/f_s)$	$\tan((\pi \cdot f)/f_s)$	$1/\tan((\pi \cdot f)/f_s)$
d	$c^2 + \sqrt{2} \cdot c + 1$	$c^2 + \sqrt{2} \cdot c + 1$	$1+c$
b_0	$1/d$	$1/d$	$1/d$
b_1	$2/d$	$-2/d$	0
b_2	$1/d$	$1/d$	$-1/d$
a_1	$2 \cdot (1-c^2)/d$	$2 \cdot (c^2-1)/d$	$(-c \cdot 2\cos(2\pi f / f_s))/d$
a_2	$(c^2 - \sqrt{2} \cdot c + 1)/d$	$(c^2 - \sqrt{2} \cdot c + 1)/d$	$(c-1)/d$

Implementation of the filter code is straightforward. We can optimize the program by reusing values that have already been calculated. When used as a dynamic filter for subtractive synthesis, we can check the cutoff frequency and only recalculate the coefficients when the frequency changes. If needed for performance reasons, we can also ignore very small frequency changes.

```
sqr2 = 1.414213562;
if (lowpass) {
    c = 1 / tan((PI / sampleRate) * cutoffFreq);
    c2 = c * c;
    csqr2 = sqr2 * c;
    d = (c2 + csqr2 + 1);
    ampIn0 = 1 / d;
    ampIn1 = ampIn0 + ampIn0;
    ampIn2 = ampIn0;
    ampOut1 = (2 * (1 - c2)) / d;
```

```
    ampOut2 = (c2 - csqr2 + 1) / d;
} else if (highpass) {
    c = tan((PI / sampleRate) * cutoffFreq);
    c2 = c * c;
    csqr2 = sqr2 * c;
    d = (c2 + csqr2 + 1);
    ampIn0 = 1 / d;
    ampIn1 = -(ampIn0 + ampIn0)
    ampIn2 = ampIn0;
    ampOut1 = (2 * (c2 - 1)) / d;
    ampOut2 = (c2 - csqr2 + 1) / d;
} else if (bandpass) {
    c = 1 / tan((PI / sampleRate) * cutoffFreq);
    d = 1 + c;
    ampIn0 = 1 / d;
    ampIn1 = 0;
    ampIn2 = -ampIn0;
    ampOut1 = (-c*2*cos(twoPI*cutoffFreq/sr)) / d;
    ampOut2 = (c - 1) / d;
}
out = (ampIn0 * in)
    + (ampIn1 * dlyIn1)
    + (ampIn2 * dlyIn2)
    - (ampOut1 * dlyOut1)
    - (ampOut2 * dlyOut2);
dlyOut2 = dlyOut1;
dlyOut1 = out;
dlyIn2 = dlyIn1;
dlyIn1 = in;
```

The bi-quad filter can also be used to produce a resonant filter with constant gain. The frequency response for this filter has a single resonant peak, similar to a band-pass filter. The coefficients are calculated as follows.

$c = 2r \cdot \cos((2\pi / f_s) f_c)$

$a_1 = -c$

$a_2 = r^2$

$b_0 = 0.5 - (r^2 / 2)$

$b_1 = 0$

$b_2 = c$

The filter is specified with a cutoff frequency (f_c) and a resonance (r) in the range [0,1]. High values for r produce a narrow peak, while small values produce a flatter curve. The b coefficients are calculated to normalize the gain.

If the center frequency (f_c) is set to 0Hz, this filter acts as a low-pass filter with the resonance value effectively controlling the cutoff frequency and roll-off rate. Likewise, if the cutoff frequency is set to one-half the sampling rate, this filter acts as a high-pass filter. In both cases, the *cos* value is a constant, making calculation of the coefficients much faster.

All-Pass Filters

As we saw at the beginning of the chapter, a digital filter affects both the amplitude and phase of the output. As we will see later, there are times when we would like to shift the phase without affecting the amplitude. If we combine a FIR low-pass filter and a IIR high-pass filter, we can produce a filter with a flat frequency response. But, because of the delayed samples, we have a frequency dependent phase shift at the output. Such a filter is called an *allpass* filter.

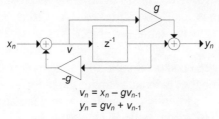

$$v_n = x_n - gv_{n-1}$$
$$y_n = gv_n + v_{n-1}$$

Figure 31 - Allpass Filter

When the coefficient is calculated as shown in the following code, the allpass filter produces a phase shift equivalent to a fraction of a sample. The delay parameter d represents a portion of a sample time.

```
g = (1.0 - d) / (1.0 + d);
out = dly;
dly = in - (dly * g);
out = out + (dly * g);
```

An alternate implementation using two delay buffers is also possible. The performance is essentially the same as when only one sample delay is used.

```
out = (g * in) + dly1 - (g * dly2);
dly1 = in;
dly2 = out;
```

Dynamic Filters

Λ common technique in subtractive synthesis is to sweep a low pass filter cutoff frequency with an envelope generator in order to produce a dynamic variation in the signal spectrum. The filters shown above can be used in that manner by initializing the cutoff frequency with the output of an envelope generator on each sample. However, this requires recalculation of the tangent and other values on each sample and can result in slow performance.

We can improve the speed of the filter by using a table lookup for the tangent value, just as we did with oscillators. A tangent is equivalent to the value of the sin divided by the cosine. Both the sine and cosine values can be retrieved from the sine wave table maintained by the wave table set object. The cosine is located at an offset of one-fourth the table length added to the sine value index. Thus we do not need a special table for tangents, but can do two table lookups and divide the two values to get the tangent.

In addition, we can combine an envelope generator with the filter code and pre-calculate the table index range for use as the envelope generator level values. This avoids calculating the table index from the frequency on each sample. We can also compare the current table index with the last table index and only recalculate the coefficients when the integer portion of the index value changes.

Using table lookup will produce a slight error in the cutoff frequency, but, for a dynamic filter, the error in frequency should not be apparent. It is the constant change in filter frequency, more than the specific frequency that is used, that produces the synthesizer effect.

Example Code

Example code for this chapter is in the *Example05* directory. The program generates one-second sounds passing a noise source and a square wave signal through each filter.

BasicSynth Library Classes

The BasicSynth library contains a variety of filter classes. Some filters are derived from the bi-quad filter, while others implement filters by averaging or convolution.

BiQuadFilter – Base class for filters using bi-quad form.
FilterLP – Butterworth low-pass filter.
FilterHP – Butterworth high-pass filter.
FilterBP – Butterworth band-pass filter.
Reson – Constant gain resonator.
DynFilterLP – Time-varying LP filter
AllPass – all-pass filter
FilterFIR – one-sample delay FIR filter
FilterIIR – one-sample delay IIR filter
FilterFIRn – *n*-sample convolution of the impulse response
FilterAvgN – *n*-sample averaging filter

Files:

```
Include/AllPass.h
Include/BiQuad.h
Include/Filter.h
Include/DynFilter.h
```

Chapter 11

Delay Lines

A delay line is used to store samples and then retrieve them for use some number of sample times later. Delay lines have a wide variety of uses in synthesizers. We have already seen one use in the development of filters. We accomplished a phase shift in the waveform by storing a sample in a variable and using it one and two sample times later. A more generic delay line allows storing samples for any number of sample times. Figure 32 shows the structure of a delay line.

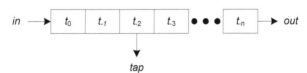

Figure 32 - Delay Line

Input samples are stored into the buffer at one end and taken out from the other. In programming terminology, a delay line is a FIFO queue.

In acoustical terms, a delay line produces an echo. If we add an attenuator at the output position of the delay line we can model the loss of signal energy in the echo. Loss of amplitude can be caused by absorption in the reflecting surface and by propagation through the air. In either case, a single attenuator at the output represents the total loss and we do not need to calculate the loss for each sample time individually.

The total time delay accomplished by the delay line is equal to the length multiplied by the sample time. Since the sample time is the reciprocal of the sample rate, the delay is also the length divided by the sample rate, $d = n / f_s$. Given the delay time, the length of the delay line is $n = d \cdot f_s$.

In addition to taking samples from the end of the delay line, we can set multiple taps that remove samples from the middle. This allows us to get multiple delay times from one buffer. The delay time for a tap is equal to one sample time multiplied by the tap position.

A delay line is implemented by allocating an array equal to the number of sample times and then shifting the contents on each sample, adding the new sample and removing the oldest sample in the process. The existing sample must be removed first before we overwrite the position with the new value.

```
delayLen = delayTime * sampleRate;
delayBuf = new float[delayLen]
...
out = delayBuf[delayLen-1] * decay;
for (n = delayLen-1; n > 0; n--)
   delayBuf[n] = delayBuf[n-1];
delayBuf[0] = in;
```

The loop that shifts the values in the buffer can be accomplished more efficiently with a specialized memory copy function, such as *memmove* from the standard C library. When using a block memory move function, we must be sure that it can handle overlapping source and destination. The loop shown here does that by starting at the end of the buffer rather than the beginning.

For short delay buffers, this code will work fine. However, as the length of the delay buffer increases, we spend an increasing amount of time shifting the samples in the buffer. We will have a more efficient implementation if we leave the samples in place and move a buffer index that indicates the current input/output position. Every time we add a sample to the buffer, we first extract the oldest sample, store the new sample back in its place, then increment the index modulo the buffer length. We must increment any tap positions as well. The result is a ring buffer.

```
out = delayBuf[delayIndex] * decay;
delayBuf[delayIndex] = in;
if (++delayIndex >= delayLen)
   delayIndex = 0;
```

To further optimize the program, we can implement the delay line using pointer arithmetic rather than array indexing.

```
ptrIn = delayBuf;
ptrEnd = &delayBuf[delayLen-1];
...
out = *ptrIn * decay;
*ptrIn = in;
if (++ptrIn > ptrEnd)
   ptrIn = delayBuf;
```

The delay line can be defined for use with any data type, including data structures. For example, if we want to store two channel audio, we can use a data structure with values for left and right outputs. When using a programming language that supports template base classes (e.g., C++) we can define a template base class that will implement a delay line for any abstract data type that includes support for an assignment operator.

Resonators

A delay line can also be set up to provide a regenerating signal. If we add the input value to the current contents of the delay buffer rather than replacing the value, the signal in the delay line will re-circulate.

```
out = delayBuf[delayIndex] * decay;
delayBuf[delayIndex] = in + out;
if (++delayIndex >= delayLen)
   delayIndex = 0;
```

The attenuator at the output of the delay line is applied each time the sample travels through the delay line and is equivalent to the dampening, or decay, of a signal over time. The input sample will be reduced in amplitude on each cycle through the buffer and slowly fade to an inaudible level. The acoustic effect is the same as multiple echoes of the signal combining together. In other words, this kind of delay line acts like a resonator. We can calculate the decay value so that the samples are attenuated with an exponential decay curve in a manner similar to the envelope generator. The exponent is the ratio of the delay time to the decay time. The base value is chosen as the level of attenuation after the decay time has passed. A value of 0.001 is equivalent to -60dB.

```
decay = pow(0.001, delayTime/decayTime);
```

The decay value must be chosen carefully to avoid overflow. Furthermore, since we are adding the input to the attenuated output, we can easily produce out of range samples. It may be necessary to attenuate the input sample before adding it to the delay line.

Allpass Delay

In the discussion of filters we saw that mixing a delayed sample with the current input sample produces a comb filter. Each additional sample time delay adds another tooth to the comb filter. If we take the output of a delay line and combine it with the input sample, the result will be filtered, coloring the sound somewhat. In those situations where we don't want to color the sound, or we need better control of the sound coloration, we can use the allpass configuration for a delay line just as we did with a one-sample delay allpass filter. When the feedback coefficient is the negative of the feedforward coefficient, the frequency response is kept flat.

```
val1 = delayBuf[delayIndex];
val2 = in - (val1 * decay);
delayBuf[delayIndex] = val2;
if (++delayIndex >= delayLen)
   delayIndex = 0;
out = val1 + (val2 * decay);
```

Varying the ratio of the two coefficients (i.e., using different *decay* values for input and output) will allow us to vary the filter frequency response.

Variable Delay

A variable delay line allows us to vary the delay time while adding and removing samples. Changing the total length of the delay line is not practical since that would require reallocating and copying the buffer each time the delay length changed. Instead, a variable length delay is accomplished by moving a read tap. The overall length of the delay line is constant, but the read point is constantly changing. The change in read index produces the varying delay.

The following figure shows the starting position for a delay line with one read tap set at four sample times delay. The numbers above the boxes show the index value. The numbers inside the boxes show the relative sample delays. The write position represents a ten sample delay prior to writing the current value, and a zero sample delay after the new value is written.

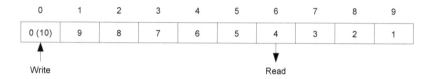

The next figure shows the relative positions after some number of samples have been added to the delay line. The write index has moved four positions, but the read index has moved six positions and the delay time for the read tap is now only two sample times.

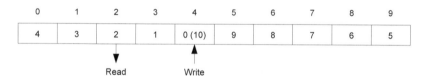

The different increment values for the read and write indexes cause the delay line to resample the input signal. The result is a frequency shift between the input and output signals. When the read increment is positive and greater than 1, the read index increments faster than the write index producing a decreased delay time and higher frequency. When the read increment is less than one (including negative values), the read index lags, producing an increased delay time and a lower frequency. When the value of the read increment is fixed, but a value other than 1, the frequency shift is constant. A more typical use is to vary the read increment on each sample. As the distance between the two indexes varies, the delay time shifts and produces a continuous frequency shift.

Different increment values for the read and write indexes will cause them to eventually pass each other. When that happens there will be a discontinuity in the output samples. Although there are techniques to blur the discontinuity, we would still need to detect the collision and the logic for that comparison is not trivial. To make effective use of the variable delay line, the read index value should never pass the write index value. When one limit (minimum or maximum delay) is reached, the delay switches direction. A typical implementation would use some kind of oscillator that varies between the minimum and maximum delay times. For example, we could use the *sin* function multiplied by the range of delay times to calculate an offset to the read position.

The total length of the delay line must be set to a value greater than or equal to the maximum delay time. Assuming we read before write, the maximum delay occurs when the read index is equal to the write index. However, if we write before read, a delay of zero occurs when the read index is equal to the write index. Thus we will typically want the overall delay length to be one sample greater than the maximum delay, or restrict the minimum delay to 1 sample time. Alternatively, we can test for the boundary conditions and either read before write, or write before read, as appropriate.

The following code implements a variable delay line. The delay range and initial delay values are in samples. This code does not show the calculation of the oscillator phase, which is the same as the oscillator code shown earlier.

```
delayBuf[delayWrite] = in;
if (++delayWrite >= delayLen)
   delayWrite -= delayLen;
delayOffset = delayMid + (delayRange * sin(phase));
if ((delayRead = delayWrite - delayOffset) < 0)
   delayRead += delayLen;
out = delayBuf[delayRead];
```

The delay range is a positive value representing the maximum positive or negative displacement to the delay time. The values for *delayMid* and *delayRange* can be set directly, or calculated from minimum and maximum values.

```
delayRange = (delayMax - delayMin) / 2;
delayMid = delayMin + delayRange;
```

There is a problem with this implementation that is not immediately obvious. The read index will almost always change by a non-integer value and the round-off of the index results in a quantization error on most samples. For some waveforms, the error is minimal and may be masked by the overall signal. However, for most signals, the effect is quite noticeable. The resulting distortion of the waveform is called zipper noise. To minimize zipper noise we must interpolate between the current and previous samples. Linear interpolation of a delay line is similar to the interpolation we used with wavetable oscillators. We extract two samples and calculate a weighted average using the fractional portion of the read index.

```
delayOffset = delayMid + (delayRange * sin(phase));
delayRead = delayWrite - delayOffset;
if (delayRead < 0)
   delayRead += delayLen;
readInt = floor(delayRead);
readFract = delayRead - readInt;
if (delayOffset < 1)
   delayBuf[delayWrite] = in;
out = delayBuf[readInt] * (1 - readFract);
if (--readInt < 0)
   readInt += delayLen;
out += delayBuf[readInt] * readFract;
if (delayOffset >= 1)
   delayBuf[delayWrite] = in;
if (++delayWrite >= delayLen)
   delayWrite -= delayLen;
out *= decay;
```

To perform the interpolation, we first separate the read index into integer and fractional parts. Because the write index is incrementing, prior samples are at negative offsets from the write index. In other words, a delay time of one sample means the read index is one position less than the current write index. We have subtracted only the integer portion of the delay to produce the read index, thus the second sample for interpolation is one position less than the calculated read index. Before reading the delay buffer, we check to see if the delay offset is less than one sample. In that case we need to set the current sample into the delay buffer so that we will use it and the previous sample to calculate the output. If the delay offset is equal to the length of the delay line, the write index points to the oldest sample, and we want to use that value before setting the new value into the delay buffer. Thus, when the delay time is more than one sample, we wait to write the new value into the delay buffer until after we have performed the interpolation. This method allows the delay time to vary from 0 to the total delay line length. An alternative strategy is to prevent the delay offset from reaching one of the extremes. This can be done by limiting the maximum delay value to *delayLen-1*. Note also that the maximum delay time can contain a fractional portion. When allocating the delay line, it is important to round up the number of samples.

Linear interpolation will only work if the change in the read index is less than two sample times per sample. For greater delay increments, there is no easy way to interpolate with two samples. We would need to take an average of multiple values. However, for most uses of variable delay lines, the delay time increment will be small and two sample interpolation will work. Note that the actual delay time is not a problem, only the change in delay time per sample.

Echo

One of the easiest things we can do with a delay line is to produce an echo. We must allocate a delay line equal to the echo time, add each generated sample to the delay, and add each delayed sample to the current sample before writing the output. We can produce multiple echoes by adding taps to the delay line, or by using multiple delay lines.

```
delayLen = echoTime * sampleRate;
// allocate and zero delayBuf
for (n = 0; n < totalSamples; n++) {
    in = samples[n];
    out = delayBuf[delayIndex];
    samples[n] = in + out;
    delayBuf[delayIndex] = in;
    if (++delayIndex >= delayLen)
        delayIndex = 0;
}
```

Because the delay line adds additional samples to the output, the input sample buffer must be padded with zeros equal to the length of the delay line. Optionally, we can continue to read delayed samples until we have emptied the delay line, using 0 as the input value.

```
for (m = 0; m < delayLen; m++) {
    samples[n++] = delayBuf[delayIndex];
    if (++delayIndex >= delayLen)
        delayIndex = 0;
}
```

Because we are adding two samples to produce the output, there is a likelihood that the output value will overflow and we need to reduce the output amplitude in some manner. We can take the average of the two values, but a more flexible method is to use a *mix* variable to control the blend of direct sound and echo. If *mix* is considered the amount of the echo to blend, normalized to [0,1], we have the following code.

```
samples[n] = (in * (1 - mix)) + (out * mix);
```

Karplus-Strong Plucked String

The Karplus-Strong algorithm[8] is another interesting application of a delay line. As we saw with wavetable oscillators, cyclic scanning of a table of values can produce a periodic signal. Suppose we initialize a recirculating delay line with one cycle of a waveform and then only read the delay line instead of adding new values. The signal circulates through the delay line but is attenuated on each cycle. The result is a dampening waveform, much like applying an envelope generator to the waveform, and is a good model of a dampened oscillation.

Rather than initializing the delay buffer with a coherent waveform, we can initialize the buffer with an initial impulse, such as a burst of noise. If we add a lowpass filter into the feedback of the delay line, we reduce the high-frequency content of the sound on each cycle. This models what happens when we strike or pluck a physical object.

---

[8] K. Karplus, A. Strong, "Digital Synthesis of Plucked String and Drum Timbres." *Computer Music Journal* 7(2), pp.43-55 (1983).

The initial pluck produces a noisy transient that is filtered by the physical structure of the object, air and/or resonator.

The fundamental frequency of the resulting sound is calculated by the following equation, where N is the delay line length in samples.

$$f_o = \frac{f_s}{N + 0.5}$$

Thus we can calculate the delay line length for a given frequency as:

$$N = \frac{f_s}{f_o} - 0.5$$

```
delayLen = (sampleRate / frequency) + 0.5;
totalSamples = duration * sampleRate;
for (n = 0; n < delayLen; n++)
   delayBuf[n] = (rand() - 16383) / 16383;
out = 0;
for (n = 0; n < totalSamples; n++) {
   in = delayBuf[delayIndex];
   out = (in + out) / 2;
   delayBuf[delayIndex] = out;
   if (++delayIndex > delayLen)
      delayIndex = 0;
   samples[n] = out;
}
```

Because the delay line length (N) must be an integer value, the frequencies available are limited, especially as the frequency is increased. The accuracy of the frequency can be improved by incorporating an allpass filter into the code, thus extending the delay by a portion of a sample time.[9] The delay time for the allpass filter is equivalent to the fractional portion of N.

---

[9] D.A. Jaffe, J.O. Smith, "Extension of the Karplus-Strong Plucked-String Algorithm." *Computer Music Journal* 7(2), pp. 56-69 (1983)

Example Code

An example of using a delay line to produce echoes is in *Example07*. An implementation of the Karplus-Strong plucked string is in *Example07c*.

BasicSynth Library Classes

The *BasicSynth* library classes for delay lines implement each of the following.

DelayLine implements a basic delay line and is the base class for other delay line classes.

DelayLineR implements a recirculating delay line.

DelayLineT implements a multi-tap delay line.

DelayLineV implements a variable delay line with interpolation.

AllPassDelay implements a delay line using the allpass difference equation in place of the single decay attenuation value.

Files:

```
Include/DelayLine.h
```

Chapter 12

Reverb

An instrument with a resonator (such as a drum or violin) produces a sound that is a mix of direct vibration and multiple reflections of the sound. Likewise, when we hear a sound in a room, we hear both the sound source and reflections of the sound mixed with it. We call this mixture of reflected sound reverberation. Sounds that lack reverberation will usually sound dull and lifeless and even a small amount of reverberation can make the sound more natural. In addition, we can use reverberation to simulate the sound of a large room, even when listening to the sounds in a small room or on headphones.

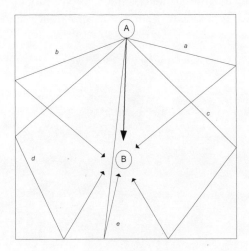

Figure 33 – Direct and Reflected sounds

In a physical space, sounds are being continuously reflected and mixed together from many surfaces similar to what is shown in Figure 33. Both the size and surfaces in the space affect the sound. Different kinds of surfaces reflect different amounts of sound at different frequencies and thus act as filters. Furthermore, a reflected sound does not simply bounce once and quit. It continues to reflect off different surfaces until the energy in the sound dissipates. What we hear is a complex set of reflections that die out over a period of time, potentially several seconds, combined with a subtle change in spectrum. In addition, as the amplitude of the reflected sound decreases, the density of the reflections increases.

We can model a continuing reflection using a feedback (i.e., re-circulating) delay line. The length of the delay line should be initialized to a value that represents some average delay in the reflected sounds. The decay value should be set so that the signal is attenuated below the audible level after the total reverberation time. The reverberation time is defined as the amount of time it takes for the sound to drop below the level of audibility (about 60dB reduction). A 60dB reduction is a ratio of 1/1000 (0.001 = 20 $\log_{10}(60)$). Thus the feedback coefficient is $0.001^{Lt/Rt}$ where Lt is the initial delay (usually called the loop time) and Rt is the reverb time.

To estimate the initial delay time, we can model the delay of a signal reflected from a nearby surface as shown in Figure 34.

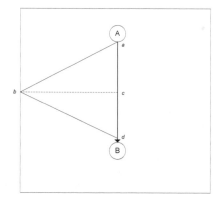

Figure 34 – Reflection Delay

Using the Pythagorean theorem, we can calculate the distance along the reflected sound path.

$$R = \sqrt{(c-a)^2 + (c-b)^2} + \sqrt{(d-c)^2 + (c-b)^2}$$

The delay time of the reflected sound is the difference between the direct path *a-c-d* and the reflected path *a-b-d* multiplied by the speed of sound (~340m/s). Varying the lengths of the triangle height and base to simulate different points of reflection will give us a range of values that are typical for various room sizes. The resulting values range from ~30ms delay for a nearby source and reflection (5m), up to ~500ms delay for a distant source and reflecting surface (100m). Typical reverberation times range from 1 to 1.5 seconds. Shorter reverb times represent a relatively "dead" room, while longer times represent a "live" room, such as a cathedral. These are the ranges we want to use to calculate the delay time and decay values of the resonator.

```
loopTime = 0.04;
rvrbTime = 1.5;
delayLen = loopTime * sampleRate;
decay = pow(0.001, loopTime / rvrbTime);
mix = 0.1;
atten = 1.0; // adjust to prevent overflow

for (n = 0; n < totalSamples; n++) {
   in = samples[n];
   out = delayBuf[delayIndex] * decay;
   delayBuf[delayIndex] = (in * atten) + out;
   if (++delayIndex >= delayLen)
      delayIndex = 0;
   samples[n] = (in * (1-mix)) + (out * mix);
}
```

The *mix* variable controls the mixture of reverberated signal (the "wet" signal) and original signal (the "dry" signal). Typically, the mix value would be 10% or less, although higher values can be used to produce an almost pure reverb sound, such as the sound heard when the direct path is blocked in some way.

In a real room, the high frequencies will tend to dissipate faster than low frequencies and later reflections will sound slightly muffled.

The reverberator will automatically act as a comb filter, but we can insert additional filters into the feedback loop to modify this effect. A simple averaging filter will further attenuate the high-frequencies, but more complex filters can be used as well.

```
out1 = delayBuf[delayIndex] * decay;
out2 = (out1 + prev) / 2;
prev = out1;
samples[n] = (in * (1-mix)) + (out2 * mix);
```

A single delay line as shown above will provide some reverberation and works well to simulate the resonance of a musical instrument. The delay time should be short, 1-10ms, and the reverb time less than one second. Adding the resonator to the output of an oscillator can often change an obvious electronic sound into a much more pleasing sound.

We know from the discussion of digital filters that a delayed signal that matches the phase of the input signal will reinforce that frequency. For example, if the delay time is set to 0.0023s the length of the delay line very nearly matches the wavelength of a frequency of 440Hz. The natural frequency of the delayline, and all harmonics of that frequency, will be amplified causing some frequencies to stand out more than others. Consequently, the reverberator will have a metallic "ring" to the sound.

Furthermore, room reverberation requires a buildup of reflected sounds over time. For that we need to combine multiple resonators at different time delays. When the delay lengths differ, their combination produces an increasing density of sounds and will also tend to mask the ringing effect. When the delay times are relative primes, the resonant peak of one delay line is different from the others and will attenuate the frequencies that the other resonators amplify.

A classic reverb design based on this principle is the Schroeder reverb.[10] This reverb uses a set of parallel comb filters plus two all-pass filters in series.

---

[10] M. Schroeder, "Natural Sounding Artificial Reverberation," *J. Audio Eng. Soc.*, vol 10, p. 219 (1962 July).

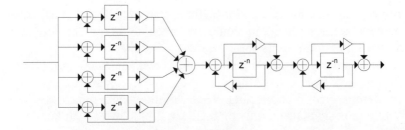

Figure 35 - Schroeder Reverb

The parallel comb filters provide different amounts of delay and in combination produce an effect similar to the multiple reflections in a real room. The two allpass filters further spread out the reflections. The delay times for the comb filters and allpass filters are given in the following table and are the ones commonly used in synthesis software. RT is typically in the range of 1 to 1.5 seconds, but can be set to longer times in order to simulate larger spaces.

Filter	Loop Time	Reverb Time
C_1	0.0297	RT
C_2	0.0371	RT
C_3	0.0411	RT
C_4	0.0437	RT
A_1	0.09638	0.0050
A_2	0.03292	0.0017

Using these values, the resulting sound is a fairly good simulation of reverberation in a medium sized room. Nevertheless, the short loop times tend to produce an overall metallic sound due to the relatively high resonant frequency. At low levels of reverberation mix, up to about 10%, and reverberation times of one-second or less, the sound is not objectionable. However, as the amount of reverb and the reverb time increase, the metallic ringing sound becomes more noticeable.

Another noticeable effect of this design is a fluttering sound that shows up when very short sounds with sharp attack transients are used. Varying the reverb and loop times can often minimize these effects. To make the reverb easy to use, we should build-in a set of preset delays that work well in general cases. But it is often best to tweak the reverb times by ear to fit the specific sounds in the music rather than relying on a single fixed set of values. Thus, when creating the reverberation code, we need to allow the loop and reverberation times to be variable.

Reverb design is an on-going area of research. Many other reverb designs have been created and are described in journals and textbooks on digital signal processing. The variations are almost endless. Different designs use more comb filters, pre-delay to simulate initial reflections, low pass and band pass filters to simulate frequency attenuation, more allpass filters to create more density, nested delay lines, splitting and mixing different delays into multiple channels, etc. In fact, there may be as many reverb designs and parameter settings as there are synthesizers. For the synthesizer we develop in this book, we will only create two reverb types, one that uses a single comb filter with low pass filter, and one based on the Schroeder design. These will be sufficient for a basic synthesis system. We can always extend the library with additional reverb types at any time.

We have been considering reverberation as a means of simulating natural room acoustics, as that is the most common use. Typically, reverberation is added to the generated sound as the last step before output, or as a separate step when mastering the sound file for reproduction. Thus the most natural place for incorporating reverb is in the mixer. However, we don't have to limit the use of reverb to simulation of room acoustics, but can treat reverberation as a sound generation technique in its own right. A highly reverberant sound can be treated as a unique timbre and used compositionally to create contrast and tension, just as we might use different instruments compositionally. We should design our reverb code to be independent of the mixer or other processing steps and allow it to be plugged-in anywhere during sound generation.

Example Code

A program demonstrating reverberation is in the directory *Example07a*. Sounds are produced using an allpass delay line, feedback delay line with low-pass filter, and Schroeder reverb.

BasicSynth Library

Two reverberation classes are implemented in the library.

Reverb1 – delay line with low-pass filter
Reverb2 – Schroeder reverberator

Files:

Include/Reverb.h

Chapter 13

Flanging and Chorus

Flanging is a technique developed in analog recording that adds a delayed signal to the original signal by running two tape recorders in parallel. The speed of each tape recorder is alternately varied by touching the flange of the tape reel, momentarily slowing down the recorder. The effect of flanging is to blend two signals that are slightly offset in time and also varying in pitch. The variable frequency shift between the two signals causes phase cancellation at different frequencies producing the classic "swoosh" sound.

We can emulate flanging using a variable delay line controlled by an oscillator. Figure 36 shows the basic structure for a flanger.[11]

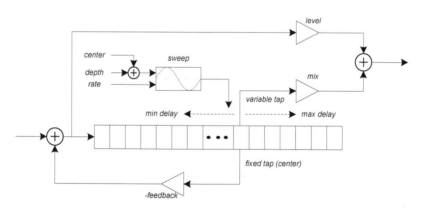

Figure 36 - Flanger/Chorus

---

[11] J. Dattoro, "Effect Design Part 2: Delay-Line Modulation and Chorus." *J. Audio Eng. Soc.,* vol. 45, pp. 764-788 (October 1997).

This setup provides several variable parameters. Depending on the settings, the flanger can produce vibrato, chorus, flanger, or siren-like warble effects. Depth values for a flanger effect will typically vary from 1 to 10ms with a center delay of 10ms or less and a very slow (.15 Hz) sweep rate. Chorus typically uses very small *depth* values but greater *center* values and faster sweep rates. Longer delays, and wider range of delay, produces a more dramatic effect, as does increasing the mixture of the delayed signal. As the center delay time increases, the sound acquires a distinct echo.

The sweep oscillator is used to move the variable tap back and forth around a nominal delay time (*center*) as shown in Figure 37. A typical sweep rate is slow, around 0.1 to 0.5Hz, but can vary from 0.01Hz up to around 10Hz at the maximum. (Beyond 10Hz the oscillator begins to introduce an audible FM effect.)

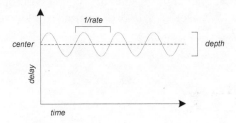

Figure 37 - Flanger sweep control

The maximum delay will be *center+(depth/2)* and the minimum delay *center-(depth/2)*. Obviously, the minimum delay must be zero or greater. Thus the *depth* parameter must be less than or equal to twice the *center* delay value and the delay line must be created with a length equal or greater than the maximum delay.

The relative settings of the *level* and *mix* values will control the strength of the flanger effect. Setting the two values equal produces the typical phasing effect of a flanger. Decreasing the *mix* value relative to the *level* creates a more subtle flanger effect. A *level* setting of 0 takes all output from the delay line and produces a vibrato.

The optional feedback signal is used to affect the coloration of the flanger. From the discussion of filters, we know that mixing a delayed version of a signal with the original signal produces a comb filter with zeros at the phase cancelation points. The number of teeth in the comb filter increases with the number of delays. As the delay shifts back and forth, the comb filter expands and contracts producing a variable frequency low-pass filter effect. This adds to the flanger effect, and is generally beneficial. However, the low-pass filtering effect can create a muffled sound and there may be times where we want to limit the frequency coloration. Just as the *mix* and *level* variables create a FIR filter, the *feedback* variable creates a IIR filter. When the *feedback* value is the negative of the *level* setting, the result is an allpass filter. Varying the *level, feedback* and *mix* settings changes the sound from low-pass to all-pass to high-pass filtering effects and varies the coloration of the sound. In short, the *feedback* controls the brightness of the resulting sound.

We can implement the flanger using the oscillator and variable delay line code shown previously. We need to calculate the delay time on each sample and set the delay line appropriately. In the following code, the oscillator and delay line are shown as functions rather than with in-line code.

```
OscilInit(sweep);
maxdelay = center + (depth / 2);
DelayInit(maxdelay);
...
if (feedback != 0)
   in -= DelayTap(center) * feedback;
DelaySet(center + (depth * Oscil()));
out = (in * level) + (Delay(in) * mix);
```

Example Code

An example program that uses the *BasicSynth Flanger* is in the *Example07b* directory. The *FlangerExplorer* program allows experimenting with the flanger parameter settings.

BasicSynth Library

The *Flanger* class implements the flanger/chorus unit.

Files:
```
Include/Flanger.h
```

Chapter 14

Synthesis System Architecture

The *BasicSynth* library classes that we have developed so far provide the sound generation and processing building blocks for many synthesis functions. It is possible to stop at this point and implement a synthesizer directly with software programs, each one written for a specific composition or application. However, our goal in developing the synthesis library is to provide not only sound generation objects that can be used in any program, but also to provide a foundation for a complete synthesis system.

Whereas implementation of the signal processing routines is largely a matter of converting the equations to code and then optimizing the code, development of a synthesis system architecture cannot be done by a simple step by step conversion. Software architecture development involves analysis of requirements, functionality, ease of use and implementation constraints. In other words, how the musician wants to use the synthesizer and the capability of the computer system are the determining factors in the system architecture.

A software architecture is defined by a set of components and their interfaces. The architecture does not directly specify how the system is to be used, or the kind of user interface that will be developed. The architecture is an abstract map of how the required functionality will be organized as a set of software modules. Once the architecture is defined, the specific functionality is implemented using the interfaces defined by the architecture. The architecture must be flexible enough that we can add functionality as needed without having to redesign the rest of the system. Thus we must think in abstract functionality that will be needed, not specific functionality of any one synthesis technique. If the architecture is flexible, we can adapt it to new functionality easily. On the other hand, if the architecture is too abstract, it will not be able to provide an effective framework for further development.

Consequently, development of a software architecture is an iterative process. We choose an initial structure then analyze the structure to determine if it meets all requirements while providing sufficient flexibility for further enhancement. After analysis, we modify the structure accordingly and perform the analysis again. This can be a lengthy process and may require development of several prototype systems for the purpose of analysis.

Rather than going through the steps of developing a synthesizer architecture, we will look at an architecture and then describe how it can be used. The architecture of the *BasicSynth* system is shown in Figure 38.

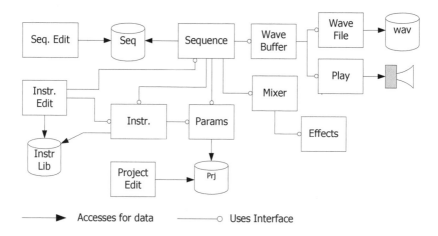

Figure 38 - BasicSynth System Architecture

This system is intended to be used as a compositional environment. Thus it centers around the sequencing of a series of events defined by the score and allows a variable set of instrument definitions. The sequencer reads the score and invokes one or more synthesis instruments to generate samples. Samples are passed through a common mixer and then to the output, either a wave file or a sound output device (DAC). The project information and parameters component contains general synthesizer information and also allows the sequencer to discover the available instruments and scores that are to be used. Editors are provided to create the score, instruments, and project parameters.

Module	Description
Sequence	Generates sample output based on a sequence of events. Events can be read from a file, added directly by a program, or added interactively through a user interface.
Seq. Edit	Editor (or generator) for sequencer files. Multiple formats can be defined by adding the appropriate file loading code to the sequencer.
Instr.	An Instrument, or sound generation and modification module. Instruments use generator, filter and effects objects to control sound generation.
Instr. Lib	File containing instrument configuration.
Instr. Edit	Editor for instrument definitions. This can be a simple text editor or a complex graphic interface.
Wave Buffer	Buffer for sample output.
Wave File	Output to a sound file, usually in WAV format, but possibly in other formats as well.
Play	Immediate output of samples to the computer's sound output device.
Mixer	Mixes sounds and applies effects.
Effects	Processing effects such as reverb, echo, flanger, etc.
Params	System wide parameters, such as sample rate, wave table length, input and output directories, etc., along with lists of instrument and sequencer files
Prjoject Edit	Editor for project parameters.

Chapter 15

Sequencer

The sequencer is the synthesizer component that cycles through events, dispatching each event in the proper order and at the proper time. Originally a sequencer was a module on an analog synthesizer that could step through a series of control voltages and produce a trigger at each step. When applied to an oscillator and envelope generator in combination, the sequencer played a short tune. The addition of microprocessor control allowed the sequencer to store any series of synthesizer control parameters and playback the control signals automatically. In a software synthesis system, the sequencer is expanded to provide the ability to automate timed control of any synthesizer function.

Timing

Timing information can be specified as either absolute or relative time. An absolute time system specifies the starting time and duration for each event. A relative time system specifies the offset from the previous event with duration implied by the offset to some later event. Events in both systems must be sorted by time. For the absolute time list, new events must be inserted into the event list at the proper position, but do not affect the start and end times of other events. This allows us to store sequencer events in a file in any order. We can break up the composition into separate sections of the file (i.e., into voices) and merge the sections by sorting the events by starting time. In contrast, a relative time system is dependent on the position of each event in the sequence. Inserting an event into the list pushes all subsequent events forward. Thus to merge multiple event lists requires adjustment of the start time of successive events, or the multiple event lists must be kept separate and processed independently during sequencing.

Absolute time event lists are typically used for scoring systems where we know the start time and duration of each note in advance. Relative event lists are typically used when events are recorded from a music instrument keyboard. In the case of recorded sequences, the recorder does not know in advance when an event will occur or how long an event will last. Thus it is easier to count ticks until the next event is received and store the relative time. However, we can always convert a relative time list into an absolute time list if we keep a running start time and calculate the start time for each event as the event list is loaded or generated. Likewise, an absolute time list can be converted into a relative time list by calculating the difference in start time between successive events.

In terms of the sequencer design, either strategy works about as well as the other. For absolute time, the sequencer keeps a running tick count and compares the start time of the event with the current time. For relative time, the sequencer counts down the start of the next event. If we need to maintain separate event lists for a relative time system, the sequencer loop processes each list in turn, counting down the next event for each list separately.

An example of an absolute time loop is shown in the following code. The *event* array holds the event structures with the member *start* containing the start time.

```
index = 0;
currentTime = 0;
while (playing) {
   while (index < numEvents
     && event[index].start <= currentTime){
     Start(event[index++]);
   }
   Tick();
   currentTime++;
   playing = Finished();
}
```

The *Start* subroutine represents the actions needed to initialize an event. For sound generation, we must allocate and/or initialize an instance of a synthesis instrument using the event parameters and then add the instruction to a list of active events. During the *Tick* subroutine, all active events are processed to generate the next sample or alter synthesizer settings. The length of the event can be explicitly set as a duration, or can be determined dynamically. The *Finished* function tests to see if all active instruments have completed and if there are events remaining to be processed. When an active event is finished it is removed from the active list. When all events are processed the sequencer can stop.

A relative time loop is shown in the following code. In this case the *start* member of the event holds the offset to the next event, which may be zero for simultaneous events.

```
index = 0;
offset = event[0].start;
while (playing) {
   if (index < numEvents) {
      if (offset == 0) {
         do {
            Start(event[index]);
            if (++index >= numEvents)
               break;
            offset = event[index].start;
         } while (offset == 0);
      }
      offset --;
   }
   Tick();
   playing = Finished();
}
```

Event Objects

The most common sequencer event is one to play a note. Each note is defined by a start time, duration, pitch and loudness. However, if we only playback notes with fixed sound generation parameters, the synthesizer will sound like a machine, not something musical. For example, if volume levels are fixed, we cannot produce a crescendo. If envelopes or instrument timbre are fixed, we cannot produce the subtle variations in articulation that are typical of an expressive musical performance. The more instrument parameters we can change during playback, the more expressive the synthesizer can become. Our events must be more than just note-on and note-off. We need to allow an event to represent anything that can potentially affect a synthesizer function during sound generation.

We could accomplish this by creating a large number of events, each one representing a different function. However, the synthesis system would be limited to the event types known by the sequencer. If we wanted to add new functions to the synthesizer we would have to add code to the sequencer as well. This is poor design since it tightly couples the sequencer to all other modules in the system. A better strategy is to attach a variable list of parameters to each event. The parameters can represent frequency, envelope, spectrum, volume level, panning, etc. The sequencer does not need to have knowledge of the use of the parameters, nor does it need to know in advance how many parameters are associated with the event. All the sequencer needs to do is ensure the event is dispatched to the proper synthesis module. The receiver of the event can then interpret the parameters appropriately. Event objects can contain information required by both the sequencer and instruments, without the sequencer having to know what parameters are associated with the event, if we define a base class that contains the sequencer specific information and then allow each instrument to derive its own event object from that base class.

The only event type that is required is a *start* event. Once an instrument has been activated with a *start* event, we need to know when to stop the instrument. The simplest strategy is to poll the instrument on each tick and continue until the instrument returns an indication it is finished. If the event includes an explicit duration, we can run the instrument until the duration is complete and then poll the instrument. The *stop* event is implicit in the event duration, in other words. However, an explicit *stop* event allows an instrument to be switched on for an indeterminate time and then turned off at a specific place in the sequence without having to pre-calculate the appropriate duration. This is most useful for live performance systems, but also useful for controllers or effects units that are started at the beginning of playback and run until playback ends. Rather than calculate the total duration of the sequence and set the controller duration, we can set the duration to some large value and then put a stop event at the end of the sequence.

If we want to be able to modify the instrument parameters without stopping and re-starting the instrument, we also need a *change parameters* event. In order to connect a change event to the original instrument instance, we store an event id value. The event id is then used to locate the instrument that is to receive the new parameter values.

Another very useful event is a *restart* event. This event is similar to the *start* event in that it instructs the instrument to adjust its parameters and then prepare to generate samples. It differs from the *start* event in that the instrument does not shut off, but merely restarts the sound generation. This event type can be used to simulate plucking or striking a string or percussion instrument that is already sounding.

A channel number is also included in the event definition. For sound generation instruments, this value is used to indicate which mixer input should receive the samples. For control functions, the channel number can be used to identify which channel is to receive the control change.

```
class SeqEvent {
   int16 type;
   int16 inum;
   int16 chnl;
   int16 xtra;
   int32 evtid;
   int32 start;
   int32 duration;
 };
```

Events that represent notes also include pitch and volume values. Although we can include those values in the *SeqEvent* base class, we can just as easily derive a class specifically for notes.

```
class NoteEvent : public SeqEvent {
   int16 pitch;
   FrqValue frq;
   AmpValue amp;
};
```

Each synthesis instrument will also need to include space for instrument specific parameters. Some instruments have only a small number of parameters and can derive a class directly from *NoteEvent*, adding on the additional values. For instruments with a large number of parameters or a variable number of parameters, we prefer to only allocate space for the parameters that are used during sequencing. We can define a third base class that handles a variable number of parameters. It will store both the actual parameter number and value as a pair. This allows the code that creates the events to map a small number of parameter values onto the complete set of values for the event.

```
class VarParamEvent : public NoteEvent {
  int16 maxParam;
  int16 numParam;
  int16 *paramNums;
  float *paramVals;
};
```

Instrument Management

The sequencer must do more than time events. It must also be able to play multiple sounds on different instruments (i.e., polyphony). Consequently, the sequencer must be able to send events to a variety of different instruments without knowing in advance what instruments are to be used or how the instrument will process the event. As with events, we could build this knowledge into the sequencer but would then limit the sequencer to a fixed number of instruments. The ability to define as many instruments and patches as we have memory to hold is one of the major advantages of a software system over a hardware synthesizer.

In addition, the samples produced by instruments can potentially be sent to a variety of outputs. For example, if the sequencer has built-in knowledge of output devices, it must include code to produce WAVE file output and send samples directly to a DAC for interactive listening. Furthermore, sound generation hardware differs between computers and operating systems. We need to be able to link to different sound output devices without building that knowledge into the sequencer.

We can allow an unlimited variety of instruments and sound output devices by separating the instrument management and sound output functions into separate objects. The instrument management object keeps a list of known instruments and allocates those instruments as needed. All instruments must derive from a common interface, but otherwise can implement different sound generation methods without affecting the sequencer or instrument manager code.

When the instrument manager, instruments and sample output functions are decoupled from the sequencer, they can also be used without a sequencer. For example, an instrument editor can invoke the instrument manger to create an instrument instance for editing rather than for sound playback. Likewise, a live performance system can allocate instruments and invoke instrument sound generation functions, copying the output samples directly to a sound output device. The instrument manager functions as the router between instruments and sound output for both sequenced and immediate sound output.

Finally, the instrument manager can be replaced with a completely different implementation without affecting the sequencer event processing. This allows customized instruments to be used with a common sequencer implementation if desired.

Sequencer Design

To produce a sequencer with all of these capabilities, we first create an abstract model of the sound generation process. This model does not define the actual sound generation functionality, only how those functions work together. We push the details of sound generation down into derived objects that implement a common interface. This decouples the sound generation knowledge from the sequencer and allows the sequencer to be used with virtually any set of instruments, processors and controllers. Figure 39 shows the internal architecture of the sequencer and its interfaces to other parts of the synthesizer. Lines with a circle at the end show the interface methods that are used.

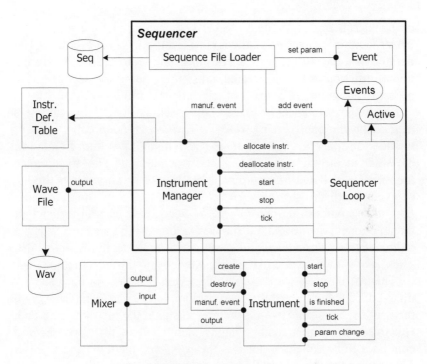

Figure 39 - Sequencer

The *Sequence File Loader* implements functions to read a list of events and event parameters from a file. Each event includes a unique identifier that indicates which instrument will process the event. As each event is loaded, the loader calls the *Instrument Manager* to instantiate an *Event* object specific to the target instrument. The *Instrument Manager* uses the instrument identifier to locate information about the instrument in the *Instrument Definition Table*. The *Instrument Manager* then calls a method on the *Instrument* interface to instantiate the event object. Parameters from the file are added to the event object by calling the *set parameter* method on the event object. The *Event* object is then added to the *Sequencer Loop* event list.

The *Instrument Definition Table* contains entries to identify each instrument in the synthesizer. This list can be dynamically created when the synthesizer is loaded, or can be compiled into the program. Typically, the table is loaded from a file containing instrument types and default settings. The table contains the address of a *factory* for each instrument and event type. The factory is the code that "manufactures" (i.e., instantiates) the instrument or event, and is defined as a part of the instrument object implementation. By storing the information in a table created at runtime, the synthesizer can have access to an unlimited number of instrument definitions.

Once the sequence is loaded, playback is started by calling a method on the *Sequencer Loop*. The *Sequencer Loop* calls the *start* method on the *Instrument Manager*. This allows the *Instrument Manager* to pre-allocate instruments if needed and also to initialize the *Mixer* and *Wave File* outputs. The *Sequencer Loop* scans the list of events until the start time of an event is reached. The *Sequencer Loop* then invokes the *Instrument Manager* to allocate an instance of the instrument identified by the *Event* object and receives back a reference to the *Instrument* interface, which is stored in the *Active* list. The *Event* is then passed to the instrument using the *start* method.

The instrument associated with the event is called for each sample time until the duration of the event is completed. The *Sequencer Loop* then calls the instrument *stop* method to signal the instrument to end. However, the instrument remains active, and the *tick* method continues to be called, so long as the *isfinished* method returns false. This allows the instrument to produce samples beyond the limit of its event duration if necessary. For example, the instrument can wait to begin the release portion of the envelope until a stop signal is received, and processors such as delay lines can empty the delay line before terminating. When the instrument indicates it has finished, the *Sequencer Loop* removes the instrument from the active list and notifies the *Instrument Manager* that the instrument is no longer in use by invoking the *deallocate* method. The *Instrument Manager* can then either destroy the instrument instance, or recycle it if possible.

When the *tick* method is called on an instrument, the instrument produces a sample and passes it to the *Instrument Manager* which then adds the sample to the appropriate *Mixer* input. However, an instrument does not need to produce samples. An instrument can also be defined to control other synthesizer functions, such as panning, mixer levels, etc. When all active instruments have been processed, the *Sequencer Loop* calls the *tick* method on the *Instrument Manager*. The output of the *Mixer* is then retrieved and passed to the *Wave File* output buffer.

Once all events have been completed, the *stop* method on the *Instrument Manager* is called to close out the wave file and discard any pre-allocated instruments.

This design allows for nearly unlimited flexibility in the sequencer. We only need a few event types and can sequence any number of instruments, processors and controllers without having to build the knowledge of the instruments into the sequencer. Any synthesizer function that can be performed with the *stop, start, change,* and *tick* signals can be sequenced. The key to this design lies in the flexibility of the event object, the dynamic allocation of instrument instances, and the abstract instrument interface.

Sequencer File Format

The sequencer file format can be as simple as a binary dump of the sequencer events and as complex as a programming language. Binary files are usually faster to load and require less disk space. However, with the large storage capacity of current computers, this is no longer an important concern and there is no advantage to a binary file format for most applications. In addition, a binary file requires a specialized editor to create and modify the file. If we use a text file, we can create sequences with any available text editor, or create a special editor that displays the events graphically.

An obvious file format is one where each line of the file defines one event. This format is similar to the MUSIC *N* languages and can represent any series of sounds desired. It is somewhat tedious to use, but for some applications the simple event-per-line format is sufficient. This simple format also has the advantage that we can easily generate the sequence files from another program, such as an algorithmic composition system, an import utility that reads other sequencer formats, etc.

Each event line in the file must start with the values required by the sequencer event base class but can include instrument specific parameter values as well. The format of one event line in the sequence file is as follows:

```
[+|-|&]inum chnl time duration { param }
```

A line beginning with a plus (+) will generate a PARAM event. Lines beginning with a minus (-) will generate a STOP event. A line beginning with ampersand will generate a RESTART event. All other lines will produce a START event. PARAM event lines must immediately follow the event that is to be modified. However, since the start time determines the ultimate sequence of events, the '+' lines can have any start time needed. The parameter change will be applied based on the start time, not the position in the sequence file. In the case of the RESTART event, the duration of the initial note must be less than the delta time to the RESTART event. Otherwise the original note will no longer be playing and the RESTART event will be treated the same as a START event.

Fields are separated by one or more spaces and may be either a number or a character string. Numbers (other than the *inum* field) may be entered as a real or integer value and may also include a leading negative sign (-). Character strings are enclosed in either single or double quote marks. The maximum length of any one field is 256 characters.

The first four fields are required. The *inum* field is an integer value that matches an entry in the instrument definition table. The *chnl* field indicates the output channel, usually a mixer input. The *time* and *duration* fields are numbers that specify the event time and duration in seconds. These will be converted to number of samples by the event object.

The *params* are optional and specific to the instrument *inum*. Any number of *param* fields may be included, up to a maximum line length.

As each field is parsed, it is passed to the event object as a character string. The object can either use the string or convert to a number as appropriate. Number fields are in a form that can be passed directly to the C++ *atof* or *atoi* library functions.

By default, each parameter is passed to the event object using the parameter's position on the line as the parameter identifier. This mechanism is simple, but can be cumbersome when an instrument has a large or variable number of parameters. For example, if we want to set the 10th parameter, we must specify, at a minimum, all parameters up to the 10th parameter even if the first nine parameters are equivalent to default values. Furthermore, if we later decide to change the instrument number, the parameter values must be edited to match the parameters of the new instrument. In order to make parameters more flexible, the sequence file loader provides a parameter mapping function. A parameter map is a list of actual identifiers that should be passed to the event object along with the parameter index. A parameter map is a line beginning with an equal sign (=) followed by the instrument number and parameter ID numbers.

```
=inum id0 id1 id2...
```

This map would pass *id0* as the identifier for the first parameter for instrument *inum*, *id1* for the second, etc. For the *BasicSynth* library implementation, the first parameter for a *NoteEvent* is the pitch, the second the volume, with variable instrument parameters following. (See *SeqEvent.h* for the default parameter numbers.)

Comments may be included in the file by beginning the comment with either the C++ style comment (//) or with a semi-colon (;). The comment continues to the end of the line. Blank lines are ignored as well.

Example Code

The program in the *Example08* directory creates a sequence from in-memory statements and plays them using the sequencer.

BasicSynth Library

The sequencer is implemented using a combination of classes.

SeqEvent – core sequencer event parameters
NoteEvent – event structure for notes
VarParamEvent – event structure for notes with instrument variable parameters
Instrument – abstract base class defining an instrument
InstrMapEntry – entry in a table of available instruments
InstrManager – class to manage a set of instruments during playback
SequenceFile – class to load sequence files and add events to the sequencer object.

Sequencer – class to loop through and process events.

Files:

```
Include/SeqEvent.h
Include/Instrument.h
Include/SequenceFile.h
Include/Sequencer.h
Src/Common/Sequencer.cpp
Src/Common/SequenceFile.cpp
```

Chapter 16

MIDI Sequencer

The *Musical Instrument Digital Interface* (MIDI) is a specification for interconnection of synthesis equipment. The specification defines the physical connection, transmission protocol, and message format. Because MIDI was developed primarily for the purpose of linking keyboard synthesizers, the message format mimics the actions of a performer at a keyboard. Messages are generated whenever a key is pressed or released, when the volume or pitch control is changed, the patch is changed, etc. MIDI is designed to allow use over a relatively slow data link (31.25k bps) and message data is compressed to a minimal size. MIDI defines sixteen different channels of data with each channel roughly equivalent to one synthesis instrument. Multiple notes may sound on a channel so long as all notes on the channel are played with the same patch. Furthermore, controller changes (e.g., volume pedal) apply to all notes on the channel and only one message needs to be sent to change all sounding notes on the instrument.

As a message protocol for instruments, MIDI provides the rudimentary features needed to link synthesizers together for performance. It has been adopted by virtually every synthesizer manufacturer and is in wide use today. Because it was successful as a synthesizer communication protocol, the MIDI specification was later expanded to include a sequencer format known as Standard MIDI File (SMF). This file format is widely used by commercial software synthesis systems.

Unfortunately, MIDI is not the best possible sequencer format for a software synthesizer. Remember that the message protocol is oriented to live performance on a hardware synthesizer. If the software system is designed to mimic a keyboard synthesizer, MIDI works reasonably well. However, the MIDI specification does not define all of the things we would like to control in a software synthesis system. MIDI messages contain a small, fixed amount of data. For example, a note-on or note-off event can only indicate the key number and velocity. In other words, we cannot specify a change to the envelope attack or decay rate in addition to a peak amplitude level, but must spread the parameters out over several control change messages. Control changes apply to all notes on the channel. Thus we cannot dynamically change the volume, panning, timbre, or other aspects of the sound on a per-note basis. The note start and end are defined by separate messages with no explicit duration information available. Consequently, instruments that could use the duration value to calculate dynamic parameter changes cannot be used unless we pre-process the SMF to match note on and note off events. Because note information applies to a channel, it is impossible with MIDI to duplicate the same pitch on the same channel. The note-off event for the first sound would also cancel the second sound. Normally that is not a problem, but it is an example of an unnecessary limitation for a software synthesizer.

These criticisms don't mean we can't use MIDI for a software synthesizer sequencer, only that there are some limitations. Nevertheless, because MIDI is widely used, and because at the present time it is a de-facto standard, it is worth the effort to be able to read and process SMF.

MIDI Messages

MIDI messages can be broken down into two basic categories: channel messages (note on/off, control change, etc.) and system common messages (global parameter changes). MIDI messages begin with a byte where the high order bit is set followed by up to two data bytes with the number and meaning of data bytes defined by the message. The two exceptions to this rule are the SYSEX message and META event, both of which can have a variable number of data bytes following. The real-time SYSEX message data is terminated by a byte with the value 0xF7, but when stored in SMF an explicit byte count is included. META events have an explicit byte count following the message value.

The message byte is divided into two four-bit fields. For channel messages, the high nibble defines the message and the low nibble is the channel number. Since the high bit is always set, there are three bits left to define the actual message and thus only 8 possible messages in MIDI when the channel is specified. However, when the high nibble has all bits set, the message is a system common message and the low nibble defines the message rather than the channel. Thus we have 7 channel voice messages and 16 possible system common messages for a total of 23 different real-time event messages. In a SMF, the reset message (0xFF) is redefined to indicate a META event. The META event is followed by a byte that defines the actual message, followed by a variable number of data bytes. This expands the available range to include 256 additional messages for use by a sequencer. Most of the META events are optional and informational (e.g., song title) and don't affect sound generation.

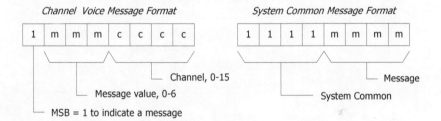

MIDI Event Messages

Since a MIDI message is defined by a byte with the high bit set, data values must be less than 0x80 (0-127). For most messages, this range is sufficient. For example, we can represent pitch over a ten-octave range with values 0-120. Likewise, we can represent volume level in dB with values in the range 0-120. In order to use a data value greater than 127, the value must be split into multiple bytes with each byte containing 7 bits of information. To reconstruct the actual value, the byte with the high order bits is shifted left by 7 and added to the byte containing the low order bits. This is one of the oddities of the MIDI protocol.

Channel voice messages and the number of data bytes for each are shown in the following table. Remember that the message value is contained in the high nibble with the high bit set and the channel number in the low nibble. For example, a note-on message for channel 1 would be a byte with a value of 0x91.

Message	Data	Description
0	*key* *velocity*	Note Off. This is rarely used.
1	*key* *velocity*	Note On. If velocity is set to zero, this is treated as a note-off message.
2	*key* *value*	Polyphonic Key Pressure (after-touch).
3	*controller* *value*	Controller change. MIDI supports 128 different controllers (0-127).
4	*program*	Program (patch) change.
5	*value*	Channel pressure (after-touch).
6	*lsb* *msb*	Pitch wheel change. The value is a 14-bit value in two bytes with the low order 7 bits contained in the first byte and the high order 7 bits in the second byte. A value of 0x2000 is considered a center value indicating no pitch variation.

One of the features of a MIDI data stream that we must also consider is called *running status*. Using running status, when the message is a channel message it only has to be sent if the message is different from the last channel message. For example, once a note-on message is sent, only the key and velocity values need to be sent until some other message needs to be sent. This is part of the data compression scheme for MIDI transmission.

The note off message is rarely used since a note on message with a velocity of zero indicates a note should stop playing. Using a running status allows a synthesizer (or sequencer) to send a single note on message followed by key and velocity information for multiple notes. When the velocity is non-zero, a note is initiated. When the velocity is zero, the note is stopped.

For note on and note off messages, the key value is typically used to indicate pitch and the velocity value indicates volume. However, a synthesizer may interpret the values otherwise. For example, pitch for a drum kit instrument can represent which drum sound is to be played. Likewise, velocity could be applied to envelope rate instead of volume level.

Control change messages are used to dynamically alter the sound of the instrument. The most common control messages are for modulation (1), overall volume (7), and panning (10). Modulation is commonly used to indicate vibrato depth. Of the remaining 128 different controllers, many are not used or only vaguely defined. For example, controllers 16-20 are designated *General Purpose* controllers without any specifics of how they should be used. Others such as 72 (release time) and 73 (attack time) do not indicate the range of operation, only the function that is to be modified. A large number of controller numbers are used to specify a LSB value. Since only one byte is provided for the controller value, a second message must be used to produce values greater than 127. For fine grained control, the synthesizer can send a second byte using the associated LSB control number. Together the messages allow for 14-bit resolution. If an instrument intends to use the LSB, it must be capable of splicing the two message values together when they occur and also be able to function properly if the LSB value is missing.

The after-touch messages are used to indicate variations in key pressure while a key is held down. These messages are often ignored by event recorders since they can result in a flood of messages that quickly fill up the recorder memory.

Program change allows indication of up to 128 different instruments. However, control #0 can be used to select from 128 different patch banks, or up to 16,384 if the LSB for control 0 (#32) is used as well. Both the program number and bank numbers are specific to the synthesizer. As a result, a sequence from one synthesizer might sound completely different on another synthesizer. For this reason, the MIDI specification was expanded to define the General MIDI (GM) patch numbers. GM defines a set of common instrument assignments on bank 0 so that a sequence recorded on one synthesizer will sound similar when played on another synthesizer. When implementing a software synthesizer we should attempt to match bank 0 program changes to sound similar to those defined for GM and use other banks for non-standard instruments.

Looking at the events listed above, we can see that some of the events apply to individual notes while others apply to all notes on a channel. The note on/off and polyphonic after-touch apply to individual notes. The control change, program change, channel after-touch and pitch wheel change apply to all notes on a channel. Events that apply to an individual note need to be sent to the instrument that is generating sound. Events that apply to all sounding notes must be handled by a channel object that has knowledge of all active notes. In addition, when a new note is started, all current channel values must be applied to the new note.

Sequencer Design

The sequencer for MIDI is slightly different from the sequencer in the previous chapter. Since SMF can contain multiple tracks and each track contains multiple events, we expand the structure to use a track object to store the event list. Likewise, instruments are associated with a channel and some events must be applied to all active notes on the channel. We add a channel object to maintain the list of active instruments for each channel.

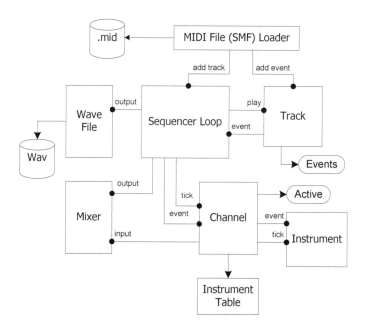

Figure 40 - MIDI Sequencer Structure

The file loader requests a track object from the sequencer when a new track is encountered in the file. The file loader builds an event structure for each event and stores the events with the track. During playback, the sequencer loop calls *play* on the track object. The track object determines when the event should be executed and sends the event notification back to the sequencer where it is dispatched to the appropriate channel object. The sequencer maintains control of the master mixer and those events that affect the mixer are processed directly as well as being passed to the channel object. The channel object is responsible for allocating instances of instruments when needed and dispatching events to the appropriate instrument. Control change events must be sent to all active notes on the channel while note on/off and pitch bend are sent to the instrument that is playing the indicated pitch. Samples are generated by calling the *tick* method on the channel object. The channel object combines all active notes by passing the generated samples to the appropriate mixer input.

Standard MIDI File Format

A SMF is a type of IFF file, similar to the WAVE file discussed in an earlier chapter. Blocks of data are stored as chunks where each chunk has a 4-byte ID followed by a 4-byte length value. Unlike a RIFF file, the SMF does not have a file header, but starts with the first data chunk. Note that the SMF file stores binary values in big-endian byte order rather than the little-endian order of the WAVE file.

The first chunk in the SMF has an ID of 'MThd' and a size of six bytes. The six data bytes of the header chunk represent the file format (two bytes), the number of tracks in the file (2 bytes) and the time division value (2 bytes). Altogether, the 'MThd' chunk has 14 bytes.

```
struct MTHDchunk {
    uint8  chnkID[4]; // MThd
    uint32 size;
    uint16 format;
    uint16 numTrk;
    int16  tmDiv;
};
```

Note that many compilers will pad a data structure to a four-byte boundary by default. Consequently, the in-memory structure size may not be exactly the same as the on-disk size and we must not assume *sizeof(MTHDchunk)* is 14 bytes.

The *format* value can be 0, 1 or 2. A type 0 file contains a single track with all channels merged into one stream. A type 1 file contains multiple tracks that should be played simultaneously. A type 2 file is used to store independent sequences. Type 2 files are typically used for patterns such as drum loops.

The *numTrk* value indicates the number of track chunks that follow. For a type 0 file, there is only one track. For type 1 files track 0 is typically used to contain general information such as song title, copyright, program changes, tempo, etc. The remaining tracks store the events that are to be played. However, this is only a convention, not a requirement.

The *tmDiv* value is used to calculate timing information. If the high-order bit is clear, *tmDiv* represents the number of divisions of a quarter note. The actual length of a quarter note is determined by the tempo event embedded in the track data. If no tempo event is found, then the tempo is assumed to be 120 bpm. When the *tmDiv* value has the high-order bit set, it is used to indicate SMTPE time. The lower seven bits of the upper byte represents frames per second while the lower byte represents number of ticks per frame.

The 'MThd' chunk is followed by one or more track chunks. The track chunk has an ID of 'MTrk' and a variable size indicated by the 4-byte chunk length value. The data content of the chunk is a stream of MIDI events and timing information. To load a SMF, we read and store the header values, then loop through the file looking for track chunks until the total number of tracks have been processed.

When reading binary values, such as the chunk size, we can read the values directly into the appropriate size variable and then rearrange the byte order if needed. However, it is just as easy to read the value one byte at a time and build the value from the bytes. The same code can then be used on any processor architecture. The following function reads a 32-bit quantity in a portable manner.

```
uint32 ReadLong() {
   return (fgetc(fp) << 24)
       + (fgetc(fp) << 16)
       + (fgetc(fp) << 8)
       +  fgetc(fp);
}
```

Similar code is used to read a 16-bit quantity.

```
uint16 ReadShort() {
   return (fgetc(fp) << 8) + fgetc(fp);
}
```

The track data stream consists of interspersed time and event information. Each event is preceded by a relative time that indicates how long the sequencer should wait before executing the event. The timing values are stored with a variable number of bytes where all but the last byte has the high bit set. The lower seven bits of each byte contain the value. To reconstruct the timing value, we must process bytes until we locate the byte without the high bit set, accumulating the 7-bit quantities into the value in the process. The following code constructs the time value from an in-memory buffer (*inpPos*).

```
uint32 GetVarLen() {
   uint32 value = 0;
   do
      value = (value << 7) + (*inpPos & 0x7F);
   while (*inpPos++ & 0x80);
   return value;
}
```

MIDI timing values represent a somewhat arbitrary value called a *delta time*. The actual length of the delta time is controlled by two other values contained within the file, the tempo event and division value from the header chunk. The tempo event is a META event containing three bytes of data. Unlike other MIDI data values, these are full eight bit values. The tempo value indicates the number of microseconds per quarter note. Calculation of actual time for an event is discussed below.

The delta time value is followed by one of the MIDI events described above. To process the event stream we first read the delta time then examine the next byte to determine the message. Depending on the message, we process the data bytes appropriately. However, we must watch for a *running status*. We need to check the byte to see if it really is a message and reuse the last channel message if the high bit is not set. Note that system common messages do not change the running status.

Many of the MIDI events do not affect sound generation. These events can be discarded if we only want to play all the notes in the file, but we have to check each event in order to skip the appropriate number of bytes. Likewise, we can ignore most META events since they only provide information about the sequence such as title, copyright, time signature, etc. The two META events that are essential are end of track and tempo.

The events that are of most concern for sequencing are the channel messages. These include the note on, note off, control change, program change, and pitch bend events. These events need to be stored for playback.

Note that we use *unsigned char* type for the input buffer. Otherwise, the messages will get sign-extended when stored in an integer value.

```
FILE *fp;
unsigned char *inpBuf;
unsigned char *inpPos;
unsigned char *inpEnd;
MTHDchunk hdr;
short trkNum;
short lastMsg;
long deltaTime;

LoadFile(file) {
    char chunkID[4];
    short msg;
    long trackSize;
    fp = fopen(file, "rb");
    fread(hdr.chunkID, 4, 1, fp);
    hdr.size = ReadLong();
    if (memcmp(chunkID, 'MThd', 4) == 0) {
        hdr.format = ReadShort();
        hdr.numTracks = ReadShort();
        hdr.tmDiv = ReadShort();
        trkNum = 0;
        while (trkNum < hdr.numTracks && !feof(fp)) {
            fread(chunkID, 4, 1, fp);
            trackSize = ReadLong();
            if (memcmp(chunkID, 'MTrk', 4) == 0) {
                inpBuf = malloc(trackSize);
                fread(inpBuf, 1, trackSize, fp);
                inpPos = inpBuf;
                inpEnd = inpBuf + trackSize;
                while (inpPos < inpEnd) {
```

```
            deltaTime = GetVarLen();
            msg = *inpPos;
            if ((msg & 0xF0) == 0xF0) {
                inpPos++;
                if (msg == 0xFF)
                    MetaEvent();
                else
                    SysCommon(msg);
            } else {
                if (msg & 0x80) {
                    inpPos++;
                    lastMsg = msg;
                } else
                    msg = lastMsg;
                ChannelMessage(msg);
            }
        }
        free(inpBuf);
        trkNum++;
    } else
        fseek(fp, trackSize, SEEK_CUR);
    }
}
fclose(fp);
}
MetaEvent() {
    long tempo;
    short meta = *inpPos++;
    long metalen = GetVarLen();
    switch (meta) {
    case 0x2F: // end of track
        AddEvent(0xFF, meta, 0, 0);
        break;
    case 0x51: // tempo
        tempo  = (*inpPos++ << 16);
        tempo += (*inpPos++ << 8);
        tempo += *inpPos++;
        AddEvent(0xFF, meta, tempo);
        break;
    default:
        inpPos += metalen;
        break;
    }
}
```

```
SysCommon(short msg) {
   long datalen;
   switch (msg) {
   case 0xF0: // SYSEX
      datalen = GetVarLen();
      inpPos += datalen;
      break;
   case 0xF1: // MIDI time code
   case 0xF3: // Song select
      inpPos += 1;
      break;
   case 0xF2: // Song position
      inpPos += 2;
      break;
   default: // remaining values have no data
      break;
   }
}

ChannelMessage(short msg) {
   short val1, val2;
   switch (msg & 0xF0) {
   case 0x80: // Note Off
   case 0x90: // Note On
   case 0xA0: // After Touch
   case 0xB0: // Control change
      val1 = *inpPos++; // key/controller
      val2 = *inpPos++; // velocity/pressure/value
      AddEvent(msg, msg & 0x0F, val1, val2);
      break;
   case 0xC0: // Program Change
   case 0xD0: // Channel Pressure (Aftertouch)
      val1 = *inpPos++;
      AddEvent(msg, msg & 0x0F, val1, 0);
      break;
   case 0xE0: // Pitch bend
      val1 = *inpPos++;
      val1 = (val1 << 7) + *inpPos++;
      AddEvent(msg, msg & 0x0F, val1, 0);
      break;
   }
}
```

The *AddEvent* function is a place-holder for the code to create an appropriate sequencer event and add the event to the event list for the current track.

Looking at the messages, we see that no channel message has more than two associated data bytes. We can create an event structure that represents the data with byte values where the channel value is located in the low nibble of the *msg* member and the meta event code is stored in a third value member when needed. However, some messages represent a 14-bit value in two bytes, and one META event (tempo) needs to store a 24-bit value. That means we have to pull bits out and combine them during playback. Furthermore, accessing byte values on odd-byte boundaries, masking off bits, and extending bytes to word or double word values takes extra execution time. During playback we are more concerned with speed than saving a few bytes of memory. Most likely the compiler will pad the structure to a four byte boundary anyway, so we might as well make the values 16-bit, separate out the various pieces, and include a 32-bit value for tempo to make a full 16 bytes. On some microprocessors it might be beneficial to make all members 32-bit values.

```
struct MIDIEvent {
    uint32 deltat;
    uint16 msg;
    uint16 chnl;
    uint16 val1;
    uint16 val2;
    uint32 lval;
};
```

MIDI Sequence Playback

The sequencer playback loop for MIDI events is similar to the sequencer shown in the last chapter. Unlike before, we must loop through all tracks looking at the next event on each track. We then loop over the active notes on each channel to generate samples. Playback continues until all tracks are at the end and all channels are inactive.

Events are timed by the delta time value. We can decrement the remaining delta time for the next event in the event list to determine when the event should be executed. However, a delta time unit is not the same as a sample time. For sample generation, the delta time value needs to be converted into the number of samples for one tick. The delta time ticks are in units of *pulses per quarter note* (PPQN) with the duration of a quarter note defined by the tempo meta event. The tempo value represents microseconds per quarter note, thus the time of one tick in microseconds is calculated as the tempo divided by the PPQN value. The number of equivalent samples is the tick value multiplied by the sample rate in microseconds.

$$srTick = \frac{sampleRate}{10^6} \cdot \frac{tempo}{ppqn}$$

We must recalculate the *srTick* value when the tempo change event is encountered. On each MIDI time tick, we loop over the active notes for the calculated number of samples. The *srTick* value will most likely contain a fractional value and we must accumulate the fractional portion so that the timing is correct.

```
Sequence() {
    samples = 0;
    while (playing) {
        trkOn = 0;
        trkNum = 0;
        while (trkNum < numTrk)
            trkOn += tracks[trkNum++].Play();
        samples += srTick;
        while (samples >= 1.0) {
            chOn = 0;
            chNum = 0;
            while (chNum < MAX_MIDI_CHNL)
                chOn += chnls[chNum++].Tick();
            // output the current sample
            samples -= 1;
        }
        playing = trkOn > 0 || chOn > 0;
    }
}
```

The track *Play* method must keep a count of the remaining time before the next event. When the count reaches zero, the event is executed. Since multiple events may follow with a delta time of zero, the code will loop until it either reaches the end of the event list or finds an event with a non-zero delta time.

```
Track::Play() {
    if (eventNum < numEvents) {
        while (deltaTime == 0) {
            switch (event[eventNum].msg) {
                // execute the event
            }
            if (++eventNum >= numEvents)
                break;
            deltaTime = event[eventNum].deltaTime;
        }
        --deltaTime;
    }
}
```

The track object executes events by calling an appropriate method on the sequencer object. One method is defined for each event. The sequencer uses the channel value stored in the event to locate the associated channel object and then passes the event to the channel. The channel object then executes the event. Note on events result in activation of a new note. Note off events cause the note to stop or begin its release cycle if appropriate. The program change event indicates which instrument should be used for all subsequent note on events. Control change messages must be passed to each active note.

The channel *Tick* method must process all active notes and combine the value into the appropriate mixer input.

```
Channel::Tick(mixer) {
    count = 0;
    while (count < active) {
        note[count++].Tick(mixer);
    return count;
}
```

MIDI Instruments

Instruments for the MIDI sequencer must contain methods to handle all channel messages, including note on, note off, after-touch and pitch wheel change. In addition, the instrument may need to process some control change messages.

The MIDI specification does not fully describe the use of parameter and controller values. For example, interpretation of key velocity for note-on and note-off is left to the instrument developer. However, these values usually indicate a volume level. More problematic are the values for pitch wheel and controllers such as modulation wheel. The instrument could simply ignore these messages and play all sounds the same, but much of the musical expressiveness available with MIDI lies in the ability of the instrument to produce varying sounds based on controller changes.

The pitch wheel change message is a good example of the kind of problems that can be encountered when designing MIDI instruments. Although the pitch bend sensitivity can be defined using the RPN messages, the speed of the pitch change is not defined. Because the pitch wheel values arrive at a relatively slow sample rate, merely adding the pitch wheel value to the current pitch may result in a series of steps between pitches. It may be necessary for the instrument to integrate between the current pitch and the bend value over some amount of time.

Example Code

The *Example09* program implements an example MIDI sequencer. The input MIDI file and output wave file can be specified on the command line. If files are not specified, the code generates a short sequence internally.

BasicSynth Library

The MIDI sequencer classes provide a framework for a MIDI sequencer, but do not fully implement all MIDI capabilities. In order to make use of the MIDI classes, a program must define one or more instruments that inherit from the *MIDIInstrument* base class. In addition, the program should derive a class from the *MIDIChannel* class and implement the *Allocate* and *Deallocate* methods to manage instrument instantiation.

Files:

```
Include/MIDISequencer.h
Src/Common/MIDISequencer.cpp
```

Chapter 17

Immediate Sound Output

The *BasicSynth* system is intended for producing sound files as output. However, it is also useful to be able to hear sounds immediately rather than write them to disk and then play back through a media player. For example, we might want to preview a portion of a composition while it is being written. In addition, instrument design is much easier when we can hear the changes to the instrument settings immediately. In both cases, we need some way to copy the output samples directly to the DAC rather than to a disk file.

Immediate sound production is similar in many ways to writing samples to a file. We must allocate instruments, generate samples, and pass the samples to an output buffer. For playback of a sequence, we can easily adapt the sequencer developed earlier by replacing the wave file output object in the instrument manager with an object that copies values to the DAC. However, we need to be able to interact with the sequencer to start and stop playback. This requires that our program manage two threads of execution. The first thread monitors user input while the second thread generates samples. In response to user input, the first thread passes messages to the sound generator thread. The messages can be as simple as setting member variables on the sequencer object, or can use an IPC mechanism such as a semaphore or queue to notify the sequencer. The messages we need are *start*, *stop*, and *change*.

Playback timing in the sequencer is automatic. Typically, we write samples to the DAC through an input buffer managed by the operating system sound device driver. The input buffer can vary in length from a few milliseconds up to several seconds. However, when the input buffer to the DAC is filled, we must wait until the block of samples is consumed before writing new samples into the buffer. The sample rate clock in the sound output device controls how fast samples are consumed. This effectively causes the sample generation code to execute synchronously with sample output at the sample rate output speed multiplied by the block length. As long as we can generate a new block of samples and copy them into the output buffer as fast or faster than the playback of the last block, sound output will be continuous and properly timed.

Dynamic Note Playback

In addition to playback of sequences, we need to be able to create note *start*, *stop* and *change* events dynamically. Doing so allows us to hear the sound of an instrument without first creating a sequence. Using either a musical keyboard attached to the computer, or an on-screen virtual keyboard, we can play the instrument directly. This could be used for live performance, but is mainly intended for use as an instrument or sequence editor. We can tweak the parameters of a sound, play a few notes, and then make any adjustment to the sound that is desired. The delay between changing parameters and hearing the effect is eliminated. This is a far more effective method of editing synthesizer sounds than having to modify an instrument definition file, convert the file to a sound file, and then playback the file to hear the changes.

An interactive playback module is similar to the sequencer already developed. The main difference is the way the play list is managed. For interactive playback, the play list must accept new events while sample generation is on-going. Each time an event is encountered on the play list, it is removed and executed immediately. The start time and duration values are ignored. In addition, when no events are present on the play list and active list, the playback routine does not halt, but continues to monitor the list for new input. When no sounds are active, output samples with 0 amplitude must be produced to keep the DAC buffer filled with silence.

Sample Output

Sound device output is specific to each operating system and separate implementations for each are needed. On some systems, management of the output buffer is contained in the device driver code and the application code only needs to pass a buffer of samples to the driver. The driver will block execution when needed. On other systems, the output buffer is shared between the driver and the application, and the application code must check to insure it does not overwrite samples that have not yet been played. This is the case with the Windows *DirectSound* interface.

In the case of a shared buffer, we cannot simply fill in the complete buffer and then wait until the read position reaches the end of the buffer to overwrite the buffer with new samples. This might produce a glitch in the sound at the point where the buffer is rewritten. Instead, the general strategy for a shared buffer is to divide the buffer into multiple blocks. In the simplest case we have two blocks. While one block is being read for playback, the other block can be written. However, the output routine must insure that it does not overwrite samples that have not been played. The process is further complicated by the fact that the buffer is circular. When the read or write position reaches the end of the buffer, it is moved back to the beginning. Thus we cannot simply write to a block that is not currently being played, but must keep track of which blocks represent areas that contain samples that have already been played. The following diagrams show how this is done.

Initially, the read position is at the beginning of the buffer and we may write to any position in the buffer.

Initial write

Once we have written block 0, we can start the playback running. We can still write to block 1.

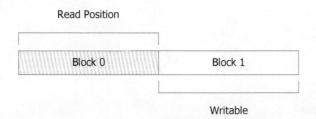

Block 0 reading, Block 1 writable

Once we have filled block 1 with samples, we wrap the write position back to the beginning of the buffer. If the read position is still within the range of block 0 when we attempt to write to block 0, we must wait before writing additional samples to the buffer.

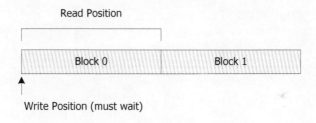

Block 0 reading, Block 1 filled

When the read position moves into block 1, we can once again write to block 0.

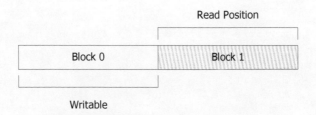

Block 1 reading, Block 0 writable

Once block 0 has been filled with samples, we must once again wait for the read position to move from block 1 into block 0 before writing block 1.

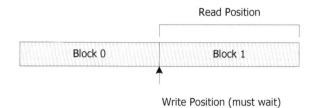

Block 1 reading, Block 0 filled

Once the read position moves back into block 0 we can write to block 1 again. At this point we are back to the beginning and repeat the procedure for following blocks.

```
int bufLen = 44100;
int blkLen = bufLength / 2;
SampleValue *blk0 = outBuf;
SampleValue *blk1 = outBuf + blkLen;
int outState = 1;

SoundOut(SampleValue *blkOut) {

    switch (outState) {
    case 1:
        // initial write
        memcpy(blk0, blkOut, blkLen);
        StartPlayback();
        outState = 2;
        break;

    case 2:
        // block 0 filled/playing
        n = GetReadPos();
        while (n > blkLen) {
            Pause();
            n = GetReadPos();
        }
        memcpy(blk1, blkOut, blkLen);
        outState = 3;
        break;
```

```
case 3:
    // block 1 filled/playing
    n = GetReadPos();
    while (n < blkLen) {
        Pause();
        n = GetReadPos();
    }
    memcpy(blk0, blkOut, blkLen);
    outState = 2;
    break;
    }
}
```

The *Pause* function is used to release the CPU for a short time so that we do not consume CPU cycles until the desired output block is available. This is not always possible, however. If the playback thread does not restart execution before playback reaches the end of the current block, we can miss seeing the read position move to the next block and end up waiting an entire buffer cycle. It may be necessary to spin, waiting on the read position in that situation and accept the wasted CPU cycles.

Once all samples have been generated we need to allow playback to continue until the samples have been played. We do this by continuing to write blocks of zeros into the buffer until both blocks contain zeros. At that point we can safely stop the playback without cutting off any remaining sound.

Even using the split buffer there is the possibility that we can get behind if it takes more time to generate a block of samples than it takes to play them. The read position will have moved more than one block forward and we will wait for it to wrap around again before writing. The result is two blocks of samples that get repeated. If this happens, it indicates that the processor is too slow, or the sound texture too complex, to produce immediate playback at the current sampling rate. The only option in that situation is to lower the sampling rate. If we use a sampling rate of 22050 rather than the standard 44100 we double the time we have available to generate samples, but only lose a little fidelity in the sound output. The slower sampling rate is usually sufficient for auditioning sounds, and in many cases is good enough for live performance systems as well.

The purpose of the playback buffer is to allow sample generation to take place simultaneously with sound output. When performing a sequence, the sequencer must switch between initialization of new notes and sample generation. During the time that instruments are allocated and initialized, no samples are generated. Using a buffer allows sample output to occur simultaneously with other operations and thus allows the program time to setup for new sounds. A longer buffer gives more lead time and is less likely to result in missed samples. However, a longer buffer means we must potentially wait longer for the writable block to become available. At some point there is a diminishing return where we spend as much time waiting on the buffer to become available as we do generating samples. We can minimize the wait time by dividing a longer buffer into several shorter blocks rather than two longer blocks. Our wait time is only the length of one block, but our lead time is still the total length of the buffer.

```
SampleValue *outBuf;
int bufLen = 44100;
int blkLen = bufLength / numBlk;
int nextWrite = 0;
int lastBlock = blkLen * (numBlk - 1);
int outState = 1;

SoundOut(SampleValue *blkOut) {
   SampleValue *blkPtr = bufOut + nextWrite;
   switch (outState) {
   case 1:
      // initial write
      memcpy(blkPtr, blkOut, blkLen);
      StartPlayback();
      outState = 2;
      nextWrite = blkLen;
      break;

   case 2:
      // fill to buffer length
      memcpy(blkPtr, blkOut, blkLen);
      nextWrite += blkLen;
      if (nextWrite >= bufLen) {
         nextWrite = 0;
         outState = 3;
      }
      break;
```

```
case 3:
   // wait for read to move into next block
   m = nextWrite + blkLen;
   n = GetReadPos();
   if (n >= nextWrite) {
      while (n < m) {
         Pause();
         n = GetReadPos();
      }
   }
   memcpy(blkPtr, blkOut, blkLen);
   nextWrite += blkLen;
   if (nextWrite >= lastBlock)
      outState = 4;
   break;

case 4:
   // wait for read to move into block 0
   n = GetReadPos();
   while (n >= blkLen) {
      Pause();
      n = GetReadPos();
   }
   memcpy(blkPtr, blkOut, blkLen);
   nextWrite = 0;
   outState = 3;
   break;
   }
}
```

When using the system for live performance, a long buffer creates an unacceptable latency in sound initiation. We may have to wait for the read position to wrap completely around before the samples we just wrote are sent to the DAC. As a result, the synthesizer does not respond immediately to user input. For interactive use, we need a fairly short buffer, in the range of 50-100ms. Fortunately, the instrument that we are playing can be allocated once and we do not need as much lead time for sample generation. In summary, for sequencing we want as much lead time as possible so that we can handle setup for complex textures, but for interactive playback, all we are doing is generating samples and we want those samples sent to the DAC as soon as possible.

Examples

The utility programs all contain code that sends samples directly to the sound output device. These can be studied for methods to implement the same functions in a synthesizer.

BasicSynth Library

The current version of the library includes two classes for immediate sound playback or output to a DAC. These are Windows-only classes.

WaveOutDirect – output buffer using *DirectSound*

Player – event player

For other platforms, the *WaveOutBuf* class can be used as a base class for sound output as the instrument manager uses the interface of this class for sample output. The *FlushBuffer* method of this class should be overridden with a method to copy the last block of samples to the output device.

Files:

```
Include/WaveOutDirect.h
Include/Player.h
Src/Common/WaveOutDirect.cpp
Src/Common/Player.cpp
```

Chapter 18

Instrument Design

Synthesis instruments combine audio signal generators, control signals and triggers to produce a specific sound. The synthesis technique used to design the instrument defines what signal gerators are needed and how the various generators are combined. To design an instrument we must select the signal generators, specify the parameters for each, and specify the signal paths between them.

First, we need to decide whether we want to produce one all-inclusive instrument or multiple instruments, each implementing one specific synthesis technique. A single all-inclusive instrument may at first seem to offer greater functionality to the musician. However, such an instrument would limit the musician to the synthesis methods built into the instrument, or would require a multitude of parameters for all possible functions of the instrument.

Along the same lines, we can decide to implement the instrument or instruments by compiling the generator functions into a single module. Alternatively, we can specify the combination of generators using a language written specifically for that purpose. The synthesizer must then interpret the language to produce sounds, a potentially much slower method. The second method is generally referred to as the "unit generator" approach. A unit generator is defined as "a software module that emits audio or control signals (envelopes) or modifies these signals."[12] A middle-of-the-road approach is to create our instruments using unit generators, but use C++ as the unit generator language and compile the instruments rather than interpret a script. This is, in fact, the purpose of the *BasicSynth* library. However, this approach does not preclude creating an interpreted

---

[12] Curtis Rhodes, *The Computer Music Tutorial,* p. 787

language that uses the unit generators defined in the *BasicSynth* library.

We also need to consider how much flexibility the instrument will have. The more variable the instrument, the greater the range of sounds it can produce. However, greater flexibility requires more effort to configure the module connections and parameters. We have to decide which is more important, flexibility or ease of use, and trade-off features to meet the desired goal. To understand this trade off, we can think of the development of synthesizers over the years.

Early synthesizers were completely modular. To create a sound, the musician had to set the controls on each module and connect the modules together with short electrical cables called patch cords. To this day, a synthesizer instrument setup is called a *patch,* even though we no longer connect circuitry together with patch cords. Creating a good patch required considerable time and an in-depth knowledge of the synthesizer's operation.

Eventually it was realized that some combinations of modules were more common than others and recurred in almost any patch. For example, a basic tone can be produced by connecting the keyboard to an oscillator to control frequency and connecting the output of the oscillator to an amplifier controlled by an envelope generator triggered by a key press. Eventually manufacturers began producing synthesizers with commonly used connections pre-wired for convenience. The musician had only a few patch options, selectable with switches, but could still vary the sound by changing the settings of the modules.

With the addition of micro-processor control, the user could store synthesizer patches in a memory device and reload them at the push of a button. The available connections between modules were mostly defined by the manufacturer, but many settings were variable by the musician. This made it possible to create a wide variety of sounds, but more quickly than by changing patch cords. Some synthesizer manufacturers went a step further and made all the patches preset, providing the musician with a wide variety of well-designed sounds at the touch of a button.

This provides us with a good taxonomy for synthesis instruments. We can divide instruments into three main categories:

1. Modular with no preset connections
2. Pre-patched with variable settings
3. Preset

All three instrument categories have advantages in certain situations. A modular system allows for the greatest variety of sounds, but requires the most configuration prior to hearing a sound. A pre-patched system has less flexibility, but is quicker to configure and less prone to mistakes. A preset system allows quick selection of sounds, and with a large enough library of presets may be all that many musicians need.

The *BasicSynth* library that we have been developing is a toolkit of unit generators, in effect, a modular synthesis system. In order to produce sounds, we must combine some set of objects together in software, forming the equivalent of a hardware synthesizer patch. Just as with early hardware synthesizers, some combinations are more useful than others and are common to many different sounds. We can create objects that contain these common patches so that set-up of a sound can be done by changing the default values of the synthesis objects. Going one step further, we can load the settings of the objects from a file and have the equivalent of a preset synthesizer available without losing any of the flexibility of the instrument.

A synthesis system can be built using only one instrument, provided that instrument has a sufficient range of sounds. However, the sequencer designs we have developed allow dynamic selection of instruments and there is no reason we can't have multiple forms of all three instrument categories available. We can produce a modular instrument to be used for developing new or unusual sounds, one or more pre-patched instruments that implement common synthesis methods, and a set of presets so that we can quickly load sounds and easily reuse the sounds that we like best.

Instrument Patch Diagrams

When developing an instrument it may be difficult to visualize how the unit generators connect. A diagram that shows the generators, their connections, and the necessary settings will make instrument design easier and less prone to programming errors. Synthesis instruments are typically described using a directed graph indicating the flow of signals. The nodes in the graph represent unit generators and the lines between them show the data flow.

There are no formal standards for the instrument diagram, but there are some conventions that are useful. Inputs are typically placed on the top or left of the symbols and outputs on the bottom or right. Oscillators are usually indicated by a circle or half-ellipse, amplifiers by a triangle, and other processing elements by rectangles. The following symbols will be used to describe synthesis instruments developed in this book. A square connector is used to indicate a control signal while a round connector indicates an audio signal. When the word "signal" is used without a qualifier in the following figures, it refers to an audio signal.

Symbol	Use
Frequency / Phase / Waveform → Signal	An oscillator or other source of periodic waveforms.
Signal / Amplitude → Signal	An amplitude modifier or a multiplier. This can also be represented by a multiplication of two signals.
Signal / Mix / Signal → Signal	A balance control. The mix signal is applied directly to one signal while the compliment (1 − mix) is applied to the other.
Level(s) / Rate(s) → Envelope	An envelope generator. The graphic shows the number of segments. To simplify the diagram, all levels are combined into one input and all rates are combined into another input.

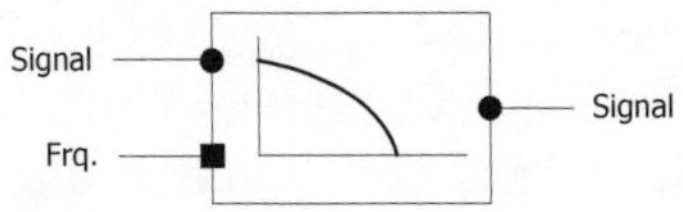 Signal ———• Frq. ———■ ⟶ Signal	A filter. The frequency response graph shows the type of filter: low-pass, high-pass, band-pass, FIR, etc.
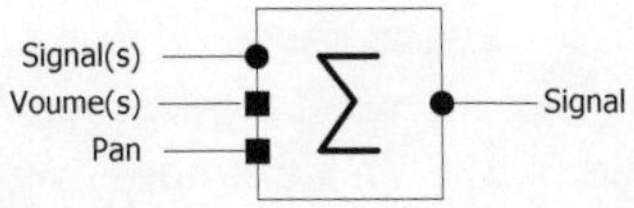 Signal(s) ———• Voume(s) ———■ ∑ ⟶ Signal Pan ———■	Mixer or addition of multiple signals. This does not necessarily represent a mixer object. The mixer may be implemented directly by adding signals.
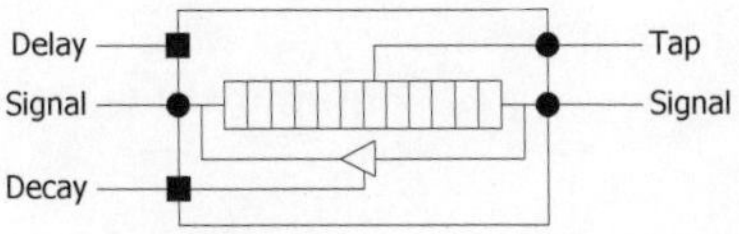 Delay ———■ ⟶ Tap Signal ———• ⟶ Signal Decay ———■	Delay line (comb filter) with optional feedback path and tap positions.
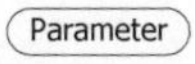 (Parameter)	A value set by the user or during the sequencer playback.
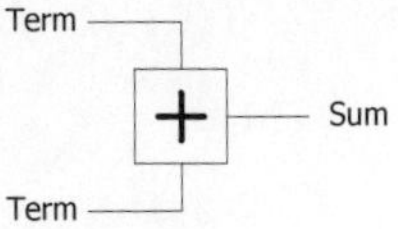 Term ——┐ + — Sum Term ——┘	Addition (or subtraction) of values.
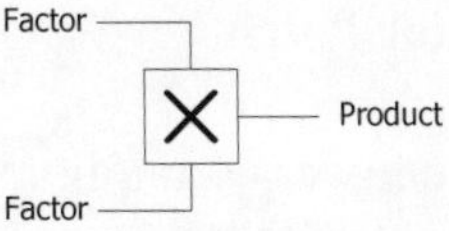 Factor ——┐ ✕ — Product Factor ——┘	Multiplication (or division) of values.
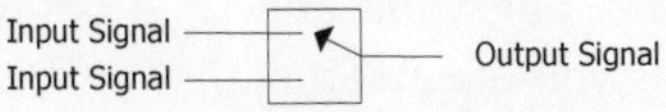 Input Signal ——— Input Signal ——— — Output Signal	A switch. Used to indicate a selection between two or more signal paths.
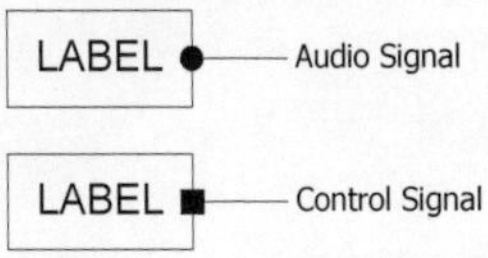 LABEL •— Audio Signal LABEL ■— Control Signal	A box with a label and output represents any signal source not listed above.

Synthesizer patch diagrams may also include trigger signals to show the connection from a keyboard or gate signal used to initiate the envelope generator attack or release cycles. Our software instruments have an implied trigger signal from the sequencer that is not shown on the diagrams. The *Start* (or *NoteOn*) method represents the rising edge of the trigger while the *Stop* (or *NoteOff*) method represents the falling edge of the trigger. Likewise, these diagrams do not show the clock signal. This is the signal that causes the calculation of a sample and is represented by the *Tick* method.

The diagram in Figure 41 shows a simple tone generation patch. An oscillator is used to produce an audio signal which is then given an amplitude envelope with an envelope generator. This patch is so commonly used that it can be treated as a basic building block for many instruments.

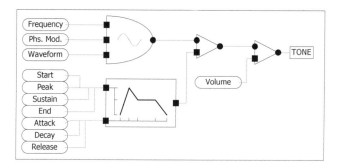

Figure 41 - Tone Generator Patch

Some synthesis diagramming systems include an amplitude input to the oscillator. This can simplify the diagram somewhat since the amplifier is implied within the oscillator and the amplifier symbol can be eliminated. Other synthesis diagrams place the envelope control directly on the output of the oscillator, implying a signal path through the envelope generator. The *BasicSynth* oscillators and envelope generators can be used in either manner by calling the *Sample* method. The oscillators and envelope generators also provide a *Gen* method that returns the current amplitude value directly. This gives us several options for how we write the program.

```
EnvGen eg;
GenWaveWT osc;

out = osc.Gen() * eg.Gen() * vol;
out = eg.Sample(osc.Sample(vol));
out = osc.Sample(eg.Sample(vol));
out = osc.Sample(eg.Gen()) * vol;
out = osc.Sample(eg.Gen() * vol);
etc...
```

Since the library uses normalized floating point values for amplitudes, all the variations shown above should produce the same output value. Although round-off errors might accumulate in some instances, which form is chosen is a matter of preference and coding style, and possibly the compiler optimization capability. Since the example instruments generally use the first form, the diagrams in the following chapters show the amplitude control at the output of the oscillator and envelope generator.

The diagram above shows all the inputs to the envelope generator. Since different envelope generators have varying numbers of inputs, and to make the following diagrams easier to read, we will combine the level parameters into a single input and the rate parameters into a single input.

To implement the patch, we first define a class with an oscillator and envelope generator as class members and define methods to set the parameters for each. Parameters may be set through a sequencer event, passed to the object by the instrument manager, loaded from a file, or set by an interactive editor. The number of parameters available via sequencer event will determine how dynamic the sound of the instrument can be. The more parameters that are variable, the more control we have over the expressiveness of the instrument.

The patch diagram shows how values flow from one unit generator to the next. We implement the patch by tracing along the diagram and converting each link into a program statement. Output signals are obtained by calling the appropriate method on the object (*Gen* or *Sample*). Input connections represent passing a value to an object as a method parameter or a property setting. We don't have, and don't need, an amplifier object. Whenever an amplifier is seen in the diagram, we multiply the inputs to produce the output.

```
class Tone {
    GenWaveWT osc;
    EnvGenADSR env;
    AmpValue vol;
    int wt;

    void Tick() {
        Output(env.Gen() * osc.Gen() * vol);
    }
}
```

A low-frequency oscillator (LFO) used to produce vibrato and similar effects is another common patch. The patch is similar to a tone generator in that it includes an oscillator and amplitude control. However, we don't need a complex envelope for the LFO. A single amplitude scale value is often sufficient, but in some cases we would like to delay the vibrato and then have it fade in. A single envelope segment generator producing an exponential rise curve can be used for this purpose.

The frequency range for the LFO is typically 0-10Hz. The amplitude range depends on the application. For vibrato, the peak amplitude determines the depth of the vibrato and is usually set so that it produces a few cents deviation in pitch. The LFO can also be used for panning and other sound effects.

The LFO waveform is typically a sine wave, but a sawtooth, triangle or square wave have uses as well. Because we want a smooth waveform, it would be better to implement the LFO with wavetables built by direct calculation of the waveforms rather than by summation of sinusoids. As explained before, a wavetable built with a sum of sinusoids will have a wiggle. In this case we need the waveform to have true straight lines.

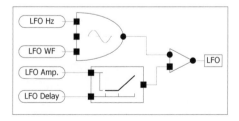

```
class LFO {
    GenWave32 osc;
    EnvSegExp atk;

    AmpValue Gen() {
        return atk.Gen() * osc.Gen();
    }
};
```

When used for vibrato, the LFO amplitude value will be set to the desired frequency variation and we can add the LFO output directly to the frequency input of other oscillators. However, the *BasicSynth* oscillator classes also includes a method that directly modifies the phase of the oscillator. For example, to add vibrato to the basic tone generator above, we can use the following code.

```
void Tick() {
    osc.PhaseModWT(lfo.Gen() * frqTI);
    Output(env.Gen() * osc.Gen() * vol);
}
```

In order to maintain the same level of frequency variation across all pitches, we must calculate the LFO peak amplitude based on the frequency of the audio oscillator. If we let the LFO depth setting represent semi-tones deviation, we can calculate the LFO amplitude as follows. The *f0* variable is the frequency of the audio signal.

```
f1 = f0 * pow(2.0, depth / 12.0);
amp = fabs(f1 - f0);
```

Loading Parameters from a File

Before we can generate sound with an instrument we must set initial values for all of its parameters. We can initialize all values directly from the sequencer start event, but for a complex instrument this is impractical. A sophisticated instrument might have dozens of settable parameters, but most of them will be the same for all notes. We would like to be able to set some parameters during playback while allowing others to be initialized automatically when a new instance of the instrument is created. The initial settings to the instrument can be compiled into the program and for some instruments that might make sense. For most instruments we need to be able to load the initial settings from a file.

The file format should be chosen so that it is portable, extensible, and easily edited. In addition, it is helpful if the file format has a hierarchical structure. A hierarchical structure allows each component of an instrument to store its own information without name collision with other parameters. It also allows the instrument definitions to be included as child nodes of another document, such as a project file.

The XML standard meets all of these requirements. Values can be stored as node attributes, node content, or child nodes. Using XML allows each instrument to define element tags and attributes specific to its parameters and embed that information into the file such that other instruments do not see it. Furthermore, the XML document object model has several available implementations and it is not necessary to create an XML parser. Unfortunately, there is no standard C++ binding that is the same on all implementations. We can, however, create a wrapper class for the parts of XML we need and then implement the wrappers for each system specific library.

All well-formed XML documents contain a root node that encloses all the content of the file. In addition, we need to define a tag to identify the start of an instrument configuration. XML files are fully specified by a document type definition (DTD).[13] The DTD is used by a validating XML parser to insure that the file is well-formed and that only valid entries are passed to the program. However, DTD files are difficult to read and understand. In place of a formal DTD, we will use a template to describe the instrument parameters file.

```
<?xml version="1.0" >
<instrlib>
 <instr id="" type="" name="" desc="">
  <param />
 </instr>
</instrlib>
```

The first tag is the required XML processing instruction that identifies the file as XML. This tag can include additional information such as character encoding. The *instrlib* tag is the document node and identifies the content of the file as a collection of instrument

---

[13] See: http://www.w3.org/TR/REC-xml/ for the official XML specification.

definitions. If we embed the instrument definitions into another file, this node will be a child of the document root node and identify the start of the instrument definition section.

Each instrument is identified by the *instr* tag. The *id* attribute is used as the instrument number value in the instrument definition table and must be unique. The *type* attribute is used to locate the code for the instrument and should be a symbolic name for the instrument factory. The *name* attribute is a text string that provides an easy to use method to identify the instrument. The *desc* attribute contains a description of the instrument. It is optional, but should be included to help readers of the file understand the content.

The instrument parameters are contained within the *instr* node as child nodes. When loading or storing an instrument configuration, the *instr* node is passed to the instrument implementation. If desired, the instrument can store additional attributes in the *instr* node.

The *param* tag is a placeholder for the instrument specific child nodes. Generally, the instrument should define a tag for each unit generator that it uses and store the information for that unit generator as attributes of a child node. For example, the *Tone* instrument includes an oscillator, envelope generator, and LFO. We can store the required parameters as follows.

```
<instr id="" type="Tone" name="" desc="">
  <osc frq="" wt="" vol="" />
  <env st="" atk="" pk="" dec="" sus="" rel=""
       end="" ty="" />
  <lfo frq="" wt="" atk="" amp="" />
</instr>
```

Each parameter is associated with a number used to identify parameter values in the sequencer event. Parameter numbers fall into two categories, general and instrument specific. General parameters, such as duration, frequency, and volume, are defined by the sequencer implementation and should be reused by the instrument when possible. The first 16 parameter numbers are reserved for use by the sequencer, and instrument specific parameters should start at 16 or above.

The following table shows the parameter numbers and the equivalent XML tag and attribute values for the *Tone* instrument.

Since frequency and volume are standard parts of the *NoteEvent* class, we can reuse the identifiers for those parameters.

Parameter	Tag	Attribute	Use
5	*osc*	*frq*	Frequency of the oscillator
6		*vol*	Overall volume level
16		*wt*	Wave table
17	*env*	*st*	Start level for envelope
18		*atk*	Attack rate in seconds
19		*pk*	Peak amplitude level after attack
20		*dec*	Decay time to sustain level
21		*sus*	Sustain level
22		*rel*	Release rate in seconds
23		*end*	End level for envelope
24		*ty*	Envelope curve type: 1 = linear 2 = exponential 3 = log
25	*lfo*	*frq*	LFO frequency
26		*wt*	LFO wave table
27		*atk*	LFO envelope attack time
28		*amp*	LFO amplitude (depth)

Instrument Editors

Because the instrument definition files are in XML format, they may be edited with either a XML editor or text editor. To make configuration easier and more intuitive, most synthesizers include a graphic editor (GUI) that uses simulated knobs, sliders, and switches to set parameters. Graphic and user interface programming is specific to the operating system, and GUI editors must usually be rewritten for each platform. Although full treatment of GUI design and implementation is beyond the scope of this book, there are some general concepts that can be used as a starting place for instrument editor design on any operating system.

The simplest GUI editor is one where each parameter is edited using a text entry field. The user must select each field in turn and type in the value as a number. This kind of interface is easy to program and allows precise specification of values. Because of its relative simplicity, a simple text entry form would be a good starting point for initial editor development. The instrument can be tested, and the overall editor design developed first without having to worry about the complexity of the graphic programming parts. Later, the text entry fields can be replaced as needed with more functional input controls.

Some typical display elements used for synthesizer editing are:

- Knobs
- Sliders
- Switches
- Graphs

Knobs display a round object that can be manipulated with the computer mouse. As the mouse moves around the knob, the knob appears to turn, indicating the entered value. Programming a knob that will work effectively can be difficult. The program must translate the X and Y movements of the mouse into an angle of rotation and use that angle to update the knob position on screen. However, knobs are one of the most useful input controls for a synthesis editor. A knob uses a small amount of display space to represent a wide range of values, the movement of the knob gives visual feed-back of the current value during data entry, and the position of the knob provides an easily perceived view of the current setting. When multiple knobs are arranged in a row or column, they can be nearly as effective as a graph of values.

Sliders are similar to knobs in that the position of the slider on the display represents the current value and the slider value can be manipulated easily with a mouse or keyboard. Sliders are somewhat easier to program since they only require movement in a horizontal or vertical axis. However, sliders usually require more display area than knobs to be usable. For instruments with a large number of parameters, the total number of sliders required may not fit on the display.

Switches are used to select between multiple options, such as a wavetable for an oscillator. A switch can be represented with a multi-state image, or a simulation of a multiple position switch. A set of switches where only one option is allowed (radio button group) is another possibility when multiple values are allowed for a parameter.

Values can also be entered using direct manipulation of a graph. A graph displays a set of values as lines and allows the user to drag the end-points of the lines to change the settings. This is most effective with envelope generators, but can be used for other unit generators as well. For example, a set of harmonics used to create a complex waveform could be presented as a bar graph.

When drawing the controls on the screen, we can either make direct calls to the graphic library or use a pre-drawn bitmap. Direct calls take less memory and always display at the correct resolution, but are slower to update and may flicker during screen updates. Bitmaps are of a fixed size and may either be too small or too large for the user's display, or may not be in the correct pixel depth for the user's display. Typically, a combined strategy is used. When the program is loaded, it can interrogate the system to determine the screen size and resolution and then generate a set of bitmaps for knobs, sliders, and switches that are of the appropriate size, color depth, and pixel format. Once these bitmaps are created, screen updates are a simple matter of copying the image to the screen. Since bitmaps are difficult to rotate, elements of the display that must be rotated can be drawn on top of fixed background bitmaps.

Managing the large number of parameters that must be configured can present a difficult problem during instrument editor design. For example, the simple tone instrument shown above has 15 values that can be configured. For a sophisticated synthesis instrument, the number of parameters can be 100 or even more. Displaying all the parameters at once on the screen can result in a crowded display where each element is so small it is impossible to manipulate the inputs. Furthermore, a screen full of display controls can become nearly incomprehensible to the user.

One solution to a crowded display is to use pop-up windows for sliders or knobs, similar to the technique widely used for context menus and other optional data entry elements. When the user clicks on the screen element a window is displayed on top of the input form that shows a menu, slider or knob. The pop-up window can be significantly larger than the display control so that when clicked, the knob or slider appears to magnify in size ("zoom in") and allows a greater range of movement for manipulation with the mouse.

Another and more general solution is to use tabbed displays. On a tabbed display, only a portion of the instrument configuration is shown at one time. In order to view the rest of the configuration, the user presses a tab on the display and the display is redrawn with another part of the configuration. This is a commonly used technique and most windowing systems provide tab controls that make it easy to switch between different parts of the display. Scrolling windows are another option, but are not as effective for dialog type input as they are for text displays.

The color, texture, detail, and overall appearance of the GUI is largely a matter of personal preference. Some users prefer a simple, clean look, while others prefer an exact replica of a piece of electronic equipment. We also have to decide whether or not to follow the default look and feel of the operating system. Generally, it is easier to program the GUI if we select only controls that are made available by the operating system. In addition, if we use the standard controls, the software will automatically adapt the look-and-feel to display settings chosen by the user. A custom GUI can end up looking awkward and antiquated as the operating system changes over time. Most systems supply text entry fields, menus, buttons that can be used for switches, and slider controls. However, few systems provide knobs and direct entry graphs, and those elements must be programmed separately.

Finally, when choosing the look of the display it is important to remember that simulation of a hardware device has disadvantages as well as advantages. A close simulation of a commonly used device makes it easy for experienced synthesizer users to understand the display. However, the design of most hardware synthesizers is limited by physical space, cost and range of movement. There is no need for a software system to be constrained in that manner. With software, it costs no more to put a big, colorful knob on a display than a up/down button. Unlike a piece of hardware, it is also easy to add a numeric text display to each object, allowing for both mouse and keyboard input for each value.

BasicSynth Library

Two XML wrapper classes provide methods to open, read and write XML files.

XmlSynthDoc - class that wraps the XML document.

XmlSynthElem – class that wraps one element node in the XML document.

The instrument implementations are contained in a separate library located in the *Instruments* directory.

ToneInstr – implementation of the Tone instrument.

LFO – implementation of the general purpose LFO generator

LoadInstrLib – Function to load an XML file containing multiple instruments

LoadInstr – Function to load one instrument from a node in an XML file

Files:

```
Include/XmlWrap.h
Src/Common/XmlWrapW.cpp
Src/Common/XmlWrapU.cpp
Src/Instruments/Tone.h
Src/Instruments/Tone.cpp
Src/Instruments/LoadInstrLib.h
Src/Instruments/LoadInstrLib.cpp
```

Chapter 19

Additive Synthesis Instrument

Additive synthesis creates a sound by adding the outputs from multiple audio signal generators. In a previous chapter we created a complex waveform by adding sine waves together. The resulting waveform is static over the duration of the note. To produce a more interesting sound, and more closely duplicate the transient spectrum of natural sounds, we need to vary the amplitude of each partial over time. We do that by duplicating the basic tone generator for each partial, giving each its own envelope.

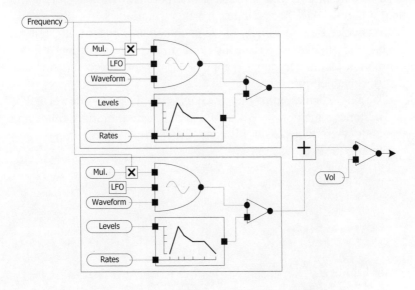

Figure 42 - Additive Synthesis Patch

The tone generator block can be duplicated as many times as desired to achieve the required complexity of the spectrum. However, as more generators are added, it will take longer to generate one sample. Using eight to sixteen generators is a good compromise between performance and functionality when using this instrument to create complex waveforms by summing partials.

We can also use this patch to implement wavetable synthesis. While the classic additive synthesis method uses wavetables containing sine waves for all oscillators, wavetable synthesis uses wavetables containing complex waveforms. Blending the waveforms produces a time-varying spectrum much like adding individual partials. However, the number of waveforms that must be added is much smaller. As little as two or three tone generators can produce an effect similar to a dozen tone generators using sine waves.

An additive synthesis instrument can also be used to produce doublings, much like a combination of stops found on a pipe organ. Furthermore, if the oscillators are slightly detuned, and the envelopes given slightly different rates, we can produce a chorus effect.

In order to produce all these variations, some tone generators may need to fade-in over the duration of the note and we will need more than a simple ADSR envelope. A better solution is to fully specify each envelope as a series of segments using the multi-segment envelope generator class. This will make configuration of the instrument parameters more complicated, but the added functionality justifies that complexity.

The implementation of the *AddSynth* class is straightforward. The simple tone generator shown above is duplicated multiple times and the code then loops over all tone generators, adding the outputs together to produce a sample.

```
struct AddSynthPart {
    GenWaveWT osc;
    EnvGenSeg env;
    FrqValue  mul;
    int wt;
};
class AddSynth {
    AddSynthPart *parts;
    int numParts;
    LFO lfoGen;
};
```

```
void AddSynth::Tick() {
   PhsAccum vib = lfoGen.Gen() * frqTI;
   AmpValue oscval;
   AmpValue envval;
   AmpValue signal = 0;
   for (int n = 0; n < numParts; n++) {
      parts[n].osc.PhaseModWT(vib * parts[n].mul);
      oscval = parts[n].env.Gen();
      envval = parts[n].osc.Gen();
      signal += oscval * envval;
   }
   Output(signal * vol);
}
```

Because of the variable number of oscillators and envelope generators, the XML format for the *AddSynth* instrument must implement a hierarchy of nodes with variable number of children at each level. The general structure is shown below.

```
<instr id="" type="AddSynth" name="" parts="" >
   <part pn="" mul="" frq="" wt="" />
   <env segs="" st="" sus="">
    <seg sn="" rt="" lvl="" ty="" />
   </env>
   </part>
   <lfo frq="" wt="" atk="" amp="" />
</instr>
```

The *instr* node contains an additional attribute, *parts*, to indicate the number of partials in the instrument. Each partial is specified by a child node with a *part* tag and contains attributes to specify the partial number and frequency multiplier. Likewise, the *env* node indicates the number of segments in the envelope. A child node of *env* is included to define the values for each envelope segment. The *lfo* node contains the LFO values and is identical to the tone instrument shown above.

Because the number of parameter values varies, parameter ID numbers must be calculated based on the partial and envelope segment index. The parameter ID numbers are formed from three bit fields.

```
[PN(7)][SN(4)][VAL(4)]

PN = (partial + 1) * 256
SN = segment * 16
```

This layout allows for 126 partials, 16 envelope segments per partial, and 16 parameter values for each partial or envelope. A value of 0 for PN indicates a parameter index used to specify parameters that affect the entire instrument (e.g., fundamental pitch, master volume, LFO).

Parameter	Tag	Attribute	Use
16	*lfo*	*frq*	LFO Frequency
17		*wt*	LFO wave table
18		*atk*	LFO envelope attack time
19		*amp*	LFO depth
	part	*pn*	Partial number
PN+0		*mul*	Frequency multiplier. The frequency of this partial is the base frequency of the instrument multiplied by this value.
PN+1		*frq*	Oscillator frequency. This is optional since the frequency will be recalculated based on the multiplier.
PN+2		*wt*	Wave table index
	env	*segs*	Number of envelope segments.
PN+3		*st*	Starting envelope value
PN+4		*sus*	Sustain-on flag, 1 or 0.
	seg	*sn*	Segment number
PN+SN+5		*rt*	Segment rate
PN+SN+6		*lvl*	Segment end level
PN+SN+7		*ty*	Segment curve type

BasicSynth Library

The additive synthesis instrument described in this chapter is implemented by the *AddSynth* class.

Files:

```
Src/Instruments/AddSynth.h
Src/Instruments/AddSynth.cpp
```

Chapter 20

Subtractive Synthesis Instrument

Subtractive synthesis passes a waveform rich in harmonics, and/or noise, through a filter. To produce a varying spectrum, one envelope generator is applied to the signal to control amplitude while a second envelope is used to vary the cutoff frequency of the filter. Usually, a LFO is included to produce vibrato. A basic subtractive synthesis patch is shown in the following diagram.

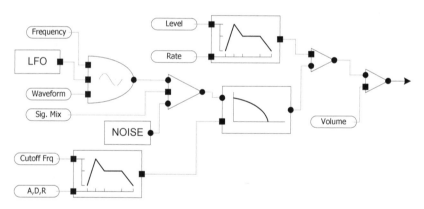

Figure 43 - Subtractive Synthesis Patch

More sophisticated subtractive synthesis instruments include multiple oscillator/filter combinations as well as a variety of filters. They may also include AM or FM inputs to create complex waveforms through modulation. However, the simple patch shown above will duplicate the sound of many classic analog synthesizers.

To implement the instrument, we define a class with members for the oscillator, noise generator, filter, and two envelopes along with the necessary parameters. The *Tick* method invokes each of the modules in turn, passing the values through to the appropriate input of other modules.

```
class SubSynth {
GenWaveWT osc;
GenWaveNoise noise;
FilterLP filt;
EnvGenADSR envSig;
EnvGenADSR envFilt;
LFO lfo;

    void Tick() {
        AmpValue sigVal;
        osc.PhaseModWT(lfo.Gen() * frqTI);
        sigVal = osc.Gen() * mixVal
                + noise.Gen() * (1 - mixVal);
        filt.Init(envFilt.Gen(), filtGain);
        Output(filt.Sample(sigVal)*envSig.Gen()*vol)
    }
}
```

The XML format and parameter ID values for the *SubSynth* instrument are shown below.

```
<instr id="" type="SubSynth" name=" ">
  <osc frq="" wt="" vol="" mix=""
       fg="" ft="" ft="" />
  <egs st="" atk="" pk="" dec=""
       sus="" rel="" end="" ty="" />
  <egf st="" atk="" pk="" dec=""
       sus="" rel="" end="" ty="" />
  <lfo frq="" wt="" rt="" amp="" />
</instr>
```

Parameter	Tag	Attribute	Use
5	*osc*	*frq*	Sets the initial frequency for the oscillator.
6		*vol*	Sets the overall volume level.
16		*mix*	Sets the mixture of oscillator output and noise output. 1 is full oscillator; 0 is full noise.

17		*wt*	Wave table index.
18		*ft*	Filter type (LP,HP,BP,RES).
19		*fg*	Filter gain
20		*fr*	Filter resonance/bandwidth
21	*egs*	*st*	Volume envelope start level.
22		*atk*	Volume envelope attack rate
23		*pk*	Volume envelope peak level
24		*dec*	Volume envelope decay rate
25		*sus*	Volume envelope sustain lvl.
26		*rel*	Volume envelope release rate
27		*end*	Volume envelope final level
28		*ty*	Volume envelope curve type
30	*egf*	*st*	Filter envelope start value.
31		*atk*	Filter envelope attack rate
32		*pk*	Filter envelope peak level
33		*dec*	Filter envelope decay rate
34		*sus*	Filter envelope sustain level
35		*rel*	Filter envelope release level
36		*end*	Filter envelope final level
37		*ty*	Filter envelope curve type
40	*lfo*	*frq*	LFO Frequency
41		*wt*	LFO wavetable index
42		*rt*	LFO envelope attack rate
43		*amp*	LFO level

BasicSynth Library

The subtractive synthesis instrument described in this chapter is implemented by the *SubSynth* class.

Files:

```
Src/Instruments/SubSynth.h
Src/Instruments/SubSynth.cpp
```

Chapter 21

FM Synthesis Instrument

FM synthesis is one of the more favored techniques for digital synthesis. Only a small number of unit generators are required to produce a sound, and all are very fast to execute, yet provide a wide variety of timbres. FM synthesis instruments can be as simple as two oscillators and envelope generators, and as complex as the number of units we wish to configure. To start, we will look at the most basic FM instrument using only one modulator and one carrier. The patch is shown in the following diagram.

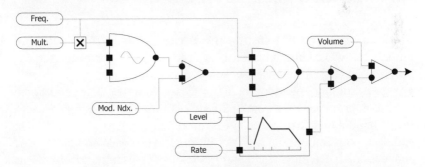

Figure 44 - Two Oscillator FM Instrument

The diagram shows the output of the modulator connected to the phase input of the carrier. We could add the modulator output to the frequency input instead. As discussed in a previous chapter, the resulting sound is the same so long as we adjust the amplitude level of the modulator appropriately. Phase modulation has a slight speed advantage during sample generation since the conversion of the modulation index from frequency to radians can be done during

205

initialization and set as the volume level on the modulator. Thus we don't have to continuously add and convert the frequencies to radians on each sample. When using wavetable oscillators, we can go one step further and convert the modulation index range to table index range. We can then directly add the output of the modulator to the table index of the carrier.

This brings up an important consideration for implementation of FM instruments. We need to make sure that the maximum modulation amplitude does not drive the carrier oscillator past the Nyquist frequency. When directly modifying the phase of a wavetable oscillator we must insure the table index does not exceed the table length. Rather than check the limit of the modulator frequency on every sample, we can check the limit during the *Start* method and reduce the modulator envelope generator settings if necessary.

The implementation of this simple FM instrument is nearly identical to the *Tone* instrument. We only need to substitute the *GenWaveFM* class for the *GenWaveWT* oscillator class and add two parameters for modulation index and modulator frequency multiple.

An Expanded FM Instrument

The two oscillator FM instrument is capable of a good range of timbres. However, the addition of a second modulator oscillator can provide a significant increase in sound generation capability with only a small amount of additional processing time. The additional oscillator provides four combinations of modulation. We can use a single modulator, two modulators in series, or two in parallel. In addition, we can modulate two carriers with one oscillator. The connections between carriers and modulators is usually reffered to as an FM *algorithm*.

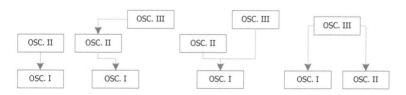

Figure 45 - Modulation Combinations

We can also improve the capability of the FM instrument by adding a LFO for vibrato. We can apply the LFO output to both modulators and carrier, or to the carrier alone. When applied to both modulators and carrier, the *c:m* ratio remains constant and produces a constant timbre. When applied to the carrier alone, the vibrato causes a slight shift in the *c:m* ratio and thus modulates the timbre along with the frequency. Both effects are useful and, if desired, we can provide an option to do vibrato either way. The example instrument applies vibrato to modulators and carrier, scaled by the frequency multiplier, so that the frequency variation is proportional on each oscillator.

Many natural sounds have a noise element, such as a transient that results from striking an object or a breath noise. FM alone cannot easily produce noise effects, but we can add a noise source to the patch and mix the noise generator output with the carrier output. We could use a filtered noise source similar to the subtractive synthesis instrument. However, the pitched noise source created by ring modulation of noise and a sine wave works very well for this purpose.

A delay line is added before the final output allowing us to add resonance to the sound. Both FM carrier output and noise signal output can be sent through the delay line. Parameters control how much of each signal is delayed and how much of the delayed signal is mixed into the final output. To minimize coloration of the sound, an allpass delay should be used.

The complete patch diagram is too large to fit on one page, so we will show each block separately. Connections between blocks are identified with labeled rectangles.

The first diagram shows the algorithm selection block. Each switch position determines the modulator signals that are sent to the inputs of the carrier and/or first modulator. The *MOD SEL 1* label represents the signals applied to oscillator I. The *MOD SEL 2* label represents the signals applied to oscillator II.

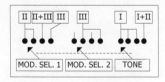

The next diagram shows the oscillator I block. This is the main audio tone oscillator and is essentially the same as the tone generator shown before. It includes a modulation input from the output of *MOD. SEL. 1.*

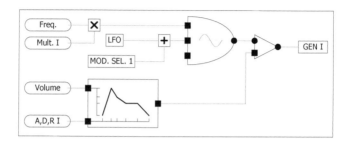

The next diagram shows Generators II and III. Oscillator II includes the input from the algorithm selection. The envelope generator levels are specified as modulation index values rather than the typical [0,1] range for amplitude envelope. This allows us to apply the output of the block directly to the modulation input of other oscillators without further calculation.

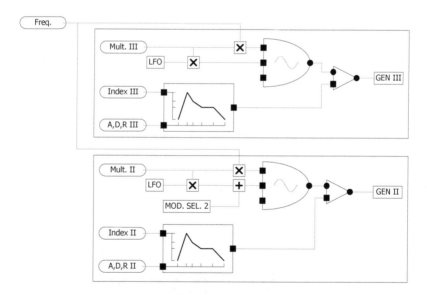

The next diagram shows the noise section.

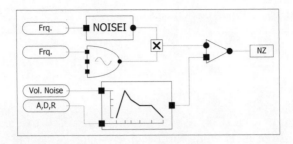

The next diagram shows the LFO block.

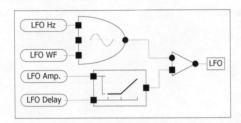

The final diagram shows the delay line block. The NZ and TONE outputs are attenuated and fed to the delay line. The final output is a mix of tone, noise, and delay signals.

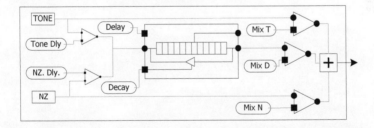

We will also add an optional internal panning function to allow the spatial location to be dynamically controlled independent of the global mixer input channel. When enabled, panning is controlled by the instrument rather than the mixer.

When initializing the envelope for the modulators, we must convert the levels into wavetable index increments. At the same time, we can check the modulation range to insure it does not exceed the maximum allowed value.

```
AmpValue CalcPhaseMod(AmpValue amp, FrqValue mult){
    amp = (amp * mult) * synthParams.frqTI;
    if (amp > synthParams.ftableLength/2)
        amp = 0;
    return amp;
}
```

The return value from *CalcPhaseMod* is passed to the envelope generator as the level value for a segment. During sample generation we only need to take the output of the envelope generator and add it to the phase of the carrier oscillator.

The implementation for the *Tick* method is shown below. The algorithm is represented with a value from 1 to 4, each representing a switch position. We can skip running the LFO, noise generator and delay line when their respective amplitude values are zero.

```
void Tick() {
    if (lfoAmp > 0) {
        lfoOut = lfoGen.Gen() * frqTI;
        gen1Mod = lfoOut * gen1Mult;
        gen2Mod = lfoOut * gen2Mult;
        gen3Mod = lfoOut * gen3Mult;
    } else {
        gen1Mod = gen2Mod = gen3Mod = 0;
    }
    gen1Out = osc1.Gen() * eg1.Gen();
    gen2Out = osc2.Gen() * eg2.Gen();
    gen3Out = osc3.Gen() * eg3.Gen();
    switch (algorithm) {
    case 2: // double stack
        gen2Mod += gen3Out;
    case 1: // single stack
        gen1Mod += gen2Out;
        break;
    case 3: // 'Y' (double modulator)
        gen1Mod += gen2Out + gen3Out;
        break;
    case 4: // 'Delta' (double carrier)
        gen2Mod += gen3Out;
        gen1Mod += gen3Out;
        gen1Out += gen2Out;
        break;
    }
```

```
osc1.PhaseModWT(gen1Mod);
osc2.PhaseModWT(gen2Mod);
osc3.PhaseModWT(gen3Mod);

sigOut = gen1Out * fmMix;

if (nzMix > 0 || nzDly > 0) {
    nzOut = nzi.Gen() * nzo.Gen() * nzEG.Gen();
    sigOut += nzOut * nzMix;
}

if (dlyMix > 0) {
    dlyIn = gen1Out * fmDly;
    dlyIn += nzOut * nzDly;
    sigOut += apd.Sample(dlyIn) * dlyMix;
}

sigOut *= vol;
if (panOn)
    Output2(chnl, sigOut*panLft, sigOut*panRgt);
else
    Output(chnl, sigOut);
}
```

The XML file format for the *FMSynth* instrument is as follows.

```
<instr id="" type="FMSynth" name="" descr="" >
  <fm mix="" dly="" alg="" pon="" pan="" />
  <gen1 st="" atk="" pk="" dec="" sus=""
    rel="" end="" ty="" mul="" wt="" />
  <gen2 st="" atk="" pk="" dec="" sus=""
    rel="" end="" ty="" mul="" wt="" />
  <gen3 st="" atk="" pk="" dec="" sus=""
    rel="" end="" ty="" mul="" wt="" />
  <nz mix="" dly="" fr="" fo="" st="" atk="" pk=""
    dec="" sus="" rel="" end="" ty="" />
  <dln mix="" dly="" dec="" />
  <lfo frq="" wt="" atk="" amp="" />
</instr>
```

The following table shows the parameter numbers for the *FMSynth* events and the associated XML tags.

Parameter	Tag	Attribute	Use
16	*fm*	*mix*	Mix of FM signal in output
17		*dly*	FM signal sent to delay line.
18		*alg*	FM algorithm
19		*pon*	Panning on
20		*pan*	Pan setting
30	*gen1*	*mul*	Gen. 1 frequency multiplier
31		*st*	Gen. 1 envelope start value
32		*atk*	Gen. 1 envelope attack rate
33		*pk*	Gen. 1 envelope attack level
34		*dec*	Gen. 1 envelope decay rate
35		*sus*	Gen. 1 envelope sustain level
36		*rel*	Gen. 1 envelope release rate
37		*end*	Gen. 1 envelope final level
38		*ty*	Gen. 1 envelope curve type
39		*wt*	Gen. 1 wavetable index
40	*gen2*	*mul*	Gen. 2 frequency multiplier
41		*st*	Gen. 2 envelope start value
42		*atk*	Gen. 2 envelope attack rate
43		*pk*	Gen. 2 envelope attack level
44		*dec*	Gen. 2 envelope decay rate
45		*sus*	Gen. 2 envelope sustain level
46		*rel*	Gen. 2 envelope release rate
47		*end*	Gen. 2 envelope final level
48		*ty*	Gen. 2 envelope curve type
49		*wt*	Gen. 2 wavetable index
50	*gen3*	*mul*	Gen. 3 frequency multiplier
51		*st*	Gen. 3 envelope start value
52		*atk*	Gen. 3 envelope attack rate
53		*pk*	Gen. 3 envelope attack level
54		*dec*	Gen. 3 envelope decay rate
55		*sus*	Gen. 3 envelope sustain level
56		*rel*	Gen. 3 envelope release rate
57		*end*	Gen. 3 envelope final level
58		*ty*	Gen. 3 envelope curve type
59		*wt*	Gen. 3 wavetable index
60	*nz*	*mix*	Mix of noise signal in output

61		*dly*	Noise signal to delay line
62		*fr*	Noise frequency
63		*fo*	Oscillator frequency
64		*st*	Noise envelope starting value
65		*atk*	Noise envelope attack rate
66		*pk*	Noise envelope attack level
67		*dec*	Noise envelope decay rate
68		*sus*	Noise envelope sustain level
69		*rel*	Noise envelope release rate
70		*end*	Noise envelope final level
71		*ty*	Noise envelope curve type
80	*dlyn*	*mix*	Amount of delay line output
81		*dly*	Delay line length in seconds
82		*dec*	Delay line decay multiplier
90	*lfo*	*frq*	LFO frequency
91		*wt*	LFO wavetable index
92		*atk*	LFO envelope attack rate
93		*amp*	LFO level

BasicSynth Library

The two oscillator FM synthesis instrument described in this chapter is implemented by the *FMTone* class. The expanded FM synthesis instrument is implemented by the *FMSynth* class.

Files:

```
Src/Instruments/Tone.h
Src/Instruments/Tone.cpp
Src/Instruments/FMSynth.h
Src/Instruments/FMSynth.cpp
```

Chapter 22

Wavefile Playback Instrument

While the main purpose of a synthesizer is to generate sounds rather than playback recorded sounds, there are some sounds that are difficult to synthesize. A door slamming and a cymbal are examples of sounds we might want to play from a short recording rather than try to synthesize. Recorded sound playback is very simple so long as we do not need to vary the pitch or envelope. All that we need to do is load the wavefile into memory and then copy the samples to the output mixer. However, we might want to repeat the sound, or stop before the entire sound is finished. Thus we need options for looping and to indicate whether to stop the sound as soon as the *stop* signal is received or to always play the sound to the end. In addition, in order to fade-in or fade-out during playback, we can include a simple AR type envelope.

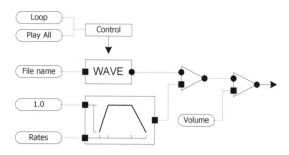

Figure 46 - WAVE File Playback Instrument

We first need to develop the code to read a WAVE file. Unlike writing the file we cannot assume the file contains only format and data chunks, or that the two chunks are the first two chunks in the file.

In order to simplify implementation, we will only accept files in PCM format with 16 bits per sample and the sample data contained in a data chunk. If other sound file types need to be used, we can pre-process the file with a wave file editor and save the sound in the format we need.

The following structures define the chunk and wave format data structures for wave file reading.

```
struct RiffChunk {
   char id[4];
   long size;
};

struct WaveFmt {
   int16 fmtCode;       // 1 = PCM
   int16 channels;      // 1 = mono, 2 = stereo
   int32 sampleRate;
   int32 avgbps;        // samplerate * align
   int16 align;         // (channels*bits)/8;
   int16 bits;          // bits per sample (16)
};
```

To load the file, we first open the file, verify that it is a WAVE file, then step forward through chunks until the two chunks we need are located. Example code to locate the wave data is shown below.

```
while (!(foundFmt && foundWav) && !feof(wfp)) {
   fread(&chunk, 8, 1, wfp);
   if (memcmp(chunk.id, "fmt ", 4) == 0) {
      fread(&fmt, 16, 1, wfp);
      if (fmt.fmtCode == 1
        && fmt.bits == 16) {
         foundFmt = 1;
      }
   } else if (memcmp(chunk.id, "data", 4) == 0 {
      dataSize = chunk.size;
      foundWav = 1;
   } else {
      fseek(wfp, chunk.size, SEEK_CUR);
   }
}
```

Once a sample block of the correct format is located we can calculate the number of samples and allocate a sample buffer. We will also need an input buffer large enough for one sample frame.

```
data = new char[fmt.align];
sampleTotal = dataSize / fmt.align;
samples = new AmpValue[sampleTotal];
```

When reading samples, we need to convert the file data into the internal type we use for samples and also scale samples to the normalized range of [-1,+1]. Many WAVE files are recorded as stereo and we may want to preserve spatial parts of the sound. However, most of the time we would rather control panning with the synthesizer mixer, and we should merge the channels into one sample by adding both channels for each sample.

```
for (index = 0; index < sampleTotal; index++) {
    fread(data, 1, fmt.align, fp);
    in = (short*)data;
    samples[index] = in[0]);
    if (fmt.channels > 1)
        samples[index] += in[1];
    if (abs(samples[index]) > peak)
        peak = abs(samples[index]);
}

for (index = 0; index < sampleTotal; index++)
    samples[index] /= peak;
```

The wave file sample rate must be matched to the playback sample rate. We can re-sample the wave file while it is loading or during playback. When the wave file sample rate is greater than that playback rate, we must skip samples. Likewise, when the wave file sample rate is less than the playback rate, we must repeat some samples. This is similar to the way we changed the frequency of a wavetable oscillator. We calculate an increment value by dividing the file sample rate by the playback sample rate to determine the index increment value. If the two sample rates are equal, the increment value is 1 and all samples are played. When the rates differ, the sample increment will be other than 1 and we will either skip or repeat samples. Although this is not the best possible re-sample algorithm, it is simple and produces reasonably good results. More sophisticated techniques such as interpolation and filtering can be added either at the time the wave file is loaded or during playback if desired.

Loading wavefiles is a potentially time consuming operation and we do not want to repeatedly load the same file every time a note is played or load multiple copies of the file. We can create a cache of files at initialization and then locate the file in the cache by its ID value. This allows multiple instances of the instrument to share the wave file and allows multiple wave files to be associated with the instrument. In addition, the wave file can be changed at any time by changing the ID parameter.

When the *start* signal is received, the sample number is set to 0 and the envelope generator is reset. We must also locate the selected wave file in the cache.

```
WaveFileIn wfCache[MAX_WAVEFILES];
int wfCacheCount = 0;

void WFSYnth::Start() {
    sampleNumber = 0;
    sampleTotal = 0;
    sampleIncr = 1;
    samples = NULL;
    for (n = 0; n < wfCacheCount; n++) {
        if (wfCache[n].id == fileID) {
            sampleTotal = wfCache[n].sampleTotal;
            samples = wfCache[n].samples;
            sampleIncr = wfCache[n].sampleRate;
            sampleIncr /= synthParams.sampleRate;
            break;
        }
    }
    eg.Reset();
}
```

Implementation of playback is simple. On each *Tick* the sample at the current index is multiplied by the envelope and output, and the index is incremented. When the increment reaches the end of the wave file and the loop option is set, the index is set back to zero.

```
void WFSYnth::Tick() {
    if (sampleNumber >= sampleTotal {
        if (!looping) {
            return;
        }
        sampleNumber = 0;
    }
    Output(eg.Gen() * samples[sampleNumber]);
    sampleNumber += sampleIncr;
}
```

The *stop* signal is handled by looking at the *looping* and *playAll* options. If we are not looping and not forcing complete playback, we can simply set the current sample number to the end. Any subsequent calls to *Tick* will produce no output.

```
void WFSynth::Stop() {
    eg.Release();
    if (!looping && !playAll)
        sampleNumber = sampleTotal;
}
```

Likewise, the *IsFinished* method can check to see if we are looping and wait on the envelope generator to finish in that case.

```
void WFSynth::IsFinished() {
    if (looping)
        return eg.IsFinished();
    return sampleNumber >= sampleTotal;
}
```

The XML format and parameter table for the *WaveFile* player are shown below. The *file* tags cause a WAVE file to be loaded into the cache and identified with the given number. Multiple *file* entries are allowed.

```
<instr>
  <wvf id="" lp="" pa="" />
  <env ar="" rr="" />
  <file name="" id="" >
</instr>
```

Parameter	Tag	Attribute	Use
16	*wvf*	*id*	ID of WAVE file
17		*lp*	Loop flag, 0 = play once 1 = loop
18		*pa*	Play all flag, 0 = stop on Release 1 = play to the end always
19	*env*	*ar*	Attack rate
20		*rr*	Release rate

BasicSynth Library

The wavefile playback instrument described in this chapter is
implemented by the *WFSynth* class.

Files:

```
Src/Instruments/WFSynth.h
Src/Instruments/WFSynth.cpp
```

Chapter 23

Eight Tone Matrix Instrument

Each of the instruments designed so far has implemented the patch such that there is little variation in how the generators are combined. Because only the parameters need to be specified, the instruments can be easily configured. In situations where we need more control over the patch, or an arbitrary synthesis patch, we need an instrument where the actual patch connections can be specified.

One option is to create a completely modular instrument where a variable set of unit generators can be combined in any order. The patch can be created using either a graphic or text configuration system, but in both cases the instrument has no built-in structure and we must specify every part of the patch directly. A good compromise that reduces the complexity of configuration is to have an instrument with a limited number of unit generators, but to allow all connections between generators to be made with a patch matrix. Depending on how the matrix is configured, the same set of generators can implement additive synthesis, FM synthesis, or a combination of the two.

Figure 47 - Modulation/Signal MatrixFigure 47 shows the overall structure of the tone generator matrix instrument. We can allocate as many tone generator units as desired, but eight is usually sufficient. Each tone generator consists of an oscillator and envelope generator combination with parameters for frequency multiple, envelope generator levels and rates, LFO input level, and output levels. All signal outputs are combined with an internal mixer before being sent to the main mixer.

Any envelope generator can be applied to any of the oscillators. This allows multiple oscillators to track the same envelope without having to enter the envelope values multiple times. The envelope levels are specified in the range [0-1], but two parameters provide multiplication of the range. One parameter provides a level for amplitude control, while the other provides a level suitable for a modulation index.

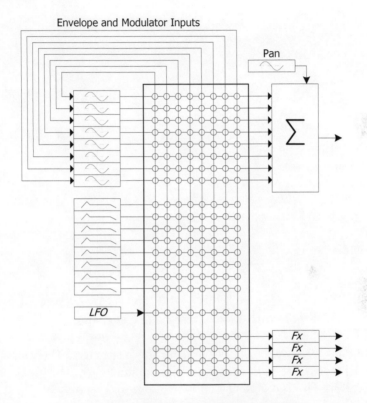

Figure 47 - Modulation/Signal Matrix

The configurable matrix does not have fixed algorithms for modulation. Any generator can be modulated by any number of other generators, or none at all, and the output of any generator can be combined into the final signal mix, potentially acting as both a modulator and signal generator simultaneously. Because the instrument is capable of producing several independent sounds simultaneously, it is especially useful for creating ensemble sounds.

Figure 48 shows the details of one tone generator. The output of the tone generator is split into modulation, audio and effects signals with each output signal level controlled independently. The volume level controls the amount of the audio signal. The modulation index level controls the level sent to the modulation inputs of other generators.

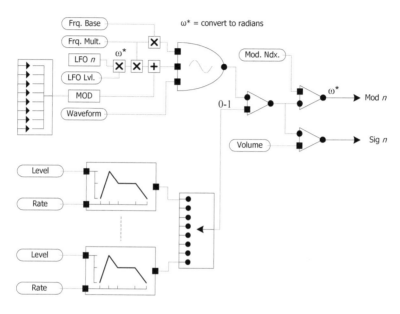

Figure 48 - Matrix Tone Generator

Figure 49 shows the LFO unit for the instrument. The output of the LFO oscillator is split into eight outputs, one for each tone generator. The same LFO rate, waveform and amplitude curve are used for all tones, but we can apply individual levels of modulation to each using the modulation level input parameter shown above.

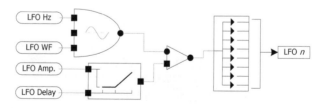

Figure 49 - Matrix LFO Unit

The audio signal can be applied to a variety of outputs as shown in Figure 50. If internal panning is set, the signal is sent directly to the left and right mixer inputs. Otherwise, the signal is applied to the mixer channel input and the mixer panning is applied to the signal. This allows the instrument to bypass mixer panning and supply dynamic panning on a note-by-note basis. A separate set of outputs is available for effects processing. Each of the four *Fx* outputs has an independent level control making it possible to vary the amount of effects processing applied to each tone generator. For example, the instrument can be set up to provide multiple sounds, some with reverb and some without.

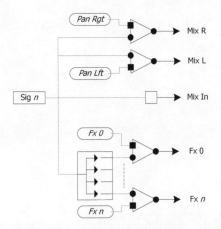

Figure 50 - Audio Signal Routing

The matrix of connections can be represented by a set of bits for each tone generator with each input or output connection controlled by one bit. One bit (MIXOUT) is used to control signal output. When the MIXOUT bit is set, the generator output is added to the audio output value. When a MODxIN bit is set, the associated modulator is applied to the generator. To optimize the instrument we also include a bit indicating if the generator is used (ON). An unused generator is skipped during sample generation. Likewise, we can test for any modulator inputs and skip the modulation code if modulation is not configured.

The *Tick* method must first invoke each envelope and oscillator to get the current output values. All generators that are indicated as an output are added to the appropriate audio signal outputs. The values are then applied to the selected modulation inputs.

```
#define TONE_ON      0x000001
#define TONE_OUT     0x000002
#define TONE_LFOIN   0x000004
#define TONE_FX1OUT 0x000010
(etc...)
#define TONE_PAN     0x008000
#define TONE_MOD1IN 0x010000
#define TONE_MOD2IN 0x020000
(etc...)
#define TONE_MODANY 0xFF0004

struct MatrixTone {
    GenWaveWT osc;
    AmpValue volLvl;
    AmpValue modLvl;
    AmpValue fxLvl[4];
    uint32 toneFlags;
    uint16 envIn;
    AmpValue panLft;
    AmpValue panRgt
};

class MatrixSynth {
    MatrixTone gens[8];
    EnvGenSegSus envs[8];

void Tick() {
    AmpValue sigOut = 0;
    AmpValue sigLft = 0;
    AmpValue sigRgt = 0;
    AmpValue lfoRad = 0;
    AmpValue out[8];
    AmpValue lvl[8];
    AmpValue fx[4];
    PhsAccum phs;
    uint32 mask;

    if (lfoOn)
        lfoRad = lfoGen.Gen() * frqTI;
```

```
for (n = 0; n < 8; n++)
   lvl[n] = env[n].Gen();

for (n = 0; n < 8; n++) {
   if (gens[n].toneFlags & TONE_ON) {
      sig = gens[n].osc.Gen();
      sig *= lvl[gens[n].envIn];
      out[n] = sig;
      if (gens[n].toneFlags & TONE_OUT) {
         sig *= gens[n].volLvl;
         if (gens[n].toneFlags & TONE_PAN) {
            sigLft += sig * gens[n].panLft;
            sigRgt += sig * gens[n].panRgt;
         } else
            sigOut += sig;
         if (gens[n].toneFlags & TONE_FX1OUT)
            fx[0] += sig * gens[n].fxLvl[0];
         if (gens[n].toneFlags & TONE_FX2OUT)
            fx[1] += sig * gens[n].fxLvl[1];
         if (gens[n].toneFlags & TONE_FX3OUT)
            fx[2] += sig * gens[n].fxLvl[2];
         if (gens[n].toneFlags & TONE_FX4OUT)
            fx[3] += sig * gens[n].fxLvl[3];
      }
   } else
      out[n] = 0;
}

for (n = 0; n < 8; n++) {
   if (gens[n].toneFlags & TONE_ON
    && gens[n].toneFlags & TONE_MODANY) {
      phs = 0;
      mask = TONE_MOD1IN;
      for (m = 0; m < 8; m++) {
         if (gens[n].toneFlags & mask)
            phs += out[m] * gens[m].modLvl;
         mask <<= 1;
      }
      if (gens[n].toneFlags & TONE_LFOIN)
         phs += lfoRad;
      gens[n]. PhaseModWT(phs);
   }
}
```

```
FxSend(0, fx[0]);
FxSend(1, fx[1]);
FxSend(2, fx[2]);
FxSend(3, fx[3]);

if (panOn)
    Output2(sigLft*vol, sigRgt*vol);
Output(sigOut*vol);
}
```

The *stop* event requires calling the *Release* method on all envelope generators in use. The *IsFinished* method tests only those envelope generators that are applied to signal outputs.

The XML format and parameter table for the *MatrixSynth* instrument are shown below. Each signal generator and envelope generator in the matrix is given a separate node in the tree. The *gen* node contains attributes for the oscillators and associated values. The *env* node contains attributes and child nodes for one envelope generator. Both *gen* and *env* may be duplicated up to eight times. The envelope segment nodes (*seg*) are duplicated as many times as indicated by the *segs* attribute. As always, the level indicates the value at the end of the segment.

```
<instr type="MatrixSynth">
  <mat frq="" vol="" />
  <gen gn="" out="" mod="" wt="" mul="" mnx=""
    vol="" eg="" lfo="" pan="" pb=""
    fx1="" fx2="" fx3="" fx4="" />
  <env en="" segs="" st="" sus="">
    <seg sn="" rt="" lvl="" ty="" />
  </env>
  <lfo frq="" wt="" rt="" amp="" />
</instr>
```

The *out* attribute contains the generator output matrix flags (bits 0-15) encoded as a text string of 1s and 0s from LSB to MSB going left to right. For example, a value of 0x03 would be '11000000' and would indicate the generator is on and applied to the output.

The *mod* attribute contains the modulator input matrix flags (bits 16-31). Modulator 0 is the first bit, modulator 1 the second, bit, etc. For example, a value of 0x12 would be '01001000' and would indicate generators 1 and 4 are applied to the oscillator as modulation inputs.

Because of the large number of parameters we use a system of IDs similar to that shown for the *AddSynth* instrument to represent parameters. The upper byte of the parameter ID contains the generator number while the lower byte contains the value index. For an envelope, 3 bits of the value index are used to indicate the envelope parameter and 5 bits to indicate the segment number. Since we have 8 oscillators and envelope generators, 3 bits of the upper byte are used to indicate the generator number. The next 2 bits are used to indicate the type, oscillator or envelope. A value of 1 for the type indicates an oscillator, while a value of 2 indicates an envelope. A value of 0 for the upper byte indicates a value that applies to either multiple generators or one of the reserved event IDs.

```
[ON(5)][val(8)] or [EN(5)][SN(5)][val(3)]

ON = (oscillator * 256) + 2048
EN = (envelope * 256) + 4096
SN = segment * 8
```

Parameter	Tag	Attribute	Use
5	*mat*	*frq*	Base frequency
6		*vol*	Overall volume
16	*lfo*	*frq*	LFO Frequency
17		*wt*	LFO wavetable
18		*rt*	LFO attack rate
19		*amp*	LFO amplitude
	gen	*gn*	Oscillator number
ON+0		*out*	Output flags
ON+1		*mod*	Mod in flags
ON+2		*wt*	Wave table
ON+3		*mul*	Frequency multiplier
ON+4		*mnx*	Modulation index
ON+5		*vol*	Audio signal volume
ON+6		*eg*	Envelope generator index
ON+7		*fx1*	Effects 1 out level
ON+8		*fx2*	Effects 2 out level
ON+9		*fx3*	Effects 3 out level

ON+10		*fx4*	Effects 4 out level
ON+11		*lfo*	LFO in level
ON+12			LFO vibrato on/off
ON+13			LFO tremolo on/off
ON+14		*pan*	Pan setting
ON+15			Panning on/off
ON+16			Oscillator on/off
ON+17			Audio signal out on/off
	env	*en*	Envelope number
		segs	Number of segments
EN+0		*st*	Envelope start level
EN+1		*sus*	Sustain on/off
	seg	*sn*	Envelope segment number
EN+SN+2		*rt*	Envelope segment rate
EN+SN+3		*lvl*	Envelope segment level
EN+SN+4		*ty*	Envelope segment type

BasicSynth Library

The synthesis instrument described in this chapter is implemented by the *MatrixSynth* class.

Files:

```
Src/Instruments/MatrixSynth.h
Src/Instruments/MatrixSynth.cpp
```

Chapter 24

Notelist

A software synthesis system needs both instruments to make sounds and a way to control the instruments. By analogy, the synthesizer includes an "orchestra" and a "score." The orchestra consists of the definition of the sound generation instruments, while the score consists of input to the sequencer. In the chapter on sequencing we created a simple score format to specify the notes to be played by the sequencer. Although easy to program and very flexible, a format of that type is tedious to use. The time and duration of each note must be calculated individually, it is difficult to insert new notes in the middle of a sequence, pitches and rhythms must be entered as numbers, and individual voices in polyphonic textures are not easily identified or synchronized. As an alternative, the MIDI file format provides a generic, widely used means to specify notes for the sequencer, but has limitations as well. It is not easy to edit MIDI files if we want to make small changes to the sequence or add or remove individual notes, and the MIDI protocol does not allow full control of the synthesizer on a note-by-note basis. To take full advantage of the synthesizer and also provide an intuitive score format, we need something else.

Traditional music notation has developed over several centuries based on the needs of musicians. A traditional music score encodes pitch, rhythm, articulation, dynamics, polyphony and timbre all at once using a relatively small number of symbols. Furthermore, music notation allows indication of dynamics and articulation at a note-by-note level and a phrase or section level simultaneously.

We could use traditional music notation as a score format for a synthesizer, but there are some features of a music score that make it unwieldy on a computer. Traditional music notation uses a graphic representation where the shape and position indicate values. Scanning shapes is difficult for a computer program and requires very sophisticated algorithms to work effectively. Computer programs work most efficiently when the input can be represented by a series of numbers or encoded text characters. Thus a traditional notation system on a computer must encode the score using a number or word for each shape and we cannot simply draw the music on the computer screen as we would with pencil and paper. Although useful for production of traditional printed scores on a computer, dragging different shapes around the computer screen and placing them on staves is not very efficient compared to drawing on a piece of paper or typing text on a computer keyboard.

Second, although music notation is concise, it is not very precise when it comes to specifying dynamics, articulation, phrasing and timbre. The score gives general clues to the performer, but the performer is expected to understand the style of the music and interpret the notation appropriately. For example, a dynamic of p is softer than f but the relative loudness depends on many factors. Musicians adjust loudness based on the ensemble, interpretation, etc. In contrast, a computer system requires an exact specification for the amplitude and we must quantize values rather than expect the computer to guess at an appropriate value. Furthermore, traditional music notation assumes that an instrument's capabilities are fixed by its construction and cannot be varied significantly. Variations in timbre are typically the result of a particular performer's touch. Thus music notation includes a minimum amount of information on variation of timbre. In contrast, a software synthesizer allows continuous and nearly unlimited variation of the sound envelope, spectrum, and processing effects. In fact, if we do not utilize these capabilities, music produced on a computer will sound mechanical and lack expressiveness. A notation system appropriate to a synthesizer must expand traditional notation in order to make full use of the idiomatic features of the synthesizer.

Finally, traditional notation uses bars to indicate measures so that multiple voices can be easily synchronized and rhythms can be counted in cyclic beats rather than a continuously increasing time value. In other words, in music notation we represent time as measure, beat, and sub-division rather than with a specific point in time. However, a computer system requires explicit and exact time in seconds or samples and does not need to use repeated spans of equal time. Thus there is no need to limit rhythm values to divisions of a beat or a portion of a measure.

Although traditional music notation is not the best representation for a computer synthesis system, it can serve as a good starting point for a synthesizer score format. After all, music notation has proven to be an effective means of describing a piece of music. If we can understand why music notation is effective, then we have a good chance of creating something equally useful for the synthesizer.

Traditional music notation provides the following information.

- Pitch
- Rhythm
- Dynamics
- Articulation
- Phrasing
- Orchestration
- Synchronization of multiple voices

Any score format for a synthesizer should provide all of these capabilities while also allowing extensions that take full advantage of the synthesizer's variable sound capabilities.

Parameters that control pitch, rhythm, dynamics, and articulation must be represented precisely by numbers, but when possible should be intuitive to a musician. For example, we should have a way to specify pitch relative to the octave rather than some arbitrary number or exact frequency. We should be able to specify start time and duration simultaneously and in a way that allows insertion and removal of individual notes without requiring manual recalculation of the values for subsequent notes. The specification of rhythm should also allow a change of tempo and easy synchronization of multiple instruments. Furthermore, we need to indicate which synthesis instrument should sound the note and how the parameters associated with a note should be applied to the instrument. Similar to staves on a musical score, we should have some means of dividing the score so that we can describe each musical voice independently of others. Finally, parameters should carry over from note to note when possible. Just as a traditional score can indicate a single dynamic or articulation for an entire section, or, place dynamics and articulation on each note, we should be able to specify parameters both on a note-by-note basis and over an entire phrase or section without explicitly repeating the values for each note.

The Notelist score format described in this chapter was designed on the basis of these requirements. It attempts to balance the need for an easy to understand, intuitive representation of music with a means to allow precise control of synthesis parameters. A Notelist score can be very simple, specifying only pitch and rhythm, or, it can be very complex, specifying any or all synthesis instrument parameters for each individual sound.

Pitch Representation

The synthesizer must eventually convert pitch into frequency in order to calculate the phase increment for an oscillator. Entering exact frequency values in a score is possible, but would be very tedious in use. Alternatively, we can encode pitch as an integer value similar to MIDI key numbers. This is easier than entering frequency, but still significantly different from the way musicians typically think of pitch.

Musicians think of pitch as a combination of pitch class and octave. This is intuitive and natural since each octave increase in pitch is considered essentially the same, or what we call *octave equivalency* in music theory. Thus a natural way to represent pitch is to use a pitch class letter and octave number combination. There are, however, two slightly different forms of pitch letters in common use. The English system uses letters C,D,E,F,G,A,B for the seven diatonic pitches, while the German system includes the letter H for B-natural and uses B to designate B-flat.

Letter names only identify the diatonic scale pitch, thus we also need the equivalent of accidentals to indicate the chromatic pitches. The '#' character looks like a sharp and can be used as such. We don't have a key that is exactly like the flat symbol, but a lower case 'b' is very similar and makes a good substitute. We can use 'x' to indicated double sharp and 'd' for a double flat.

We must also decide which octave designates Middle C. Middle C is the fourth C from the bottom on a standard 88-key piano keyboard and musicians generally refer to C4 as Middle C.

A pitch letter, accidental, and octave combination is easily converted to an integer pitch value. In order to convert to frequency for the synthesizer, we use the integer pitch value as an index into a table of frequencies. To produce an equivalent integer pitch value, we first convert the letter to the equivalent number of semitones above C, increment or decrement to take into account the accidental, then add the octave multiplied by the number of semi-tones in an octave.

```
//                       A   B   C   D   E   F   G
int letterToPitch[] = { 9, 11,  0,  2,  4,  5,  7 };
int index = letterToPitch[pitchLetter - 'A'];
if (accidental == '#')
   index++;
else if (accidental == 'b')
   index--;
else if (accidental == 'x')
   index += 2;
else if (accidental == 'd')
   index -= 2;
index += oct * 12;
```

If we want to use the German system of letters, we can alter the *letterToPitch* array:

```
//                       A   B   C   D   E   F   G   H
int letterToPitch[] = {9, 10,  0,  2,  4,  5,  7, 11};
```

Because the pitch designation is converted to an integer, we can also allow integer values for pitch. In either case, we can perform calculations with the pitch by adding or subtracting a value representing semi-tones. For example, C4+7 represents G4, 7 semi-tones above middle C.

Traditional music notation also provides a way to specify gaps in the sound by using rests and we need something similar for a computer score. We can indicate rests by using a letter 'R' for the pitch.

Rhythm

Rhythm must be specified in a way that indicates note start time, duration, and spacing between notes. Traditional music notation indicates rhythm by duration alone, modified by the tempo, with the start time of the note equal to the end of the previous note or rest. This strategy works equally well as a sequencer score format. After a note is processed, its duration can be added to a current time value.

The new current time value is then used for the start time of the next note. The sequencer event contains the calculated start time along with the note duration. This allows us to use a single list of events for the sequencer while allowing the score to specify only the note duration. For polyphonic music, we can divide notes among *voices* and keep a current time value for each voice. Because we sort sequencer events by the internally calculated note start time, the score does not need to arrange all notes sequentially by start time, only sequentially within a voice. It is also possible to switch back and forth between voices at any time.

In traditional music notation, only a small number of rhythm values are defined. Each rhythm represents an equal sub-division of the beat by a factor of two or three. Other subdivisions of a beat are indicated by using a bracket and number under a group of notes. We can create something similar for a computer system by stating that a rhythm value is a subdivision of some known duration, such as a whole note. For example, we can say that a value of 4 is one-fourth of a whole note at the current tempo, in effect the same as a quarter note. Using a number alone would make it difficult to differentiate between rhythm values and other numerical values. To avoid confusion, we will indicate rhythm values with a leading percent character (%). Thus %1 indicates a whole note, %2 a half-note, %4 a quarter note, etc.

We do not need to limit rhythm values to a small number of standard divisions of the beat. For example, a value of %10 indicates a duration equal to $1/10^{th}$ of a whole note. In addition, the value can contain a fractional part. A rhythm value of %2.5 indicates a duration of a whole note divided by 2.5, or 4/10 of a whole note. Longer rhythm values, and values that are not easily specified by a single number, can be specified by an arithmetic expression. For example, a double whole note can be entered as %1+%1 or %1*2, and a dotted quarter note %4+%8 or %8*3.

A rhythm value can be converted into seconds of duration by a simple calculation:

```
seconds = beat / rhythm * secPerBeat;
```

The value of *beat* is an integer representation of a multiple of a whole note. For example, if we want a tempo of quarter notes at 120bpm, then *beat* is 4, and *secPerBeat* is 0.5.

Rhythm values are intuitive for musicians, but there are cases where we would like to indicate duration with an explicit time in seconds. This is often necessary in order to synchronize the score with something else, such as film, video or pre-recorded music. We can state that when a rhythm is specified with a number alone (no %), the number indicates duration in seconds. We can mix rhythm values and seconds together in an arithmetic expression without any problem if we convert rhythm values into the equivalent number of seconds before performing any calculations. For example, a rhythm of %4+0.25 can be calculated by taking the duration of a quarter at the current tempo in seconds and then adding 0.25 to the value.

Although we do not need to give an explicit start time for a note, it is sometimes useful to do so. For example, if one voice is silent for several seconds, we can enter a number of rests to move the current time forward. However, it is easier to enter the score if we implement a way to indicate an explicit start time for one note with subsequent notes then calculated automatically. We can allow the explicit start time to be indicated directly in seconds, or calculated using a rhythm. For example, if we want a note to start at the equivalent of measure 20 in 4/4 time, we can write *time %1*20* and have the software calculate the next start time based on the tempo.

Even calculating explicit start time using rhythm values, it can be difficult to keep voices synchronized. If one voice is extended by adding notes, the explicit start times in other voices must be recalculated. We can eliminate this problem by using a marker to store the current start time in one voice and then reference that saved start time in another voice. Notelist includes this capability with the *mark* and *sync* keywords. The *mark* keyword stores the current start time and the *sync* keyword retrieves it. Any number of notes can then be added to the first voice prior to the mark point without having to edit the start times or number of rests in other voices.

Dynamics

Traditional music notation specifies volume levels in a relative and imprecise manner. For the synthesizer we must indicate a precise volume level. We could establish a mapping between the traditional indications of *p, mp, mf, f,* etc., but the values would need to vary based on the texture of the composition. Moreover, we need to have fine-grained control since the synthesizer will not automatically vary volume levels on a note by note basis unless we explicitly tell it to do so. For example, if we set a single volume level of 100dB, that level will apply to all notes until we change it. A human performer would most likely vary the loudness of individual notes within a phrase in order to add expressiveness, even if the composer indicates only a single volume level for the phrase. We can accomplish both goals if we include a volume level for each note and an overall volume level for the voice. This makes it easy to include note-by-note variations in volume and still balance the volume level of one voice against other voices without having to edit each note individually.

The volume level can be indicated by a simple numeric value scaled to a convenient range with 0 indicating silence and the top of the range the maximum amplitude allowed. The normalized amplitude range of [0,1] would work, but a range of [0,100] is just as convenient and avoids having to enter fractional values. We can easily divide the volume level by 100 in order to scale the value to the normalized range for the synthesizer. The volume level can be treated as either a linear amplitude value or a decibel level. The decibel scale is sometimes more appropriate, but for those not used to thinking in decibels it may be confusing. For example, if a volume of 100 is the maximum level, it is intuitive to think of 50 as half-volume. Dividing the amplitude by half does not necessarily produce a sound half as loud, but a 50dB reduction in volume is significantly softer than one-half of the maximum volume.

Articulation

In most cases the duration of a note will be identical to the rhythm value. However, there are situations were we would like to use the rhythm value to indicate distance between note start times while providing a different note duration. One example is a staccato note. We can simulate staccato by placing a short rest between notes, but this is awkward and prone to error. Staccato, legato and similar markings in traditional music notation allow varying the actual note duration without entering extraneous rests, and we can do the same thing in a synthesizer score.

In addition, a synthesizer has capabilities that traditional instruments do not have. For example, the actual duration of a note is affected by the release rate of the envelope generator, but it is more natural to think of the duration of the note in terms of the attack and sustain portion of the sound without regard to the release time. This is the way the *BasicSynth* sequencer works. It uses the duration to determine the point where the release should begin, not the total duration of the note. At times, however, it may be desirable to start the release early, much like a staccato note. At other times we may wish to delay the release in order to allow notes to overlap. Synthesizer instruments may also include playback of a recorded sound of a fixed duration. In that case, we will want to specify the rhythm value independently of the note duration.

Notelist provides the *artic* keyword to control duration of notes independently of the note-to-note rhythm. The articulation may be specified as a percentage of the rhythm, an amount added to or subtracted from the rhythm, or a fixed length independent of the rhythm.

Synthesizer Parameters

Synthesizer parameters are values that control the operation of the synthesizer. These values must be passed from the score directly to the synthesizer without interpretation.

The number of parameters used by the synthesizer will vary considerably. A simple instrument may only allow parameters for envelope rate or waveform selection while a complex instrument could easily have 100 parameters. The score must have a way to easily specify those parameters that are of interest without requiring every possible parameter to be entered.

The varying number and interpretation of parameters creates a second problem for the score design. We would like to be able to switch instruments at any time without having to worry whether or not the synthesizer parameters are the same for each instrument.

We can solve both these problems using an instrument parameter map. The parameter map translates the parameter index from the score into an instrument specific parameter number.

Since many parameters do not change frequently, we should allow parameters to hold over from note to note so that they do not need to be entered individually for each note. In addition, we should have a way to change one parameter without having to enter all other parameters.

Notelist Score Syntax

A Notelist score contains one or more *voices* and *sequences*, each containing a combination of *control statements* and *note statements.* A voice is used to group one or more notes that follow sequentially in time. A sequence defines a set of statements that can be inserted into a voice by "playing" the sequence. A control statement either changes the settings associated with a voice or controls how Notelist interprets the score. Note statements define sounds to be played by the synthesizer.

Rather than start with a formal specification, we will use examples to explain the Notelist voice syntax. In these examples, keywords are shown in lower case letters. However, Notelist does not distinguish between upper and lower case for keywords (i.e., *VOICE*, *Voice*, and *voice* are all equivalent).

The following example contains two voices that play simultaneously. The lines between the *begin* and *end* keywords specify the sequence of notes played on the voice. Each note statement consists of a pitch, rhythm and volume level.

```
tempo 4, 60;

voice 1
begin
   instrument "piano";
   channel 0;
   C4, %4, 100;
   D4, %4, 100;
   E4, %4, 100;
   F4, %4, 100;
   G4, %4, 100;
   B3, %4, 100;
   C4, %2, 100;
end
```

```
voice 2
begin
  instrument "bass";
  channel 1;
  C3, %2, 100;
  A2, %2, 100;
  G2, %2, 100;
  C3, %2, 100;
end
```

The first voice plays notes from C4 to G4, then B3, C4 in quarter notes on a piano instrument output to mixer channel 0. The second voice plays C3, A2, G2, C3 in half notes on a bass instrument output to mixer channel 1.

Notice that each note or control statement is terminated with a semicolon. To non-programmers, this may seem unnecessary, but it serves a purpose similar to punctuation at the end of a sentence. Without an explicit character to terminate the statement, the Notelist parser would need either to require a fixed number of values per note or to assume an end of line represents the end of a note. Because a note is terminated with a semicolon, a note can contain a variable number of parameters, can span multiple lines, and can place multiple notes on a single line. Blank lines can be inserted at any point to help set-off different phrases, sections, etc. Likewise, a comma is used to separate items in a list. Spaces, tabs, and end of lines (whitespace) are generally ignored by the Notelist program and can be used freely to format the score in any manner desired. Spaces are required to separate a keyword (such as *voice*) from subsequent values, but otherwise spaces can be included or left out as desired.

In most cases where a numerical value is allowed, the value can be either a single number or a calculated value. A calculated value is called an *expression*. An expression consists of one or more operands separated by operators. Operators include arithmetic operators, relational operators, logical operators, and the string concatenation operator. The arithmetic operators are + - * / ^ for addition, subtraction, multiplication, division, and exponentiation, respectively. Multiplication, division, and exponentiation have higher precedence than addition and subtraction and are evaluated first. Equal precedence operators are evaluated in order, left to right. Parts of the expression can be grouped within parentheses to override the order of evaluation. For example, the expression *5*4+2* would multiply first then add, but *5*(4+2)* would add first then multiply. The string paste operator (#) indicates the two operands should be combined into a single character string. String pasting has lower precedence than all other operators. The relational and logical operators will be listed later.

Operands can be a pitch, rhythm, number, variable, function or quoted text. Quoted text is enclosed with double quote marks (" "). A quote can be placed inside quoted text by preceding the quote with a back-slash (\). When quoted text is used as an operand in an arithmetic expression, the text is first converted to a number. Likewise, when a non-text operand is used with the string paste operator, the value is automatically converted to text.

Using expressions often makes specification of rhythms easier. For example, in the following statements the first note is equivalent to a quarter note tied to an eighth note while the second is equal to three quarter notes and an eighth note tied together.

```
voice 1
begin
   instrument "piano";
   C4, %4+%8, 100;
   C4, %4*3+%8, 100;
end
```

The *tempo* statement controls conversion of rhythm values into duration in seconds. The first number indicates the fraction of a whole note. The second number indicates beats per minute. In this case, the tempo is set to quarter notes at 60 bpm. Notice that the *tempo* statement is outside the first voice indicating it is a global control statement. This statement, and a few others, apply to all voices regardless of where the statement is located and are applied from the point where they are located in the file. A tempo statement within a voice will modify all notes in subsequent voices, not only notes within the voice.

The line beginning with *instrument* defines which instrument should be used to play the following notes. The keyword *instrument* can also be abbreviated as *instr*. An *instrument* statement is an example of a Notelist control statement. Control statements affect the evaluation of subsequent statements but do not produce any sound output. Only note statements generate sound.

The *begin...end* keywords are used to enclose multiple note statements, but are not required. However, without them each note must begin with a *voice* keyword. For example, we could have written the previous example like this:

```
tempo 4, 60;
voice 1 instrument "piano";
voice 2 instrument "bass";
voice 1 channel 0;
voice 2 channel 1;
voice 1 C4, %4, 100;
voice 1 D4, %4, 100;
voice 2 C3, %2, 100;
voice 1 E4, %4, 100;
voice 1 F4, %4, 100;
voice 2 A2, %2, 100;
voice 1 G4, %4, 100;
voice 1 B3, %4, 100;
voice 2 G2, %2, 100;
voice 1 C4, %2, 100;
voice 2 C3, %2, 100;
```

Each voice keeps track of the values used to produce a new note. These include the next starting time, and last pitch, rhythm, note volume level, and note parameters. In addition, the voice keeps track of the instrument, channel, overall volume level, and transposition. Because each voice maintains this information separately from other voices, notes in a voice do not need to be contiguous. A Notelist score can freely switch between voices, or can group all notes of each voice together with *begin...end*. A voice can also be entered using multiple *begin...end* blocks because the starting time for each block begins at the end time of the previous block.

A note must include pitch, rhythm and volume values, but, because the voice keeps track of the last used values, only the pitch needs to be entered when the rhythm and volume values are the same as the previous note. For example, the first voice above could be written as:

```
voice 1
begin
  C4, %4, 100;
  D4; E4; F4; G4; B3;
  C4, %2;
end
```

Typically, pitch and rhythm are specified for each note for clarity. The shortened form is most useful when a note statement contains a group of notes on one line. A group is indicated by enclosing values in braces with each value separated by a comma. This notation not only allows multiple notes to be easily contained on one line and avoids entering duplicate values, but is also an intuitive way to represent a musical phrase. In the following example, the rhythm value and volume value are specified once for the entire group.

```
voice 1
begin
  { C4, D4, E4, F4, G4, B3 }, %4, 100;
  C4, %2, 100;
end
```

We can provide a group for rhythm and volume values and allow the pitch value to repeat. In the following example, the pitch C4 is repeated four times followed by C4 through F4. Notice that the volume value is missing from the second note statement as it will carry forward until another value is specified.

```
voice 1
begin
  C4, { %4, %16, %16, %2 }, 100;
  { C4, D4, E4, F4}, { %4, %16, %16, %2 };
end
```

When using multiple groups on a single line, the longest group controls the number of notes that are played.

```
voice 1
begin
  { C4, D4, E4, F4 }, { %4, %4, %2 }, 100;
  C4, %4, { 50, 60, 75, 100 };
end
```

In this example, the first note statement plays C4 and D4 as quarter notes followed by E4 and F4 both as half notes. The second statement plays C4 four times with a crescendo.

A pitch group can also be enclosed in square brackets [...] to represent simultaneous pitches, (i.e., a chord). If only one rhythm value is given, it will apply to all pitches in the chord. However, it is possible to give a different rhythm value to each pitch so that some pitches have a shorter duration. The start time of the note following the chord will be equal to the longest duration in the chord. In the following example, the first note statement plays a C-Major chord for one quarter note, followed by a F-Major chord for one quarter note, but with only the C4 pitch sounding through the entire duration.

```
voice 1
begin
  [ C4, E4, G4 ], %4, 100;
  [ C4, F4, A4 ], { %4, %8, %8 }, 100;
  C5, %4, 100;
end
```

A note group can be preceded by the keywords *sus* (sustain) or *tie* in order to modify the interpretation of the duration values. The *sus* keyword causes the first note in a group to be interpreted as the total duration for all notes in the group. Subsequent note start times are interpreted as a delay from the previous note. This produces the effect of a roll or arpeggio where all the notes hold through the total duration.

```
sus { C4, E4, G4, C5 }, { %1, %8, %8, %8 }, 80;
```

In this statement the total duration is a whole note with each successive pitch played an eight-note apart. A value of 0 for a duration after the first will cause a pitch to sound simultaneously with the previous pitch.

```
sus { C4, E4, G4, C5 }, { %1, 0, %8, %8 }, 20;
```

In this case, C4 and E4 sound together followed by G4 and C5 spaced an eighth note apart.

The *tie* keyword causes the first note in the group to be interpreted as the total length of the note with subsequent values as modifications to the note. As with *sus* the rhythm value specifies the delay from the previous value.

```
tie { C4, E4, G4, C4 }, { %1, %4, %4, %4 }, 100;
```

In synthesizer terms, a *tie* alters the oscillator frequency, volume level, and other parameters without resetting the oscillator phase or re-triggering the envelope generator. Not all synthesizer instruments are capable of modifying note values in this mannter. In particular, changing parameters that alter the envelope may have no effect.

A voice can contain control statements that affect all subsequent notes within the voice. Notelist defines several of these for commonly used effects.

The *channel* control statement sets the mixer output channel for the voice. The keyword *channel* can be abbreviated as *chnl*. The single argument indicates the mixer channel number. A voice is usually associated with a specific instrument and/or mixer input channel, but is not required to do so. A voice can switch between instruments and channels at any time, and multiple voices can be played on the same instrument or channel. This is especially useful when complex polyphonic voices are used. For example, a complex rhythm with overlapping notes can be specified more easily with multiple voice lists.

```
voice 1
begin
  instrument "piano";
  channel 0;
  {C4, D4, E4, F4}, {%4, %4, %8, %8}, 100;
end

voice 2
begin
  instrument "piano";
  channel 0;
  {C3, G3, C3, G2}, {%16, %8, %16, %2}, 100;
end
```

The *volume* statement sets a volume multiplier that is multiplied by the per-note volume value to produce the actual volume for a note. The keyword *volume* can be abbreviated as *vol*. Using *volume* is similar to setting a mixer level on the synthesizer, but is applied internally by Notelist. Setting the volume on a voice can help balance the level between voices, but can also be used to generate a change in volume level within a voice without having to explicitly set each note volume. This makes it easy to produce a crescendo of notes that have varying volume levels, and to vary the range of a crescendo later without having to reenter the volume levels for all notes.

```
voice 2
begin
  volume 30;
  {C3, G3, C3, G2}, {%16, %8, %16, %2},
  {100, 80, 90, 100};
  volume 40;
  {C3, G3, C3, G2}, {%16, %8, %16, %2};
  volume 50;
  {C3, G3, C3, G2}, {%16, %8, %16, %2};
end
```

The *transpose* statement modifies the pitch of subsequent notes. The argument to *transpose* indicates the number of semi-tones to be added to the pitch value and can be positive or negative. Transposition is chromatic as there is currently no concept of key signature in Notelist.

```
voice 2
begin
  {C3, G3, C3, G2}, {%16, %8, %16, %2}, 100;
  transpose 12;
  {C3, G3, C3, G2}, {%16, %8, %16, %2}, 100;
  transpose -12;
  {C3, G3, C3, G2}, {%16, %8, %16, %2}, 100;
end
```

The *time, mark* and *sync* statements are used to synchronize time values. The *time* statement sets an explicit current time value for a voice. The *mark* and *sync* statements are used together to insure that voices playback at the same point in time.

```
voice 1
begin
  time 10;
  {C4, D4, E4, F4, G4}, {%12, %13, %14, %15, %16};
  mark "cue1";
  {C4, D4, E4, F4}, %16, 100;
  G4, %4, 100;
end

voice 2
begin
  sync "cue1";
  {C3, G3}, %4, 100;
end
```

In this example, the first voice begins 10 seconds into the playback. The initial scale has duration values that make it difficult to calculate the exact start point for voice 2. Using the *mark* and *sync* pair causes voice 2 to play the bass notes at the point where voice 1 reaches the 16th note scale. In addition, if the start time is moved, or the rhythm of the first voice is changed prior to the mark point, the second voice will still synchronize to the first voice. In effect, *mark* and *sync* serve a function similar to bar lines in music notation.

The *artic* statement modifies the actual duration of notes without changing the time between notes. The articulation value can be one of three types. A *fixed* articulation value sets the duration of the note to the articulation value regardless of the rhythm value. An *add* articulation value adds to the note duration. A *percent* articulation value extends the note by a percentage of the rhythm value.

```
voice 1
begin
  artic add 0.1;
  C4, %4, 100;
  artic percent 90;
  C4, %4, 100;
  artic fixed %1;
  {C4, C5}, %4, 100;
  artic percent param;
  {C4, G4, C5}, %4, 100, {80, 90, 100};
end
```

The first *artic* statement causes the subsequent note to be played for 1/10 second longer than the given duration and causes an overlap with the following note. The second *artic* statement causes the note to be played for 90% of the given duration, producing a short gap between notes similar to *staccato*. The third *artic* statement causes the notes to be played for the duration of a whole note even though the duration of the following note is given as a quarter note. The last *artic* statement causes the note duration to be modified using the first parameter after the volume. The first note is played at 80% duration, the second at 90% duration, and the third at 100% of the duration.

Note Parameters

Synthesizer instrument parameters can be included on a note statement by placing them after the volume value. As with other values, parameters carry over to subsequent notes and do not need to be explicitly stated except when a value changes. Since the number of parameters varies depending on the instrument, Notelist cannot know in advance how many parameters should be retained. By default, space for up to 10 values is allocated. If more or fewer parameters are needed, the *maxparam* statement can be used to extend or reduce the size of the parameter buffer. The *maxparam* statement is a global control statement and affects all voices.

Parameters are specified as numbers and passed directly to the synthesizer instrument without interpretation by the Notelist parser. With one exception, the number and meaning of the parameters is left to the synthesizer instrument. As explained above, when indicated by the *artic* keyword, the first parameter value can be used to modify the note duration.

Each parameter is separated by a comma, and parameters can be grouped in the same manner as pitches, rhythms or volume values. In the following example, the first note statement contains two parameters, 10 and 20, for the note C4. Since the next note statement does not include any parameters, the same values are applied to each note in the group. The last line plays C4 twice, once with values of 10 and 20, and once with values of 15 and 30.

```
maxparam 2;

voice 1
begin
  C4, %4, 100, 10, 20;
  { D4, E4, F4}, %4, 100;
  C4, %2, 100, {10, 15}, {20, 30};
end
```

When deciding how parameters affect synthesizer performance, it is a good idea to put the most actively changing parameters at the beginning of the list if possible. Even so, entering parameters can become tedious when a large number of parameters are in use. If only one or two parameter values change from note to note, all other parameters up to the changing value must be reentered. For this reason Notelist includes an alternative way to set parameters. The *param* statement sets one parameter for succeeding notes.

```
param 0, 1;
param 1, 2;
param 2, 3;
C4, 1, 100;
param 2, 4;
D4, 1, 100;
```

These statements are the equivalent of:

```
C4, 1, 100, 1, 2, 3;
D4, 1, 100, 1, 2, 4;
```

The second *param* statement sets the third parameter to a value of 4 and leaves other parameters at the previous value. The parameter index is zero-based (i.e., index 0 represents the first parameter).

Instrument parameters are position dependent. In other words, the first parameter must be the first value after the volume value. When passed to the synthesizer, each parameter is represented by a zero-based index indicating the position on the note statement. For instruments with a small number of parameters, using position dependent values is generally not a problem. However, when the instrument includes a large number of parameters it is often the case that we only want to give values for a small number of the possible values. Parameter maps allow selecting a sub-set of an instrument's parameters and also allow direct specification of the parameter index.

```
map "instrument" id1, id2…;
```

The values on the *map* statement specify the actual instrument parameter id values for the nth parameter on the note statement. With a map, only the parameters that are of interest need be entered on the note statement. Suppose that an instrument uses parameter 18 to set the envelope attack and parameter 22 to set the envelope decay. Rather than list all 22 parameters on the note statement, we can create a map of the two values we need. The following example sets the first parameter to the attack rate and the second parameter to the release rate.

```
map "iname" 18, 22;

voice 1
begin
  instr "iname";
  C4, %4, 100, 0.1, 0.4;
end
```

A parameter map can contain optional scaling values for each parameter. The scaling value is specified by adding *:expr* after the parameter id. The scale is multiplied by the value on the note statement when the event is generated. This allows parameters to be specified in a normalized range and also provides automatic conversion of values when the instrument changes. For example, suppose that two instruments both have a parameter to indicate a modulation of the sound, but instrument *in1* has a range of [0,100] on parameter 19 while *in2* has a range of [0,1] on parameter 20. We can specify a parameter map for each instrument so that we can change between instruments without having to change the note statement values.

The following statements play C4 on instrument 1 with a parameter value of 50 for parameter 19, and on instrument 2 with a parameter value of 0.5 for parameter 20. If we later decide to switch the order of the instruments, the note statements will still produce the correct parameter values.

```
map "in1" 19;
map "in2" 20:0.01;
voice 1
begin
   instrument "in1";
   C4, %4, 100, 50;
   instrument "in2";
   C4, %4, 100, 50;
end
```

Instrument parameter maps are global and remain in effect across voices and until another map statement is encountered for the instrument. A map with no id values removes the instrument map.

Loops

The *loop* statement is used to repeat one or more note statements. The *count* argument indicates the number of times the loop repeats.

```
loop (count) notelist
```

The *notelist* is either a single note statement or a series of statements enclosed with *begin...end* keywords. The parentheses around the loop count are optional, but must be included if the count expression could be interpreted as a part of the first statement in the Notelist. The next example plays an arpeggio five times.

```
loop 5
   { C4, E, G, C5 }, 0.25, 50;
```

The following example plays the arpeggio fifteen times, varying the volume level.

```
loop 5
begin
   { C4, E, G, C5 }, 0.25, 50;
   { C4, E, G, C5 }, 0.25, 80;
   { C4, E, G, C5 }, 0.25, 100;
end
```

Loops can be nested within loops to any level:

```
loop 5
begin
  loop 2
  begin
    { C4, E, G, C5 }, 0.25, 100;
    loop 2
      {C4, E, G, C5}, 0.125, 50;
  end
end
```

Because control statements apply to all notes from the point where they are encountered, they must be used carefully within loops. For example, a *volume* statement at the end of a loop will apply to all iterations after the first. In the following example, the first iteration will play at a volume level of 100 while iterations 2-5 will play at volume 50.

```
volume 100;
loop 5
begin
  { C4, E, G, C5 }, 0.25, 50;
  volume 50;
end
```

This feature can be useful, especially with nested loops. In the following example, the phrase is played four times, alternating between loud and soft.

```
loop 2
begin
  volume 100;
  loop 2
  begin
  { C4, E, G, C5 }, 0.25, 50;
   volume 50;
  end
end
```

Loops are expanded by the Notelist parser, not the sequencer. Although this produces a longer event sequence, it allows values within the loop to be calculated during processing and thus different for each iteration. The *count* keyword can be used inside the loop to modify a value based on the number of times the loop has played. The value of *count* varies from 0 to *n*-1, where *n* is the loop count. The following note statement plays a chromatic scale with crescendo.

```
loop (12) C4+count, %8, 40+(count*5);
```

In the case of nested loops, each loop has its own instance of the *count* value and the value will always refer to the associated loop count. In the following example, the chromatic scale is played 5 times, each time at a higher volume level. The first reference to *count* will vary from 0-4 while the second will vary from 0-12.

```
loop 5
begin
  vol 50+(count*10);
  loop (12)
    C4+count, %16, 80;
end
```

If *count* is referenced outside of a loop it has a value of 0.

Sequence Definitions

Often, it is useful to define a sequence of notes that repeat at different places in the composition. By defining the repeated phrase as a sequence, the notes can be inserted by referring to the sequence rather than repeating entry of the notes.

A *sequence* statement begins definition of a note sequence. The keyword *sequence* may be abbreviated to *seq*. The content of the sequence is enclosed in a *begin...end* block and is the same set of statements that can appear within a voice. The sequence itself must be defined outside of any voice. A sequence is identified by a name or number and is invoked by that name or number from within voices by using the *play* statement.

```
sequence "short"
begin
  { C4, D, E, F}, {%4, %16, %16, %8}, 100;
end
```

```
voice 1
begin
  play "short";
  play "short";
end
```

Since a sequence is played within the context of a voice, control statements that modify the performance of subsequent notes should be used carefully. For example, a *volume*, *transpose* or other voice control statement within a sequence would remain in effect for notes within the voice that come after the sequence is played.

Built-in Functions and Variables

Notelist includes a set of built-in functions that calculate a series of values. The *init* statement is used to initialize the function and the *fgen* keyword to produce the next value in the series.

```
init unit type start, end, steps;
```

The *unit* argument is an integer value in the range [0,9] that identifies the generator in later calls to *fgen*. Since function generators can be reused, the unit range only limits the number of generators that can be operating simultaneously within a voice.

The *start* argument indicates the starting value for the series. The *end* argument indicates the ending value for the series. The *steps* argument indicates how many discrete steps are calculated. The *type* argument must be one of the following:

LINE   Values will be linearly interpolated between start and end.
EXP   Values will be exponentially interpolated.
LOG   Values will be logarithmically interpolated.
RAND   Values will be random numbers between start and end.

The *fgen* function returns the current value of a built-in function. It takes two arguments, the unit number and the number of steps to calculate. The *unit* argument should match a previous *init* statement. The *fgen* function is especially useful within loops to provide crescendo, decrescendo, or step-wise alteration of the synthesizer parameters:

```
init 0 line 50, 100, 10;
loop 10
   { C4, D, E, F, G}, 0.1, fgen(0,1);
```

The *fgen* function is zero based. That is, on the first call it will return the start value and will only return the end value after *n*+1 steps. In the example above, volume would range from 50 to 95. Once *fgen* reaches the end of the series, the returned value will remain at the end value until another *init* statement on the same unit is encountered.

When *fgen* is invoked, the second argument indicates how many steps to move forward. The *steps* value in the *init* statement is usually an integer value and *fgen* is invoked as *fgen(unit,1)* to retrieve the next value. However, the *steps* value on the *init* statement can be set to a duration. Each call to *fgen* should then indicate how much of that duration has passed. This is useful to map a series of steps onto notes of varying duration.

```
init 0 line 50, 100, %1;
{ C4, D, E, F }, %4, fgen(0,%4);
```

In addition to *fgen,* the *rand* function can be used to produce a random value without first initializing a function with *init*. The two arguments to *rand* are optional. Without arguments, *rand* returns a value between 0 and 1.

```
loop (4)
   C4+rand(-4,4), %16, 100;
```

In addition to built-in functions, Notelist defines built-in variables that reference the current time, last pitch, duration, volume, and loop count values.

```
curpit       Last pitch value
curdur       Last duration value
curvol       Last volume value
curtime      Current time in seconds
count        Current loop count
```

The built-in variables can be used in an expression to calculate values relative to the last note in the voice. Obviously, the value of the variables will change after each note statement. The following example increments the pitch by one semi-tone and the volume by 10 on each iteration of the loop and then sets the time forward by 2 seconds.

```
C4, %4, 50;
loop (4)
   curpit+1, curdur, curvol+10;
time curtime+2;
```

Grouped note values are evaluated before synthesizer events are generated. Since the built-in variables are updated at the end of the note statement, they do not change within a group. In the following example, the statements with groups are equivalent.

```
C4, %4, 100;
{D4, E4, F4, G4};

C4, %4, 100;
{curpit+2, curpit+4, curpit+5, curpit+7};
```

Programming Statements

The primary purpose of Notelist is to specify synthesizer parameters in an intuitive manner. It is not intended as a general purpose programming language. However, the addition of some simple programming capabilities can make specification of the score easier in some cases and also allows simple compositional algorithms to be used within the score. Notelist includes variable definitions, variable assignments, *if...else* and *while...do* control statements for these purposes.

Variables are used to hold values that can change during processing of the score. Variable names begin with a letter followed by any number of letters and digits. Note that single letter variable names in the range [A-G], with or without a number following, represent pitches and cannot be used as variable names.

All variables must be declared with a *var* statement before they are used. The *var* statement must appear outside of any voice and can be repeated as many times as needed. A single statement can define multiple variables by separating the variable names with commas.

```
var val1;
var oct, step;
```

The value of a variable is set using the *set* statement. The *set* statement can appear within a voice as well as outside of a voice. The value on the right of the '=' can be any valid expression and can include pitches and rhythm values along with numbers.

```
set oct = 12;
set step = 1;
set val2 = C4 + (oct * step);
```

A variable can be used anywhere an expression is allowed. This allows calculating pitches, rhythms and other parameters based on changing values. For example, the following will produce a chromatic scale.

```
var val1;
voice 0
begin
  set val1 = C4;
  loop (12)
  begin
    val1, %4, 100;
    set val1 = val1 + 1;
  end
end
```

The *if...then...else* statement is used to conditionally execute statements. The expression between *if* and *then* controls which statement is executed. If the condition is true, the statement after *then* is executed. If the condition is false, the statement after *else* is executed. The *else* part is optional. The statement controlled by *if...then..else* can also be a *begin...end* block, allowing for a group of statements to be controlled by a single condition. In the following example *if* is used to create two endings for a repeated phrase.

```
loop (2)
begin
  {C4, E4, G4, F4, A4}, %8, 100;
  if count = 0 then
    {C5, G4, E4}, %8, 100;
  else
    {B4, G4, C5}, %8, 100;
end
```

The *while...do* statement is used to repeatedly execute a statement, similar to a *loop*. Unlike a loop, the *while...do* statement contains a condition to control the number of times the statement is executed. Whereas the *loop* statement automatically increments the loop count, the expression that controls the *while* loop must be explicitly calculated. The following example loops five times, increasing the volume level by 20 on each step.

```
set val1 = 20;
while val1 <= 100 do
begin
  C4, %8, val1;
  set val1 = val1 + 20;
end
```

The conditional expression for *if* and *while* can contain relational and logical operators in addition to arithmetic operators. The following operators are defined.

a < b	True if *a* is less than *b*.
a <= b	True if *a* is less than or equal to *b*.
a > b	True if *a* is greater than *b*.
a >= b	True if *a* is greater than or equal to *b*.
a = b	True if *a* is equal to *b*. A double equal '==' can be used instead of the single '=' if desired.
a <> b	True if *a* is not equal to *b*.
a & b	True if both *a* and *b* are non-zero. The word 'and' can be used instead of '&'.
a | b	True if either *a* or *b* are non-zero. The word 'or' can be used instead of '|'.
~a	True if *a* is false. The word 'not' can be used as well.

Multiple operators can be used and are evaluated left to right, with relational operators having a higher precedence. In other words, the relational operators are evaluated first, then the logical operators. Arithmetic operators have a higer precedence than relational and logical operators. Parenthesis can be used to override the order of evaluation.

As is typical of programming languages, any non-zero value is considered *true*, while a zero value is considered *false*.

Since they represent integer values, pitch and rhythm values can be used in conditional expressions anywhere a number is valid, including with relational operators. The following example calculates random intervals up to an octave, but insures the pitches stay within a two octave range [C3-C5].

```
var val1;

voice 0
begin
  set val1 = C4;
  loop (20)
  begin
    set val1 = val1 + rand(-12,12);
    if val1 > C5 then
      set val1 = val1 - 12;
    if val1 < C3 then
      set val1 = val1 + 12;
    val1, %16, 100;
  end
end
```

Extended Scripting

We sometimes need to perform more complicated calculations than those allowed with Notelist expressions and built-in functions. Although it is possible to embed more sophisticated programming capabilities into Notelist, there are numerous scripting languages available that can be easily embedded into another program. Rather than invent a new script syntax and embed it into Notelist, or choose one scripting language, Notelist provides hooks to invoke an external script interperter. Four keywords are defined for this purpose.

The *script* statement passes a character string to a scripting engine. The argument to the script statement can be a file of scripting language code that will be loaded into the scripting engine for later use, or it can be a statement in the script language that is executed immediately. The *script* statement is executed during parsing of the Notelist script.

```
script "file";
```

The *call* statement also passes a string to the script engine for execution. Unlike the *script* statement, the *call* statement is executed during sequence generation.

```
call "script";
```

The *eval* operator passes a string to the script engine for immediate execution. The value returned from *eval* is then used as a value within a Notelist expression.

```
voice 1
begin
  vol eval "getVol()";
end
```

Since *eval* is a unary operator, an expression used as an argument to *eval* must be placed in parenthesis. For example:

```
eval "getVol" + 10
eval ("getVol" # 10)
```

The first expression will add 10 to the value returned by *eval*. The second expression will pass the string "getVol10" to *eval*.

The string passed to *call* or *eval* is specific to the scripting engine and is not interpreted by Notelist. In order to pass Notelist variables to the script engine, the argument to *eval* can be created dynamically using the Notelist string paste operator (#).

```
loop 5
begin
  C4, %4, eval("getVol(" # count # ")");
end
```

A script engine does not need to be a programming language. We can also create an interface to a data storage system and use the script engine interface to retrieve values. For example, if values are stored in a spreadsheet, a script engine interface can be developed that reads values from the spreadsheet cells. The *call* operator could be used to put values into spreadsheet cells and the *eval* operator used to get values. Likewise, a relational database, XML file, or remote website could be used as the source of values for a Notelist script.

Additional Control Statements

Most control statements change the settings associated with a voice, but a few statements affect the way the score is interpreted.

The *include* statement includes another file into the current file. This allows reusing fragments of note lists without having to retype them every time. A typical use would be to include pre-defined settings, sequences, or notes generated by another program.

```
include "filename";
```

The *filename* argument should be a complete path to the file. Relative paths can be used, but will be relative to the current directory.

The *system* statement invokes an external program using the system command shell.

```
system "myprogam file.txt";
```

The *middlec* statement is used to move the octave number that indicates middle C. The following statement would cause C6 to refer to middle C.

```
middlec 6;
```

The value of *middlec* is processed by the parser and must be a number, not an expression. Changing the octave of middle C only affects parsing and does not change the integer value for middle C passed to the synthesizer.

The *version* statement sets the version number for the Notelist file.

```
version 1.0;
```

By default, the version number is set to the version of the Notelist program. Subsequent versions of the program may alter the default behavior of Notelist statements and it might be necessary to indicate that the prior behavior should be used instead. By setting a version number as the first statement in the file, the parser and generator will revert to the previous behavior and the score will not have to be edited to be properly interpreted.

Comments can be entered by beginning the comment with either an exclamation point (!) or a single quote ('). Text in comments is ignored. The comment extends from the comment character to the end of the line.

```
! A comment can begin with an exclamation
' or it can begin with a single quote.

voice 1 ' a comment about the voice
begin
end
```

Chapter 25

Notelist Interpreter Implementation

The description of Notelist given in the last chapter explains the rationale for the syntax and shows how to use it. However, that description is not sufficiently formal to use as a basis for the program design. In order to develop an interpreter for Notelist, we must write out the syntax as a formal grammar. A formal grammar insures that all aspects of the language are represented and guides the development of the code.

Notelist Grammar

The Notelist grammar is shown below.[14] An asterisk (*) indicates zero or more occurrences of a symbol, a plus (+) one or more occurrences, and a question mark (?) one or zero occurrences. The vertical bar is used to denote alternates, and parenthesis indicate a sub-element of a production rule. Text in quotes represents a keyword or terminal symbol that must be matched exactly.

```
score       : statement* ;
statement   : global | sequence | voice ;
global      : include | system | script | write
            | version | tempo | middlec | initfn
            | maxparam | map | declare | set ;
include     : 'include' STRING ';' ;
system      : ('system'|'sys') STRING ';' ;
```

---

[14] The grammar syntax is the one used by the ANTLR program. The RE syntax uses the format of *grep, pearl* and similar programs.

```
script       : 'script' STRING ';' ;
write        : 'write' expr ';' ;
version      : 'version' id ';' ;
tempo        : 'tempo' expr ',' expr ';' ;
middlec      : 'middlec' NUMBER ';' ;
initfn       : 'init' NUMBER fn
                 expr ',' expr ',' expr ';' ;
fn           : 'line' | 'exp' | 'log' | 'rand' ;
maxparam     : 'maxparam' expr ';' ;
map          : 'map' id mapval (',' mapval)* ';' ;
mapval       : expr (':' expr)? ;
declare      : ('variable'|'var') VAR (, VAR)* ';' ;
set          : 'set' VAR '=' expr ';' ;
sequence     : ('sequence'|'seq') id notelist ;
voice        : 'voice' NUMBER notelist ;
notelist     : 'begin' notes* 'end' | notes ';' ;
notes        : global | ifstmt | whilestmt | loop
             | instr | vol | chnl | call | play
             | artic | param | time | mark | sync
             | transpose | double | sus | tie
             | note | notespec ;
ifstmt       : 'if' expr 'then' notelist
                 ('else' notelist)? ;
whilestmt    : 'while' expr 'do' notelist ;
loop         : 'loop' '(' expr ')' notelist ;
instr        : ('instrument'|'instr') expr ';' ;
vol          : ('volume'|'vol') expr ';' ;
chnl         : ('channel'|'chnl') expr ';' ;
call         : 'call' expr ';' ;
play         : 'play' expr ';' ;
artic        : 'artic' artval ';' ;
artval       : 'fixed' artexpr
             | 'percent' artexpr
             | 'add' artexpr
             | 'off' ;
artexpr      : 'param' | expr ;
param        : 'param' expr ',' expr ';' ;
time         : 'time' expr ';' ;
mark         : 'mark' expr ';' ;
sync         : 'sync' expr ';' ;
transpose    : 'transpose' expr ';' ;
double       : 'double' dblparam ';' ;
dblparam     : 'off' | expr (',' expr)* ;
sus          : 'sus' notespec ;
```

```
tie           : 'tie' notespec ;
note          : 'note' notespec ;
notespec      : valgroup (',' valgroup)* ';' ;
valgroup      : '{' exprlist '}'
              | '[' exprlist ']'
              | expr ;
exprlist      : expr (',' expr)* ;
expr          : logical ('#' logical)* ;
logical       : relation (logop relation)* ;
relation      : term (relop term)* ;
term          : factor (addop factor)* ;
factor        : value (mulop value)* ;
value         : '(' expr ')' | NUMBER | STRING
              | PITCH | RHYTHM | VAR
              | 'fgen' '(' expr ',' expr ')'
              | 'rand' | 'count' | 'curtime'
              | 'curpit' | 'curdur' | 'curvol'
              | '-' value | 'eval' value
              | '~' value | 'not' value ;
logop         : '&' | '|' | 'and' | 'or' ;
addop         : '+' | '-' ;
mulop         : '*' | '/' | '^' ;
relop         : '<' | '>'
              | '<=' | '>='
              | '<>' | '=' | '==' ;
id            : STRING | NUMBER ;
```

The terminals *NUMBER, STRING, PITCH, RHYTHM,* and *VAR* are recognized by the lexical scanner and passed to the parser as a single token. They are best described with regular expressions (RE).

```
NUMBER     = [0-9]+(\.[0-9]*)?
STRING     = "([^"]|\\")*"
PITCH      = [A-Ga-g][#bxd]?[0-9]*
RHYTHM     = (%[0-9]+(\.[0-9]*)?)
           | (W|H|Q|EI|S|T|w|h|q|ei|s|t)(\.)?
VAR        = [A-Za-z][A-Za-z0-9]*
```

Note that the RE for *VAR* overlaps with the definitions for *PITCH* and *RHYTHM*. A single pitch letter (A-G), a pitch letter followed by a number, or a rhythm letter (WHQEST) will match multiple expressions. We can write the lexical scanner so that it looks for

PITCH and *RHYTHM* first and only recognizes a single letter as a variable name when the letter is not a pitch letter or rhythm letter.

The *note* keyword is included for completeness. It is optional since any statement that begins with an expression is considered a note. However, there are times when using *note* helps clarify the intent of the statement. For example:

```
voice 5 10;
voice 5 note 10;
```

Without the *note* keyword, the statement could appear to be missing a keyword.

The *loop* production rule shown in the grammar requires parentheses around the loop count even though they are considered optional by the parser. The grammar includes parentheses in order to avoid a conflict that would otherwise arise from statements such as:

```
loop 5 -(expr);
```

Ordinarily, a negative pitch is meaningless. However, whether or not a negative pitch value is valid will depend on the interpretation given to the pitch value by the current instrument. Thus a negative value should be allowed. The parser will allow missing parentheses since a statement such as:

```
loop 5 C4;
```

is correctly parsed without them.

Similarly, the production rule for *if* requires *then* after the conditional expression. Usually, the statement will parse correctly without *then* and the parser treats it as optional. The same is true of the *do* keyword on the *while* statement.

Class Design

A language interpreter is typically designed around three cooperating objects, *lexer, parser,* and *generator.* The lexer object scans the input stream for the next token, stores the characters in a buffer, and returns a number to identify the token. The parser object repeatedly calls the *lexer* to get the next token and then attempts to match the current token with a production rule from the grammar. When a statement in the language is recognized by the parser, the parser constructs an internal representation and adds it to the parse list maintained by the generator. Once parsing is complete, the generator object steps through the list of tokens produced by the parser, evaluating each in turn.

The three objects, lexer, parser and generator, are aggregated into a *converter* object that acts as the interface between the synthesizer and the script convertor. The converter is invoked by the generator to produce the sequencer events. This design allows for easy replacement of the output data format. If desired, a class derived from the converter class can override the appropriate methods and produce events for a completely different sequencer or synthesis system.

The overall class structure of the Notelist interpreter is shown in Figure 51. Classes are indicated by rectangles. Connections with a diamond at one end indicate aggregation and/or containment. Connections with a triangle indicate specialization (i.e., inheritance).

The *nlConverter* class provides the interface between the interpreter and the rest of the system. The caller must set sequencer, and instrument manager objects so that *nlConverter* can identify instruments and generate sequencer events. In addition, the caller should set an error output object on the converter to receive error and debugging output. The caller can optionally provide lexical scanner input and script engine objects to the converter.

The *nlLex* class provides the lexer. The *nlLex* class method *Next* skips over comments and white space and then scans the input for the end of the next token. It does not directly manage stream input, but instead relies on the *nlLexIn* class. The *nlLexIn* class provides methods to get/unget one character from a buffer. Two derived classes provide the actual implementation. The *nlLexFileMem* class retrieves characters from an in-memory buffer and is typically used from an editor where the file is already in memory. The *nlLexFileIn* class reads directly from a disk file and is typically used when the Notelist script file is not already loaded into memory.

The *nlParser* class implements the parser. The Notelist parser uses a recursive descent technique where each production rule in the grammar is matched to a method on the parser class. There are a few instances where production rules are combined for efficiency. As each input token is consumed, the parser adds a new script node to the current node list of the *nlGenerator* class. The parsed tokens are output to a single linked list rather than the more typical parse tree. Exceptions to the single list are *sequence, loop, if..else,* and *while* nodes. These nodes each contain a separate *nlSequence* pointer for the code controlled by the node.

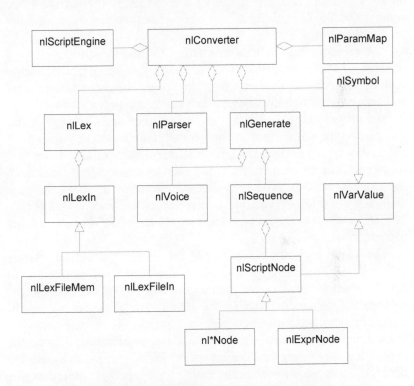

Figure 51 - Notelist Script Interpreter

As expressions are parsed, infix notation is transformed into postfix notation. Thus an expression of the form $(a+b)$ results in the node list $(a \ b \ +)$. Parentheses are also discarded since order of evaluation is preserved by the script node order. For example, the expression $(c*(a+b))$ will produce $(c \ a \ b \ + \ *)$ as output. Commas separating parameter lists are preserved since they act as a terminal symbol that will stop expression evaluation at the point where the comma node is encountered.

The *nlGenerator* class contains the list of sequences for execution, global generator values such as tempo, and the list of voice objects. Generation of the sequence is accomplished by invoking the *Play* method on the main *nlSequence* object. The *nlSequence* object steps through each *nlScriptNode* object in its list, calling the *Exec* method on each in turn. The *Exec* methods either change the current voice context or invoke the *nlConverter* object to produce another sequencer event.

The *nlVoice* class defines a structure to hold the current state of one voice. The generator maintains a list of voice objects, creating each dynamically on the first use of the voice. The current voice is set and accessed through methods on the generator object.

The *nlVarValue* class holds a variant value of *double, long integer,* and *char** types. It defines methods to store and retrieve values with automatic type conversion. Since *nlScriptNodes* inherit from this class, each can be treated as a value and copied directly to and from the evaluation stack. The *nlVarValue* class also serves as the base class for variables. A variable is represented by a *nlSymbol* object. The *nlConverter* class contains the symbol table, making all variable names global.

The class indicated as *nl*Node* represents the set of classes defining the operations performed during sequence generation. In general, there is one class for each terminal symbol in the grammar.

Expressions are evaluated by the *nlExprNode* class. An instance of this class is created for each *expr* in a production rule. Expression evaluation is performed using a stack-based calculator. Since the parser has converted the script from infix operators to postfix operators, expression evaluation with proper operator precedence is simple. When an operand is encountered, it is pushed on the evaluation stack. When an operator is encountered, the appropriate number of values are popped from the stack, the operation performed, and the result pushed back on the stack. When the expression is complete, the top of stack is copied to the expression node and made available to other script nodes through the *GetValue* method of the expression object.

The *nlParamMap* class is used to hold the parameter mapping values. When the *nlConverter* object generates a sequencer event, it maps each parameter index and value from the Notelist script onto the instrument specific parameter IDs using the information in the currently selected map.

The *nlScriptEngine* class defines the interface between the Notelist interpreter and an external scripting system. The *BasicSynth* library defines the interface but does not implement this class.

Some classes used to hold current values for a voice are not shown. They are aggregated with the *nlVoice* class and do not have a significant interface.

Extensions

The Notelist interpreter is designed and implemented in a way that allows easy extension of the syntax without the use of external parser generation tools. The procedure for extending the Notelist syntax involves the following steps.

1. Modify the formal grammar to include the extension, reusing existing rules whenever possible.
2. If needed, derive a new class from *nlScriptNode* and implement the *Exec* method to handle processing during the generator pass. Symbols that represent a constant value can use the *nlScriptNode* class directly by setting the token and value members appropriately. If the new symbol represents a value or operator, add the appropriate code to the switch in the *nlExprNode::Exec* method.
3. Define a token for the keyword or terminal symbol in *NLConvert.h* and add code to the *nlLex::Next* method to recognize the symbol.
4. For new statements, add a method to *nlParser* that represents the production rule for the statement and invoke the new method from the appropriate place, typically the switch in the *nlParser::Statement* or *nlParser::Notelist* methods. For new value symbols, add the token to the list in the *nlParser::Value* method. For new operators, add the operator to the appropriate method in the expression recognizer, or, if it requires special treatment, add a new method to handle the operator. In each case, add code to create an instance of the associated script node and add the node to the generator list when the token is encountered.

Classes derived from *nlScriptNode* have a member variable (*genPtr*) that points to the generator object. This variable can be used to gain access to other parts of the interpreter. A pointer to the current voice is maintained by the generator object and should be used by a script node to modify the current state of the voice. Values that are not specific to the current voice (e.g., tempo) should be set on the generator object. If new member variables are added to either the voice or generator classes, appropriate initialization must be added to the respective constructor. Global variables should also be avoided. Use the generator or converter objects to store information that needs to be accessible from multiple script nodes or across multiple input files. Keep in mind that the parser can be invoked multiple times before the generator is run. Any persistent values should be stored in the convertor, generator, or script node, not the parser. In addition, the lexer object can change during parsing when an include statement is encountered. A parser method can not rely on the state of member variables in the lexer and only the base class methods of *nlLex* should be used by parser code.

In addition to language extensions, the Notelist interpreter can be extended to read a script from sources other than a file or memory. For example, an extension could be developed that reads the output of another program through a pipe, retrieves the script from another computer using a network protocol, or reads the script from a database. To extend the input source capabilities, derive a new class from *nlLexIn* and implement the methods appropriately. Pass an instance of the new class to the converter as an argument to the *Convert* method.

Files:

```
Src/Notelist/NLConvert.h
Src/Notelist/Converter.h
Src/Notelist/Parser.h
Src/Notelist/Generate.h
Src/Notelist/Lex.h
Src/Notelist/ScriptEngine.h
Src/Notelist/Converter.cpp
Src/Notelist/Parser.cpp
Src/Notelist/Generate.cpp
Src/Notelist/Lex.cpp
```

Chapter 26

BSynth

BSynth is a command line program that implements a complete synthesizer using the *BasicSynth Common, Instrument*, and *Notelist* libraries. *BSynth* takes a single command line argument that specifies a project file containing instrument configurations and Notelist scripts, and produces a WAV file as output.

A *BSynth* project file is an XML format file that contains general information about the composition, synthesizer settings, instrument definitions, score files, and parameters that control the format of the output. A template project file is shown below.

```
<synthprj>
  <name>Composition name</name>
  <author>Composer name</author>
  <desc>Description of the composition</desc>
  <cpyrgt>Copyright notice</cpyrgt>
  <synth sr="44100" wt="16384" usr="" >
    <wvtable ndx="" parts="" gibbs="" >
      <part mul="" amp="" phs=""/>
    </wvtable>
  </synth>
  <mixer chnls="" fxunits="" lft="" rgt="">
    <chnl cn="" on="" vol="" pan=""/>
    <reverb unit="" vol="" rvt="" pan="" >
      <send chnl="" amt=""/>
    </reverb>
    <flanger unit="" lvl="" mix="" fb=""
      cntr="" depth="" sweep="" pan="" >
      <send chnl="" amt="" />
    </flanger>
  </mixer>
```

```
<libdir>path to libraries and scores</libdir>
<libfile>an instrument library</libfile>
<instrlib>
   <instr> instrument definition </instr>
</instrlib>
<seq name="">a sequencer file</seq>
<score name="" dbg="">a notelist file</score>
<text>file associated with the project</text>
<out type="1" lead="" tail="">
   output file path
</out>
</synthprj>
```

Tag	Attribute	Use
synthprj		Document root tag
name		Name of the composition
author		Composer's name
desc		Description
cpyrgt		Copyright
synth	*sr*	Sample rate
	wt	Wavetable length
	usr	Number of user defined wave tables, defined by *wvtable* tags
wvtable	*ndx*	Wavetable index number (0-9 are reserved for library use)
	parts	Number of partials
	gibbs	Apply adjustment for Gibbs effect
part	*mul*	Partial number (1-n)
	amp	Amplitude for this partial
	phs	Starting phase of this partial
mixer	*chnls*	Number of mixer inputs
	fxunits	Number of effects units
	lft	Master volume – left
	rgt	Master volume – right
chnl	*cn*	Mixer input channel number
	on	Channel on (1) or off (0)
	pan	Channel pan (-1 to +1)
reverb	*unit*	Effects unit number
	vol	Output volume level

	rvt	Reverb time
	pan	Pan for the reverb
send	*chnl*	Channel to send from
	amt	Amplitude sent to effects unit
flanger	*unit*	Effects unit number
	fb	Feedback amount
	center	Center delay (seconds)
	depth	Delay sweep depth (seconds)
	lvl	Output level
	mix	Mix of input to flanger output
	sweep	Sweep rate in Hz
	pan	Pan position for flanger output
libdir		Path to libraries
libfile		Instrument library file
instrlib		In-line instrument library
instr	*	See the definition of *instr* under instrument design chapters
seq		A sequencer file, may be path relative to a *libdir* entry
	name	Display name for the file
score		A Notelist file, may be path relative to a *libdir* entry
	name	Display name for the file
	dbg	Notelist debug level 0-3, values 1-3 produce increasing amounts of information from the parser
text		File associated with the project
out		Output file path
	type	1 = WAVE file
	lead	Seconds of silence at beginning of the file
	tail	Seconds of silence at end of file; when reverb is enabled, this should be RVT seconds or longer

The *name, author, desc, copyright, synth, mixer* and *out* tags should appear once. The *libdir, libfile, instrlib, seq,* and *score* tags can be repeated as many times as needed.

The synthesizer parameters must be set prior to loading instruments, and instruments must be loaded prior to processing score or sequence files. The *BSynth* program insures the proper order by making three scans of the project file. The first scan looks for *synth* and *mixer* nodes. The second scan loads instruments and instrument libraries. The third scan processes score and sequence files.

Files:

```
Src/BSynth/main.cpp
Src/BSynth/jig.xml
```

Chapter 27

BasicSynth Library

The directory structure for the *BasicSynth* source code is shown in Figure 52.

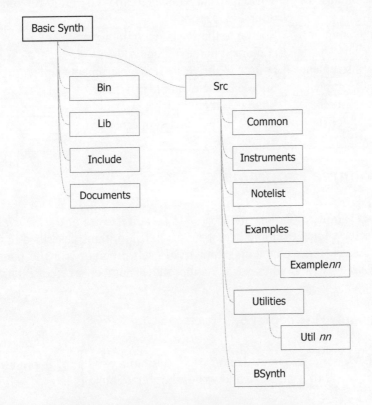

Figure 52 - BasicSynth Directory Structure

The *BasicSynth* source code described in this book is contained in a set of four C++ source code libraries. The libraries include classes for sound generation and sequencing, instruments, and the Notelist interpreter. The source distribution also contains the source code to the example programs along with reference documentation for the classes in each library and the Notelist score language.

Directory	Content
Bin	Binary files; executable images and shared libraries
Lib	Object file libraries
Include	Source include files. Most of the *BasicSynth* sound generation code is contained in these files.
Documents	Various documents including the library reference
Src	Source code root
Src/Common	Source to the *BasicSynth* library code not contained in the include files
Src/Instruments	Source to the *BasicSynth* instruments collection.
Src/Examples	Source to the example programs.
Src/Utilities	Source to the utility programs.
Src/Notelist	Source to the notelist interpreter
Src/BSynth	Source to the *BSynth* synthesizer

Example Programs

The example programs are located in sub-directories of the *Examples* directory. Each example demonstrates the algorithms described in the associated book chapter. Output from each program is a file named *exampleNN.wav* where *NN* is the same number as the example program.

Example01 (Chapter 5)

This example program demonstrates a simple oscillator. It produces one second of a sin wave and writes the sound into a file.

Example02 (Chapter 6)

These examples demonstrate envelope generators. *Example02* has in-line code, *Example02a* uses the *BasicSynth* Library, *Example02b* uses a graphics line algorithm.

Example03 (Chapter 7)

Program to calculate complex waveforms.

1. summation of first 8 partials
2. sawtooth wave
3. inverse sawtooth wave
4. triangle wave
5. square wave
6. 25% pulse wave
7. frequency modulation
8. phase modulation
9. amplitude modulation
10. ring modulation
11. white noise

Example04 (Chapter 8)

Program to calculate complex waveforms using wavetable oscillators.

Example05 (Chapter 10)

Various filters: LP, HP, BP, Reson, using bi-quad filter; FIR and IIR averaging and convolution.

Example06 (Chapter 9)

Program to demonstrate mixing and panning.

Example07 (Chapter 11)

Using delay lines to implement echo.

Example07a (Chapter 12)

Using delay lines to implement reverb.

Examle07b (Chapter 13)

Using delay lines to implement Flanger/Chorus.

Example08 (Chapter 15)

BasicSynth sequencer.

Example09 (Chapter 16)

MIDI Sequencer.

Example10 (Chapters 19-25)

Synthesizer Instruments

- Tone Generator
- Additive Synthesis
- Subtractive Synthesis
- FM Synthesis (3 oscillators)
- Matrix Synthesizer (8 oscillators)
- Wavefile Playback

Utility Programs

Several interactive utility programs are included with the library source code. These can be studied for ideas on how to use the library, and also to help better understand various synthesis techniques.

Waveform Explorer

This program allows setting each of 16 partials to construct a complex waveform using the inverse Fourier transform (sum of sine waves). The resulting waveform can be saved to disk as a WAVE file and as a graphic (EMF). Settings can be copied to the clipboard.

FM Explorer

This program implements a three oscillator FM synthesizer. Each oscillator is combined with an ADSR envelope generator. Several presets are available as examples. The program can save the sound to a WAVE file. The settings can also be copied to the clipboard.

Reverb Explorer

This program implements a Schroeder reverb. The loop times and reverb time can be set from the program to hear how they affect the sound. Sounds can be internally generated or loaded from a WAVE file. The processed sound can be saved to disk.

Flanger Explorer

This program implements a Flanger/Chorus effect. The delay times, modulation depth, and amplitudes can be set to hear how they affect the sound. Sounds can be internally generated or loaded from a WAVE file. The processed sound can be saved to disk.

Virtual Keyboard

This program displays a piano keyboard on the screen and allows playing sounds by clicking the on-screen keys with the mouse. Instruments can be loaded from either an instrument library or *BSynth* project file.

Building the Software

To build the examples or your own synthesis program with *BasicSynth* requires a C++ compiler. As much as possible, the source code was written to be independent of the compiler and any C++ compiler should work. The source code has been tested with the Microsoft® VC compiler, version 9, and the GNU compiler, version 4.1.2.

The *Include* directory and the *Common* library provide the sound generation, wave file and sequencer code. If you want to use the *BasicSynth* instruments collection in your program, you must also include the header files from the *Src/Instruments* directory and link with the *Lib/Instruments.lib* library. To include the Notelist score processor, you must include the header file *NLConvert.h* from the *Src/Notelist* directory and link with the *Lib/Notelist.lib* library.

Building on Windows

There are several solution files that can be built depending on what you want to do. All solution files are for Visual Studio 2008 (version 9). If you have a different compiler, you will have to reproduce the project and/or solution files.

To build just the libraries, use the solution files in *Src/Common*, *Src/Instruments*, and *Src/Notelist* directories.

To build the example programs, use the solution file in *Src/Examples*. This builds all the example programs and libraries.

To build the utilities, use the solution file in *Src/Utilities*.

To build the stand-alone command line synthesizer, use the solution file in *Src/BSynth*. This also builds the libraries if needed.

Each project provides four targets:

- Release Win32 - 32-bit version without debug info.
- Debug Win32 - 32-bit version with debugging.
- Release x64 - 64-bit version without debug info.
- Debug x64 - 64-bit version with debug info.

Output of the 32-bit release version is in the *Bin* and *Lib* directories. The 64-bit version produces output in *Bin64* and *Lib64*. Debug versions are written to the *Examples/Debug* directory so that they do not overwrite the Release output binaries.

Building on Linux and other Unix Variants

There is a master Makefile located in the Src directory that will build all of the libraries and programs. There is also a Makefile in each directory that can be used to build part of the source. The file *BasicSynth.cfg* in the Src directory contains the settings for the compiler and linker. Edit this file to point to the appropriate places. Usually it is only necessary to change the location of BSDIR to point to the root directory of the source tree. By default, *BasicSynth* is built with XML support using the *libxml2* library. You should install the *libxml2-dev* package first before building *BasicSynth*. If you do not need to use the project/instrument file loading code, there is a null implementation of the *XmlWrapper* class that can be used instead. The file is *XmlWrapN.cpp* in the *Src/Common* directory, and should be compiled and added to the Common library in place of *XmlWrapU.cpp*.

Output is to the directories *Bin* and *Lib* under the *BasicSynth* install directory. These directories are created automatically by the Makefile if they do not exist.

The *Utilities* programs depend on the Windows graphics system and are not available for other operating systems. The *BSynth* program is portable and should compile and run on any platform.

Library Classes

The *BasicSynth* Common library classes provide the signal generation and processing foundation for the synthesizer. The *Instruments* library contains code for the example instruments. The *Notelist* library contains code for the Notelist parser. Reference documentation is in the *Documents* directory.

Chapter 28

Further Development

The *BasicSynth* libraries developed in this book provide a good foundation for developing a synthesis system and can be used directly to develop a synthesizer system or to incorporate sound generation into your own program. However, the code shown here is only a starting point, and represents only one way among many to implement a synthesizer.

The example instruments developed in this book are fully functional, but mainly intended as working examples. There are several other instruments that a complete synthesis system might require. Two obvious additions would be instruments for sampling and waveguide synthesis methods. Understanding the techniques for those kinds of instruments will require additional study and research, but most of the program components needed are already a part of the library. Adding a waveguide instrument would be a good first step for those who want to experiment with expanding the library's capabilities.

A fully configurable modular synthesis instrument is another good extension to the instrument library. A modular instrument allows for quicker development, experimentation and variation of the synthesis method and is especially useful for education and research of synthesis techniques.

Additional processing units are another possible extension. The reverb units shown in this book will work for most applications, but there are other reverb designs available. Other processing units, such as equalizers and compressors, would make good additions to the library as well.

Although the *BSynth* program is a complete and working synthesizer, a truly useful synthesis system should be based on a graphical interface and incorporate instrument configuration, score entry, and playback into one integrated program. With the *BasicSynth* library as a foundation, creation of such a synthesizer is much easier and well within reach of anyone with a basic understanding of GUI programming. The advantage of creating such a program for yourself is the ability to customize both the functionality and the interface to match your own preferences.

The primary goal of this book was to examine and solve the practical problems in developing a music synthesizer. Hopefully, seeing how this library and programs were developed will help you to understand the problems and possible solutions needed to develop your own music programs.

References

Boulanger, Richard (editor), *The CSound Book*, MIT Press, 2000

Chamberlin, Hal, *Musical Applications of Microprocessors,* Hayden Book Co., 1985

Cook, Perry R., *Real Sound Synthesis for Interactive Applications*, A. K. Peters, 2002

Dodge, Charles, and Jerse, Thomas A., *Computer Music: Synthesis, Composition, and Performance*, Schirmer, 1997

Loy, D. Gareth, *Musimathics, The Mathematical Foundations of Music, Volume 1*, MIT Press, 2006

Loy, D. Gareth, *Musimathics, The Mathematical Foundations of Music, Volume 2*, MIT Press, 2007

Miranda, Eduardo, *Computer Sound Design: Synthesis Techniques and Programming* , Focal Press, 2002

Roads, Curtis, *The Computer Music Tutorial*, MIT Press, 1996

Smith, Julius O., *Introduction to Digital Filters with Audio Applications*, W3K Publishing, 2007

Smith, Stephen W., *The Scientist and Engineer's Guide to Signal Processing,* California Technical Pub., 1997

Online Resources

Online resources may move or disappear. These were available at the time of publication.

CCRMA, http://ccrma.stanford.edu/

CECM, http://www.indiana.edu/~emusic/

Computer Music Journal, http://www.mitpressjournals.org/cmj

CSounds, http://www.csounds.com/

DSPRelated.com, http://www.dsprelated.com/

ICMC, http://www.computermusic.org/

Harmony Central, http://www.harmony-central.com/articles/

Music-DSP Software Archive, http://www.musicdsp.org/

Puckette, Miller, Pure Data, http://crca.ucsd.edu/~msp/software.html

Smith, J.O., Physical Audio Signal Processing, http://ccrma.stanford.edu/~jos/pasp/, online book.

Smith, J.O., Introduction to Digital Filters with Audio Applications, http://ccrma.stanford.edu/~jos/filters/, online book.

Smith, Steven W., DSP Guide, http://www.dspguide.com/

Smyth, Tamara, Lecture Notes, http://www.cs.sfu.ca/~tamaras/

WikiPedia, Computer Music, http://en.wikipedia.org/wiki/Computer_audio

Index

Made in the USA
San Bernardino, CA
30 March 2013